SCIENCE AND THE STUDY OF GOD

Science and the Study of God

A Mutuality Model for Theology and Science

ALAN G. PADGETT

To Ted,
with blessings
in Christ our
Lord,
Alan Padgett

WILLIAM B. EERDMANS PUBLISHING COMPANY
GRAND RAPIDS, MICHIGAN / CAMBRIDGE, U.K.

Wm. B. Eerdmans Publishing Co.
2140 Oak Industrial Drive N.E., Grand Rapids, Michigan 49505 /
P.O. Box 163, Cambridge CB3 9PU U.K.

Printed in the United States of America

08 07 06 05 04 03   7 6 5 4 3 2 1

Library of Congress Cataloging-in-Publication Data

Padgett, Alan G., 1955-
   Science and the study of God: a mutuality model for theology and science \
   Alan G. Padgett.
     p.   cm.
   Includes bibliographical references (p.) and index.
   ISBN-10: 0-8028-3941-X / ISBN-13: 978-0-8028-3941-1 (pbk.: alk. paper)
   1. Religion and science. I. Title.
  BL240.3.P33   2003
  261.5′5 — dc21

                                       2003049468

www.eerdmans.com

To Steve, Dennis, Tom, and Richard
  With love in Christ from a grateful student

Contents

Preface

I want to thank the editors and publishers of earlier versions of a number of chapters in this book for the opportunity to circulate my ideas and arguments. All of these chapters have been rewritten for the present volume and are often longer. All of them, too, have benefited from debate and criticism. An early version of Chapter Three appeared in *The Resurrection,* a book edited by Steve Davis, Gerry O'Collins, and Dan Kendal. Chapter Five was originally read at the American Academy of Religion meeting, and I thank Bryan Stone and Tom Oord for the invitation. They eventually edited a fine book *(Thy Nature and Thy Name is Love),* in which this chapter appeared in briefer compass. An early version of Chapter One appeared in *Christian Scholar's Review,* and a shorter version of Chapter Two came out in *Perspectives on Science and Christian Faith.* Likewise, Chapter Eight appeared in different form in the *Journal for Christian Theological Research.* An earlier and shorter version of Chapter Six appeared in the Festschrift for Thomas Oden edited by Chris Hall and Ken Tanner *(Ancient and Postmodern Christianity).*

I am grateful to several institutions and societies for the opportunity to lecture on the topics developed in this book. Leeds University and Durham University in England both provided opportunities to lecture on some ideas now found in this volume. I thank my hosts there, especially Professors Nigel Biggar, E. J. Lowe, Ann Loades, and David Brown. I want to thank Steve Davis, Gerry O'Collins, and Dan Kendal for the opportunity to participate in two symposia at St. Joseph's Seminary in Dunwoodie, which provided a very stimulating atmosphere for outstanding theological dialogue. The American Academy of Religion, Western Region, and the Wesley Studies Group in the AAR also heard earlier versions of some of these chapters as lectures, and I very much enjoyed the opportunity to debate with my colleagues in these settings. Themes that went into Chapter Six were developed at the Wabash Center for Teaching Religion at Wabash College, and I thank my hosts (William Placher, Raymond Williams, and Lucinda Huffaker) and my fellow participants in the Theologians' Consultation for a very stimulating set of three summer seminars. Finally, much of the work of revising and re-thinking this material as one book was done at three summer seminars in Wycliffe Hall, Oxford (the Oxford Templeton Seminars on Science and Christianity, 1999-2001). This was a wonderful environment for serious thinking (and some fun!). Thank you to all who read and discussed ideas with me regarding this project. We are all in debt to our hosts, Alister McGrath and John Roche, as well as to the Templeton Foundation (including Sir John Templeton and Dr. Charles Harper), which funded the grant.

Several friends, colleagues, and students have read over sections of this book, and I have greatly benefited from their remarks. My heartfelt thanks to all of you, including David Brown, Sarah Coakley, John Culp, Jeanne Dahl (my excellent TA!), Steve Davis, Steve Evans, Gordon Fee, Bill Hasker, Brian Hebblethwaite, Chuck Hughes, Tom Lindell, Lynn Losie, E. J. Lowe, Randy Maddox, Ralph Martin, Ernan McMullin, Kirsten Mebust, Carey Newman, Gerry O'Collins, Tom Oord, Steve Palmquist, Sharon Pearson, Sam Powell, Bruce Reichenbach, Gary Simpson, Paul Sponheim, Richard Swinburne, Dennis Temple, and Steve Wilkens. Any remaining errors in this text should be attributed not to my friends, but to my remaining irrational doxastic practices.

I enjoyed talking over some of these chapters, in earlier forms, with the Doctoral Student Association, and with the theology Ph.D. colloquium, here at Luther Seminary. I thank all those who attended and paid such kind attention to my work. Indeed, Luther is a welcoming academic community of faith, for which this Methodist and Californian is grateful to God. Finally, I want to thank my beloved, Sally Bruyneel, a most wonderful and understanding wife. She is a gift from God to my life and heart.

I dedicate this book to four teachers and mentors in Christ whom I now count among my friends: Steve Davis, Dennis McNutt, Tom Oden, and Richard Swinburne. Thank you for all you have taught me, for your model of Christian scholarship, and for your friendship over the years.

Trinity Sunday, 2002   A.G.P.

Introduction

We are living in exciting times for those interested in the interplay between religion and science. In recent years, there has been a tremendous growth of interest in the subject, reflected in conferences, journal articles, books, Web pages, degree programs, and even new posts in universities focusing on this growing field.[1] This book is written for anyone who has done some hard thinking about both religion and science and would like to reflect more fully on conceptual issues and theological or philosophical problems that the current dialogue brings up. My participation in this movement has led to a growing conviction that philosophy has a role to play in the religion and science dialogue. Its purpose is to create a congenial philosophical atmosphere in which theology and science can go beyond dialogue to collegiality. I call my metaphor for the relationship between science and religion the "collegial metaphor" because I would like to see religion and science working together to help us understand our world and ourselves more fully. My proposal is neither descriptive of how things have been nor prescriptive of the way things must be. I write in a suggestive mood, putting forward one way of thinking about religion and science which I think will be helpful in the long run. The collegial metaphor is relevant for our work in developing a satisfactory worldview; religion and science need to work together here. Within the context of each intellectual discipline (that is, within the academy) I also call for a "mutuality model." I argue that the special sciences and theology, even though they have

1. For a good overview, with an extensive bibliography, see Jitse van der Meer, ed., *Facets of Faith and Science,* 4 vols. (Lanham, Md.: University Press of America, 1996).

their own domains as disciplines, can rationally influence each other, in special situations, without giving up their own important distinctives and methods.

In his excellent overview of the religion-science dialogue, Ian Barbour, one of the world's foremost experts in this interdisciplinary debate, discusses four models for the different ways that religion and science have come together.[2] These have become something of a standard starting place for those who wish, as I do, to think more fully about how theology and science can relate. His four models are independence, conflict, dialogue, and integration. The mutuality model we will develop here lies between dialogue and full integration. The integration I seek lies at the level of worldview, which is exactly where science and religion should work together.

Almost fifty years ago, the evolutionary ecologist L. Charles Birch made a similar argument in his article "Creation and the Creator." Birch then argued that "metaphysics is the ground on which scientist and theologian can meet."[3] The collegial metaphor, in which scientist and theologian can work together, is a development of Birch's point. Science and theology need to work together to improve our worldview. I have decided to speak of worldviews, rather than metaphysics, because the latter term is narrower. A worldview is, broadly, our understanding of who we are and of the world we live in, including our system of values and our religious beliefs. The sciences do not themselves, taken as a whole, create a worldview. Rather, various worldviews can ground and interpret the special sciences in their own unique ways. I use "worldview" in a broad and flexible way and allow that various communities of faith will develop differing worldviews. Indeed, people within the same broad worldview will have important differences among them. While Christians share a broad Christian worldview, for example, there are important differences within that larger, shared tradition. The same diversity holds true for any philosophy or religion.

Our worldview, then, is the level where we grow and develop a satisfactory philosophy of life based upon the best from religion and

---

2. Ian Barbour, *Religion in an Age of Science* (San Francisco: Harper and Row, 1990).

3. L. Charles Birch, "Creation and the Creator," *Journal of Religion* 37 (1957): 85-98; reprinted in Ian Barbour, ed., *Science and Religion* (London: SCM, 1968), where the quotation appears on p. 199.

modern science. And our world needs just such wisdom to face the challenges of the next millennium. These challenges often come from the use of new technologies, though other problems are as old as humanity itself. Hatred, racism, and poverty still plague our nations, but added to these perennial problems are the growing difficulties related to science and technology. These modern difficulties include the disappearance of the rain forests, massive extinction of species, global warming, the use of nuclear power, global capitalism, genetic engineering, and the destructive power of nuclear weapons and high-tech instruments of war. It is now possible for us to manipulate our genes directly, or even to destroy all life on this planet.

For too long the conflict or warfare model has dominated the debate between religious faith and scientific knowledge. This division has not helped our culture find truth and wisdom. My conviction is that we need both religious and scientific truth. Since we are interested in the truth and wisdom that comes from religion, I will tend to use in my comparisons with science the term "theology" rather than "religion." Both are legitimate forms of knowledge, but they are very different in the ways and means they seek the truth.

For the most part, I write as a Christian theologian and philosopher of science. What I say here I hope will be found useful by people of goodwill everywhere from any and all types of religious traditions. But my own tradition is the one I know best, and the one out of which I think most naturally. Those readers kind enough to make their way through these chapters, who worship other gods or none at all, should still find something to think about and learn from in this volume.

Perhaps a brief overview of the argument I make in this book will help set the stage for our journey into the details. The first chapter, which develops the mutuality model more fully, is really the heart of the whole book. I argue for a "levels of explanation" approach to the sciences but advocate the idea that different levels can influence each other. This influence includes, in the right circumstances, theory evaluation based upon our worldview commitments (including religious ones). I argue that such evaluation is rational in any special science where differing theories are, for the moment, epistemically equal in validity given the data and standards of that discipline.

The second chapter develops a philosophical approach to both science and religion which makes their collegial relationship most natural. This I call "dialectical realism," which in effect is critical realism that takes dialectics seriously. This brings in a communal and historical dimension to our epistemology. I also argue for a realist ontology for both theology and the sciences. This is rather unfashionable in our postmodern times, but I think there are important reasons to hold on to a sophisticated version of realism, namely, dialectical realism.

The third and fourth chapters set forth the relationship between science and worldviews more fully. In the third chapter, I argue against a modern myth that we have in the social sciences and religious studies a neutral and value-free scientific approach to the study of religion. My focus is on Jesus and the recent explosion of books about the historical Jesus. The historical claim of his resurrection is a good place to look at the role of values and presuppositions in critical historiography. In the fourth chapter I give a brief overview of the reasons why modern philosophers of science have come to reject the notion of pure objectivity and rationality even in the natural sciences. We look at Thomas Kuhn's notion of a paradigm and also discuss the nature of a worldview. I argue, against scientism, that the natural sciences cannot ground their own presuppositions and epistemic values, since those things make science possible in the first place. For these things we need to turn to our (various and different) worldviews, which themselves represent various philosophical and religious traditions. Drawing upon Wilhelm Dilthey and Ludwig Wittgenstein, I discuss the nature of worldviews and their role in everyday life. Our task, then, is to develop a scientific and religious worldview, which grounds our epistemic and moral values. As part of this latter argument, I critique the notion of "methodological naturalism" and "intelligent design" in the sciences.

Chapters Five and Six turn to focus on theological method. Having rejected scientism in the philosophy of science, I turn upon rationalism in theological method. My major conversation partner is process theology. I propose that theology is rightly ordered when it places Scripture first and then looks to tradition for criteria and norms, followed by reason and experience, which is where philosophy and science (among other things) fit in. This theological method (the so-called Wesleyan Quadrilateral) I contrast with "ontotheology" and the rationalism of some process theologians in the Methodist tradition. This leads into a chapter on the nature of theology. I argue that theology, done properly, is a form of worship. I discuss three publics for theology: God, the people of God, and all people interested in Christianity. Distinguishing theology from religious studies, I note that theology is interested in the truth about God (or Ultimate Reality), and so goes beyond social science and religious studies.

Chapters Seven and Eight give focused examples of the mutuality model. Chapter Seven looks at time from both a theological and a physical perspective. I argue that our worldview gives us good reason to interpret modern physics in a particular way, one that comes more from thermodynamics than from mechanics. I also introduce, in a popular way, some aspects of that area of science. This is a project in the hermeneutics of science and the role of religion and worldview in that process. The next chapter is an exploration of the role that historical science can and should play in Christology. In this example, science (history) is shown to influence theology (Christology). These chapters taken together illustrate the mutuality model at work.

Chapter Nine is a concluding summary. Finally, I indulge myself in a rather technical appendix on the problem of induction after the collapse of classical foundationalism. The arguments I make throughout this book are grounded, to some extent, in this proposed answer to the classical puzzle posed by David Hume.

I have written this book in a style which, I hope, is readable and clear. Any intelligent and learned person interested in the religion and science debate, of whatever specialization, should be able to read and understand it. That, at least, is my aim. If you come away with a greater appreciation for the links between theology and science, for the importance of developing a worldview that is both religious and scientific, and for the possibilities of improving our understanding of God and creation, then the effort will have been worthwhile.

1 Developing a Collegial Metaphor: The Mutuality of Theology and Science

This chapter develops the major theme of our current study, that is, the ways in which theology and the sciences interact and yet remain distinct. I call my model for interaction the "mutuality model" and distinguish it from other models, most importantly the conflict or warfare model. In later chapters, I will develop the mutuality model through two focused examples, natural science (thermodynamics) and social science (history). The leitmotiv is that both theology and the sciences, like all academic disciplines, can influence each other through larger schemes of thought, that is, through metaphysics and worldviews.

In the late Middle Ages, the relationship between theology and natural philosophy (or science) was understood as that of a queen to her handmaidens. In the nineteenth century, a warfare model was popular in many circles. As I look at the ways in which, in my view, theology and science should work together, I can see the need for a new metaphor. My proposed metaphor is that of co-workers or colleagues: theology and the sciences work together, each respecting the other, but understanding their different tasks. I will call this a "collegial metaphor," since I hope that the sciences and theology may become colleagues, listening to each other and learning from one another. The image of colleague goes beyond the image of dialogue because of the notion of work or task; both theology and science are needed in the task of developing a worldview that will meet the needs of twenty-first-century women and men.

A major intellectual issue facing religious scholars in our time, and in the next century, is the relationship between faith and our academic commitments. The natural and social sciences, in particular, can be places where our theological commitments seem out of place. Can a Christian (for example) be a good sociologist or biologist without splitting her mind into two boxes? While we often hear of the integration of faith and learning, there is plenty of room for further careful discussion of the proper relationship between faith and rational knowledge. One purpose of this book is to answer these questions. I hope to persuade you that we can integrate both theology and the sciences in a broad religious worldview. To this end, we will explore avenues in theology, philosophy, and social and natural science to ground and illustrate the mutuality of theology and science. I will argue that a two-way dialogue can and should take place between theology and the sciences in which they legitimately influence each other. In pursuing this conclusion we will canvass the nature of explanation and levels of explanation in theology and the sciences. I shall conclude that large-scale explanations of reality are the place where theology and the sciences can best learn from each other and work together as colleagues.

On what basis can theology claim to have anything in common with the sciences? To start with, I must depart from the grand tradition of calling theology a kind of "science." I will use the word "science" to indicate academic disciplines that are fundamentally empirical in nature. While I agree with (among others) Nancey Murphy that theology shares some common elements with science, I cannot agree that this makes theology a science.[1] While academic theology is a rigorous and scholarly activity yielding knowledge, it is not a merely empirical study since it is based upon special revelation. Theology arises out of religious faith and seeks to meet the needs of the human heart. It seeks wisdom about how we can live happily and well in the world, but such wisdom is also grounded in the truth about ultimate concerns. What then do theology and science have in common? As John Polkinghorne argues in many books, there is only one world.[2] Both the theologian and the scientist are concerned about the truth concerning that one world. What is real? What is true? How do things work? How can we

---

1. See Nancey Murphy, *Theology in an Age of Scientific Reasoning* (Ithaca, N.Y.: Cornell University Press, 1990).

2. See *One World* (London: SPCK, 1986), *Science and Creation* (London: SPCK, 1988), *Science and Providence* (London: SPCK, 1989), *Reason and Religion* (London: SPCK, 1991).

understand ourselves and the world? These are the kind of larger questions about reality around which theology and the sciences can build a dialogue.

Do Theology and Science Conflict?

For too long in the modern period, theology and the special sciences (that is, the natural and social sciences) were seen as being at war with one another. This perspective, called the conflict model by Ian Barbour,[3] dominated the thinking of Enlightenment rationalists. These overconfident believers in the triumph of science accepted the general cult of progress found in Western culture from the early modern period until the world wars. A good example of one such true believer in scientific progress was Andrew D. White (1832-1918), the first president of Cornell University. Cornell was the first private university founded in this country on purely secular principles, the implicit judgment being that religious bias warps the quest for scientific truth. White helped make the conflict model popular through his *A History of the Warfare of Science with Theology* (1896). In the minds of "enlightened" and truly "scientific" thinkers (as they thought of themselves), religion too often resulted in an unnecessary bias that presented an obstacle to scientific progress.

Alas, this warfare model (with science ever victorious!) is not a relic of the past. Numerous contemporary publications still advocate such a position, working from either a secular humanist or a scientific materialist perspective. A striking example is the article by Norman and Lucia Hall entitled "Is the War between Science and Religion Over?" which appeared in *The Humanist*. The Halls insist that

> While it may appear open-minded, modest, and comforting to many, this conciliatory view [that seeks harmony between religion and science] is nonsense. Science and religion are diametrically opposed at their deepest philosophical levels. And, because the two worldviews make claims to the same intellectual territory — that of

3. Ian Barbour, *Religion in an Age of Science* (San Francisco: Harper and Row, 1990), p. 4.

the origin of the universe and humankind's relationship to it — conflict is inevitable.[4]

Science and religion are not, however, diametrically opposed, as the Halls state. Their article unfortunately perpetuates the usual errors made in popular works by scientific materialists. In particular, they continue to confuse science with their own philosophy or worldview. They need to reflect on the fact that *science is not a worldview*. The relationship between science and worldview is one we will develop more fully in a later chapter. For now, it is enough to realize that natural science yields facts and theories about creation; but facts and theories alone do not constitute a worldview. The worldview of the Halls is scientific materialism or naturalism. It is this materialistic worldview — not the teachings of science, but a secular philosophy — that is deeply in conflict with religion. The ideals and teachings of modern science are in fact compatible with many religious worldviews, including a Christian one.

The warfare model misunderstands the character of both theology and science. Science simply cannot answer the questions that are addressed in religion, nor can religion hope to answer merely scientific questions from its basis of faith. Religion answers questions about ultimate concerns and spiritual or moral conundrums. The special sciences are concerned with factual issues concerning the natural and human world and with the interpretation of human actions and institutions. There is some overlap, of course, but there should be no ultimate conflict between the sciences and religion.

While it is certainly true that prejudice, in the guise of religious faith, has opposed scientific advance, the warfare model overlooks the important contributions that theology has made to science, especially at the level of presuppositions and worldview. The warfare model ignores the historical fact that there might not be any such thing as modern Western science if it were not for the intellectual influence of the

---

4. Norman F. and Lucia Hall, "Is the War between Science and Religion Over?", *The Humanist* 46, no. 3 (May-June 1986): 26. A more recent example of this same point of view is Michael Shermer (director of the Skeptics Society), *How We Believe: The Search for God in an Age of Science* (New York: W. H. Freeman, 2000). He asserts, for example, that "science is based upon the philosophy of naturalism" (p. 131), a historically false if rather common opinion.

Christian faith. In his Lowell Lectures, Alfred North Whitehead notes the contributions of theology to the development of science in our cultural history.[5] His view has been corrected by more recent historical investigation,[6] but the main point remains: Christian theology provided the intellectual environment out of which natural science was able to develop. By founding a worldview in which reason and order were understood to be built into the world by a rational God, theology helped to create the intellectual nursery in which early modern science was born and raised. The history of science contains many examples that support this conclusion. Just in physics alone, Copernicus, Kepler, Newton, and James Clerk Maxwell were all influenced in their understanding of the rationality of creation by the Christian worldview. Of course, to suggest that Christianity alone is responsible for the rise of early modern science, or that science could not have arisen without Christian faith, is too simplistic a hypothesis. Many factors were involved, but belief in a rational and mathematical Creator was certainly central. To explore the soundness of this historical conclusion concerning the helpfulness of theology to science, let us consider more fully the example of Galileo, the man adherents of the warfare model quite often refer to.

Galileo Galilei (1564-1642) was a brilliant scientist whose work has influenced human culture and fundamentally shaped our understanding of the world. He made significant advances in many areas of natural science and is justly famous for his work in physics and astronomy. His major methodological contributions to the founding of modern science were his careful experimental method and his insistence on the mathematical form of natural philosophy. While others engaged in mathematical work and in various kinds of experimentation, "before Galileo, the systematic appeal to experience in support of mathemati-

---

5. Alfred North Whitehead, *Science and the Modern World* (New York: Macmillan, 1925), chap. 1. Many other scholars have argued this same point, although some of their works are marred by apologetic certainty that science could *only* have arisen in a theistic environment (e.g., Stanley L. Jaki, *The Road of Science and the Ways to God* [Chicago: University of Chicago Press, 1978]).

6. See Ed Grant, *The Foundations of Modern Science in the Middle Ages* (Cambridge: Cambridge University Press, 1996); David Lindberg, *The Beginnings of Western Science* (Chicago: University of Chicago Press, 1992); and David Lindberg and R. Numbers, eds., *God and Nature* (Berkeley: University of California Press, 1986).

cal laws seems to have been lacking."[7] Traces of the methods Galileo embraced can in fact be found in medieval science, but Galileo was certainly decisive in the development of early modern science and the "new method" of mathematical models supported and tested by experimental data.

True, Galileo's work was opposed by Christian thinkers in his own day, and especially by conservative factions in the Roman Catholic Church. Often overlooked, however, is the fact that Galileo, like Kepler and Newton, was a Christian thinker who understood himself to be a "Catholic astronomer."[8] As Stanley Jaki notes, "Little if any effort is made, for instance, to recall the role played in Galileo's scientific methodology by his repeated endorsements of the naturalness of perceiving the existence of God from the study of the book of nature."[9]

The influence of the Christian worldview on Galileo is clear from his tract on the relationship between biblical hermeneutics and natural science, published under the title *Letter to the Grand Duchess Christina* (1615). For Galileo, the great "book" of nature and the book of Scripture equally reveal the greatness of God. Mathematical models and laws govern the physical universe because it is created by God. In turn, we can discover these laws through empirical research:

> I think that in the discussion of physical problems we ought to begin not from the authority of scriptural passages, but from sense-experience and necessary demonstrations; for the Holy Bible and the phenomena of nature proceed alike from the divine Word, the former as the dictate of the Holy Ghost and the latter as the observational executrix of God's commands.[10]

In our Western history, many factors worked together to aid in the development of natural science and technology. The Christian faith was one of these factors. From Galileo we learn that theology and science are not enemies but different ways to the truth of God.

---

7. Stillman Drake, *Galileo Studies* (Ann Arbor: University of Michigan Press, 1970), p. 44.

8. Galileo Galilei, *Discoveries and Opinions of Galileo,* trans. and ed. Stillman Drake (Garden City, N.Y.: Anchor, 1957), p. 168.

9. Jaki, *Road of Science,* p. 47.

10. Galileo, *Discoveries,* p. 182 (from the *Letter to the Grand Duchess Christina*).

What, then, do we understand the proper model of the relationship between theology and science to be? Our brief glance at Galileo would lead us in the direction of an open dialogue between theology and the sciences, in which Christian scholars seek to build a worldview consistent with both. I am calling this the "collegial metaphor." Theology must take its factual and empirical basis from the best of contemporary science, but it may offer a basis for correcting interpretations of science or preferring one view over another within a scientific discipline. In a similar manner, science can be guided or brought into question by theological conclusions. Our quest thus becomes the search for the truth in both disciplines, in order to develop a coherent worldview that meets our religious needs *and* satisfies our scientific thirst for knowledge.

The Nature of Explanation

In order to develop this mutuality model and collegial metaphor for the relationship between science and theology, we must look more closely at the nature of explanation. Explanation is an important, even central, idea in the quest for knowledge and understanding, a fact which raises the issue of the nature of explanation in science and theology. Such an approach to the theology-science dialogue will afford us the opportunity to explore theological explanation in contrast to other kinds. In this way we can develop a model of mutual learning and edification between theology and science in the development of a coherent worldview. This intellectual exploration will lead us to three conclusions: (1) Theological explanation is similar to explanation in the natural and social sciences in that it develops models for a causal explanation, positing certain entities with certain natures, powers, and relationships. (2) Theology assumes the findings of other disciplines in its explanatory scheme, and as such the natural and social sciences influence theology. In the same way the findings of theology may send us back to the other disciplines to rethink the basis of our scientific conclusions and change our minds. (3) A consideration of the nature of levels of explanations, or explanatory schemes (also called "paradigms"), leaves an open place for a two-way dialogue that can and should take place between theology and the other disciplines of the university.

First we need to reflect on just what an "explanation" is. Broadly conceived, an explanation is some answer to a "why?" question.[11] More narrowly understood, explanations tell us why the world is the way it is: why rivers run downhill, why clocks run slower in the presence of greater gravity, why the tides rise and fall, why all the members of the orchestra arrived at roughly the same time and place for the performance, and so forth. It is this sort of "explanation" of why things are the way they are, and why things happen as they do, that we are now interested in.

These short remarks lead us to another question: what counts as knowledge or *scientia* in the sense of scientific explanation? In the tradition of Aristotle,[12] perhaps it is best to see a "cause" as some reason for being, and thus an explanation will be any answer to a question about why a thing is, or how it got to be that way, or why things happen as they do. Scientific explanations, then, are (in part) causal accounts answering our "why" questions. Yet not all scientific explanation is causal. For example, neither Newton's nor Einstein's laws for gravitation are causal, because they stipulate the mathematical laws that govern gravitational interaction but do not tell us what *causes* gravitational attraction. Instead, various theories of quantum gravity are now being tested, and if confirmed they will tell us the causes. What the example of gravity indicates is this: explanation without a causal account is incomplete. Scientists will continue to seek a full scientific explanation, which will include a causal element in the explanatory theory. Not all scientific explanation is causal, but causation is an integral element in explanation in the sciences. This is, of course, not the only way to understand scientific explanation, but it is the most promising view as well as the one in accord with common sense.[13]

11. This is the view of Sylvian Bromberger, "Why Questions," in *Mind and Cosmos: Essays in Contemporary Science and Philosophy*, ed. R. G. Colodny (Pittsburgh: University of Pittsburgh Press, 1966).

12. *Metaphysics*, bk. A.

13. Those who reject the idea that causation is an integral aspect of scientific explanation do so, for the most part, because of the many philosophical problems with this concept. Some of the finest minds in Western philosophy have struggled with this difficult philosophical problem and with the related problem of induction. I discuss the problem of induction later in this book (see the Appendix). See also R. G. Swinburne, ed., *The Justification of Induction* (New York: Oxford University Press, 1974) and especially two fine books by D. C. Stove, *Probability and Hume's Inductive Scepticism* (Oxford: Clarendon, 1973), and *The Rationality of Induction* (Oxford: Clarendon, 1986).

Levels of Explanation in Science

In my view, dialogue between theology and the special sciences is best understood as taking place between different levels of explanation.[14] Before we can even begin to discuss levels of explanation in the sciences, however, we must consider the case of reductionism or "nothing-buttery," as Donald MacKay was fond of calling it.[15] My philosophical approach is post-Enlightenment, or "postmodern," which among other things implies a holistic approach to our understanding of reality. Logical positivists and other modernists often held that things must be dissected and reduced to their most simple parts in order to be understood. A post-Enlightenment philosophy will insist that the whole is more than the sum of the parts.

Let us take a concrete example of this kind of reductionism in explanation. F. H. Allport, in his discussion of the group psychology of crowds in his book *Social Psychology,* wrote that

> given the *situation of the crowd* — that is, of a number of persons within stimulating distance of one another — we shall find that the actions of all *are* nothing more than the sum of the actions of each taken separately.[16]

Now clearly there is something correct here. The action of a crowd is, ontologically, the sum of the actions of each member. But reductionism of this sort ignores an important explanatory (that is, an epistemological) dimension: even if we can explain each person's act individually, what still escapes explanation is the larger question of why these individuals all act in a like manner, together, as a unit. What needs an

14. On levels of explanation in science, see Donald MacKay, "'Complementarity' in Theology and Science," *Zygon* 9 (1974): 225-44; Polkinghorne, *One World;* Arthur Peacocke, *Theology for a Scientific Age* (Minneapolis: Fortress, 1993); J. A. Fodor, "Special Sciences," *Synthese* 28 (1974): 97-115; David Owens, "Levels of Explanation," *Mind* 98 (1989): 59-79; M. J. McDonald, "Exploring 'Levels of Explanation' Concepts, I and II," *Perspectives on Science and Christian Faith* 41 (1989): 194-205, and 42 (1990): 23-33; and Nancey Murphy and George Ellis, *On the Moral Nature of the Universe* (Minneapolis: Fortress, 1996).

15. See Donald M. MacKay, *The Clockwork Image* (Downers Grove, Ill.: InterVarsity, 1974), pp. 30-38.

16. F. H. Allport, *Social Psychology* (New York: Houghton Mifflin, 1924), p. 5, his italics.

explanation, then, are the similarities of group action or group think-ing. Such things cannot be explained by atomistic methods.

The history of physics, especially early on, illustrates a tendency toward reductionism and atomism in scientific explanations; yet even physics has been pushed into a more holistic frame of explanation in recent times. One example of this would be the physics of dynamical systems, or chaos theory; another would be thermodynamics. Perhaps the best-known example is quantum mechanics. Even though Einstein contributed to the early development of this area of physics, he did not agree with the anti-deterministic interpretation it was being given. He developed a famous thought experiment known as the Einstein-Podolsky-Rosen paradox (EPR) to show the counterintuitive nature of quantum mechanics. Recently, the EPR result has been given experi-mental verification, and the thought experiment has actually been per-formed in a lab. The entire discussion is rather complex, but it seems that subatomic particles can communicate with each other as a holistic system, even though such signals are forbidden by the Special Theory of Relativity when we consider each particle independently. The EPR result has caused us to give up "Einstein locality" for subatomic sys-tems, and to treat them in a holistic way.

Biology and psychology, as well, are disciplines that raise the is-sue of levels of explanatory schemes most clearly.[17] The activities of living organisms can be "explained" from a variety of different per-spectives. Why animals eat, for example, could be approached from a physical, chemical/thermodynamic, biological, or psychological scheme. It is not clear that any one of these points of view would nec-essarily be *the* correct one. They are all equally valid in terms of their own discipline. A physical scientist might focus on the chemical, espe-cially the molecular, need for energy. This in turn could lead to an ex-planation of the living organism in terms of a thermodynamic system. A biologist might focus her explanation on the biological organism as a whole and its relations to other living things in the ecosystem. Yet again, an animal psychologist would assume the truth of these other explanations, using them as assumptions to discuss the complex in-

---

17. See also Arthur Peacocke, *Creation and the World of Science* (Oxford: Clarendon, 1979), but his understanding of these levels sometimes conflates levels of being (scien-tific ontology) with levels of explanation (epistemology).

teractions between the individual, the group, other competitive species, and the natural environment in the description of eating habits of a particular species (say, spider monkeys) in particular environments (say, a given forest).

Once we grant that there are different sorts of schemes for explaining the same thing, and that they do not reduce to each other, this raises the question of their interrelationship. Since the sort of explanation we have in mind is causal, these schemes postulate certain causal relationships that hold between things. They develop models for the nature and powers of the things involved, their regular causal relations, laws describing the regularities in these relations, and general theories. What happens, it seems, is that some levels are more fundamental than others in the following sense: the accepted results of the scheme at the more fundamental level are used, and assumed, in the next level up. So particle physics is assumed in thermodynamics, and psychology and sociology are assumed in history.

It is also possible, although not as common as one might like, for there to be a two-way dialogue between levels of explanatory schemes. A good example of this is the case of gravity: the occurrence of gravitational force at one level has led physicists to look for gravity waves, or gravitons, at a lower level. Particle physics has also learned a great deal from solid-state physics (especially the phenomenon of superconductivity) even though particle physicists in the past have been known to disdain their "squalid-state" siblings. Another interesting example is chaos or dynamical systems theory, a view that developed in meteorology (a higher-level physical science) but that has great implications for other levels of physical, as well as biological, science.

Dialogue between levels is based not only on the fact that the more fundamental level is assumed in the higher, but also on the fact that findings in the higher levels can cause us to turn back to the more fundamental levels to rethink our results and assumptions. Chaos theory is an excellent example of this from recent science. The argument of this chapter is that the same sort of thing is possible in the theology-science dialogue.

The social sciences use causal explanations, but of course they also use other types of understanding. The general confusion as to the nature of understanding in the social sciences is in part the result of there being three types of understanding at work in the social sciences:

(1) ordinary causal explanations based on natural sciences; (2) socio-psychological causal explanations based on social and psychological forces, conventions, and complex background influences (this area deals with a quite different kind of causal "power" from the first); and (3) a hermeneutical concern for interpretation or understanding, for example, in sociology or history.[18] It is quite important for the kinds of understanding found in (2) and (3) that we deal with human beliefs, intentions, desires, drives, and the like (both for individuals and for collectives) and not merely with physical causal structures. We cannot possibly consider all the issues here, even briefly. The main point is that, while the social sciences involve more than simply causal explanation, causal explanation is an important element of social science which cannot be reduced to or subsumed under "understanding" (#3 above).

The social sciences likewise illustrate the fact that whether one explanatory scheme is more fundamental than another is not always clear. The metaphor of "levels" can and does break down as we begin interdisciplinary research, for the interrelationship may be more complex than our simple levels model. With psychology and sociology, for example, neither one seems obviously higher than the other. Both disciplines use explanatory schemes that assume the results of the other. There can be a mutuality of interaction, then, one scheme acting as fundamental to the other scheme and/or discipline in some respects but not in others. The basic point is that one science can and does influence the other because the results of one science form part of the background against which theories and explanations are created and evaluated.

Before considering the case of explanation in theology we should ponder what counts as explanation. How does a set of beliefs or ideas (the *explanans*) "explain" some phenomena (the *explanandum*)? The

---

18. I would therefore reject the view of Wolfhart Pannenberg, *Theology and the Philosophy of Science* (Philadelphia: Westminster, 1976), that the social and natural sciences are both hermeneutical, that both seek "coherence," and that these considerations alone serve to fully explicate scientific method. What such a view ignores is specifically the causal element I am emphasizing, an element quite different from the concern of "meaning" in hermeneutics. So it is not enough to simply state, as Stephen Toulmin does (*Foresight and Understanding* [Bloomington: Indiana University Press, 1961], p. 81), that natural scientific explanation amounts to placing an event in a context in which it is intelligible. Such an opinion is correct but incomplete.

view of Carl Hempel, whose work is seminal in the field, is that the *explanans* is a type of argument and must include a covering law or law of nature.[19] In this theory, the *explanandum* is deduced from the law, along with certain other facts such as initial conditions and observational sentences. This received view has, however, come under serious philosophical attack. For the most part, this view confuses logical connections (in arguments) with the kind of physical or psycho-social connections that we are concerned with in the natural and social sciences. Further, many philosophers have pointed out that equally good deductions can be made from *"explanans"* that do not explain anything. For example, given a situation in which the morning sun is casting the shadow of a flagpole on the ground, we can "explain" the position of the sun in the sky (according to the received view) by the length of the shadow! But that is absurd. Something is missing here, pointing to a problem in the received view.

What is missing from the covering-law view is a notion of causal connection. Those who were raised with logical positivism tend to have an allergy to metaphysics, even after logical positivism had been overthrown. But explanations are always attached to some metaphysical commitments, as David-Hillel Ruben persuasively argues.[20] Causation is an ineliminable element of scientific explanation.

Many of the various theories of scientific explanation are, like Hempel's, empirical and predictive. On such theories, something counts as an explanation if it yields a prediction of how events of that type will turn out. We use explanations, then, to manipulate the outcome of events. The best explanation is "empirically adequate," that is, explains observed phenomena and allows the manipulation or prediction of future observed events.[21] We are not in fact committed, intellectually, to the acceptance of nonobservable entities and relations posited in scientific theories. There are problems with such views. An emphasis on prediction and experiment seems adequate for some types of science, but in many cases explanations can be given for events that

19. Carl Hempel, *Philosophy of Natural Science* (Englewood Cliffs, N.J.: Prentice-Hall, 1966).

20. David-Hillel Ruben, *Explaining Explanation* (London: Routledge, 1990). Ruben also provides an extensive bibliography on this topic.

21. As, for example, Bas van Fraasen argues in *The Scientific Image* (Oxford: Oxford University Press, 1980).

are past (as in geology or paleontology or cosmology) or that are singular and unique (as in archeology or history or textual criticism). An explanation can tell us why a certain event occurred, even if it only happened once. An explanation, therefore, does not have to be predictive.

With respect to the empiricism common in many circles: there is no reason, other than prejudice, to limit ontology to what humans can observe. That seems, in fact, to be rather anthropocentric. Reality is not limited to observable phenomena, as we will argue more fully in the chapter on dialectical realism. Paleontologists posit the existence of nonobserved animals, for example, to explain the fossil records. I, for one, believe in dinosaurs (a bon mot I borrow from Ernan McMullin). The restriction of *explanantia* that deserve rational acceptance to observable (or observable-in-principle) things is artificial, and discredited by the actual history of science where previously unobserved things have in fact become observed (e.g., germs). The extreme empiricism of such views is an example of the futile attempt to avoid metaphysical commitments in philosophy of science.

One last theory deserves mention. According to it, scientific explanation is understood as any larger story or intellectual framework that "makes sense" of the *explananda* or makes them intelligible. The problem here is that this view is too broad; it allows too many frameworks that are pseudo-scientific or even unreasonable (astrology, for example, or voodoo, or Velikovsky) to pass as *scientific* explanations. The weakness of Pannenberg's excellent book *Theology and the Philosophy of Science* lies in his following this overly vague conception of scientific explanation.[22]

The basic problem with all of these theories can be found in two root issues: (1) the vain attempt to avoid induction in the philosophy of science and/or (2) the equally forlorn attempt to describe scientific explanation without recourse to causation. Covering laws, pragmatic usefulness, intelligibility, prediction: all these have a place in scientific explanation, but they are not the whole story, any more than causation is. The addition of induction and causation overcomes some of the prob-

---

22. Pannenberg, *Theology and the Philosophy*, pp. 143-55. Pannenberg attempts to subsume causal explanation under the banner of hermeneutical understanding — a category error that results in a mistaken notion of what counts as theological explanation (pp. 326-45).

lems of the theories we have just been covering. This leaves us, then, with a view of explanation that is causal and inductive.

Theological Explanation

Is there something like "explanation" of this sort to be found in theology? There certainly are many types of explanation and understanding, as we have just seen. All scholars should agree with the idea that theology can explain things in some sense of the term "explain." Theology can explain why people act the way they do, for example, in the same way that any ideology can be utilized in a social scientific explanation. Theology can also explain the set of beliefs that one finds in a particular religious tradition, without any commitment to the truth of those beliefs. Our entire discussion of levels of explanation, however, brings up the idea that theology might explain things in a causal way as well.[23]

Ludwig Wittgenstein and some of his followers have been persuasive in arguing that religion is not really any kind of explanation. Even if it is false, however, religion is not just a simple mistake. Surely this much is true: religion is not an explanation for something.[24] Religious belief is much more complex than that. Likewise, language is much more complex than the simple notion of conveying information. What also must be said, in the spirit of dialectics, is that language does, after all, convey information; and there is an explanatory dimension to religious beliefs as well. A religious scheme such as astrology, for example, may not be a simple mistake, but it is still mistaken — is it not? Religious believers do recognize the impact of experience and reason on their belief systems, and do not always hold on to that system come what may. So D. Z. Phillips and company misunderstand the nature of religious belief when they deny it any explanatory dimension, even though they are correct in asserting that religion is not an explanation

---

23. This point about causation in theological explanation is also made, in differing ways, by Richard Swinburne, *The Existence of God* (Oxford: Clarendon, 1979); E. L. Schoen, *Religious Explanation* (London: Routledge, 1985); and Philip Clayton, *Explanation from Physics to Theology* (New Haven: Yale University Press, 1989). Swinburne has been criticized by Rob Prevost for focusing too much on causal explanation (*Probability and Theistic Explanation* [Oxford: Clarendon, 1990]).

24. See, e.g., D. Z. Phillips, *Religion Without Explanation* (Oxford: Blackwell, 1976).

of something in the way that, say, Darwinian evolution is. Specifically, certain elements in religion, especially those collected in theologies, do explain elements in the world.

But even if some elements of religion or theology are explanatory, surely we are not looking for a causal explanation, are we? In seeking to answer this question, we turn again to the notion of levels of explanation.

One dimension of theology is that of an academic discipline. As a rigorous investigation into the truth, theology seeks to organize religious beliefs into a satisfactory paradigm or explanatory scheme. There is a lot more to theology, of course, as we shall argue later in this book; but theology does seek to know the truth, and it also seeks explanations. As such, theology is concerned with the facts about God: other things are theologically important in their relationship with him.

Theological explanation is similar in some ways to the explanatory schemes of the natural and social sciences. Theology will develop models of the Ultimate Reality, its nature and powers, as well as models of other things in relationship to the divine (e.g., humans, the cosmos, the ecosphere). Theology seeks explanations, and as such it is devoted to the truth, as Pannenberg rightly argues. Theology always takes place, however, in a religious community. There is no generic theology, only, for example, Christian, Buddhist, or Muslim theology: the theology of particular religions. Even natural theology occurs *within* a particular religious tradition. So these twin concerns, truth and community, define the horizon of the theologian. As Tillich wrote,

> Theology moves back and forth between two poles, the eternal truth of its foundation and the temporal situation in which the eternal truth must be received. . . . [F]or the church is the "home" of systematic theology. Here alone do the sources and the norms of theology have actual existence.[25]

Theological explanation involves causal explanation, but not the same kind of causation that one finds in the sciences, any more than sociology uses the causal notions found in the natural sciences. Theology can and does use both natural and social causal explanations. The-

25. Paul Tillich, *Systematic Theology,* vol. I (Chicago: University of Chicago Press, 1951), pp. 3, 48.

ology can and does involve hermeneutical, ethical, and metaphysical issues from philosophy, and some of these can indeed be understood as a
kind of "explanation" (I grant this much to Pannenberg and Toulmin).
But in addition to these things, theology posits a unique God-world relationship (or Ultimate Reality-lifeworld relationship) on the basis of
which it seeks theological explanatory schemes for certain elements of
human existence and for certain elements of our knowledge of reality
derived from extra-religious sources. Because theology understands the
Ultimate Reality to be the most basic of all realities, the divine is used
as a metaphysical principle to explain some elements of reality. Within
theistic worldviews, God is understood to be an agent, and some aspects of our world are explained on the basis of divine agency. For example, the Christian doctrine of original sin, if true, is explanatory of
certain facts known to us through history, sociology, and psychology.
The doctrine of karma in Hinduism, likewise, is explanatory if true.
Surely the divine does bring about certain facts about the world, if religious explanations are to be accepted as true. Of course, if they are
merely interesting or pragmatically useful stories, then the study of religion is reduced to social science, and theological explanation per se
cannot occur.

What Theology Learns from Science

If I am on track in my suggestions about the nature of theological explanation, then we need to consider again our view of the theological
task. Theology is not merely an exercise in making sense of religious experience and beliefs in a particular community, as some would have us
believe. Such an exercise is important, of course, but is really an aspect
of the social sciences (witness the "religious studies" departments in
most universities). Theology is not just about religious being-in-the-
world, although it includes that. Theology is about God, and about
other beings in relationship to the divine. Theology does not seek to
develop only pragmatically useful models but also accurate models
whose pragmatic usefulness is one criterion — among others — of their
verisimilitude. Theology seeks the truth about the Transcendent, or,
more modestly, theology seeks adequate, reasonably accurate models
and theological principles that are reasonably held to be true. We do

not merely seek pragmatically successful God-talk, but we seek to discover the truth about God.

What seems to have happened in American theological circles is this: the source of knowledge has been confused with the subject of that knowledge. It is surely true that what we know about the divine comes to us through the religious experiences of ourselves and others. But this does not imply that the only subject of theology is religious experience. Scientific knowledge (say, in physics) is based on ordinary human experience but it is not about ordinary human experience. Likewise the rational, explanatory element in religion (which we call theology) is not about religious experience, but about the source and subject of those experiences (God or Ultimate Reality). Theology is about God, too, and not just about the human.

In seeking the truth about the divine, theology needs the other arts and sciences. In developing its models, theories, principles, and postulated causal relationships, it assumes the results of the other disciplines. This would include such fields as philosophy, sociology, physics, history, and aesthetics: in short, the whole of the university faculty. No wonder it is so difficult to be a theologian! Theologians do not require a comprehensive view of such fields, of course, any more than a botanist need be a biochemist just because botany depends upon the results of biochemistry; yet the results and views of these disciplines will shape our understanding of the nature of creation in its relation to the Creator. This is especially true of any large-scale explanations of reality that come from the special sciences. For example, behaviorism in psychology and determinism in philosophy have important theological implications. While these disciplines do indeed influence theology, they do so through the explanatory filter of religiously interpreted and founded scholarship. In the Christian tradition, this is Christian learning, or the Christian worldview. In other words, Christian theology is dependent for its own development upon Christian scholarship in other disciplines. These things taken all together generate for us a worldview that is both Christian and scientific. This basic point, which seems so modest, will take the rest of this book to develop, explain, and illustrate.

What Science Learns from Theology

What is not as often acknowledged by those considering the dialogue between theology and science is that theology should influence, if we are rational, our beliefs in other fields. The special sciences can and should learn from theology, and not just the other way around. If on theological grounds we have good reason to affirm the free will defense, say, then this should cause us to closely examine the evidence for behaviorism and determinism. If two or more theories in another discipline are currently of equal status with respect to their reasonableness, the religious believer is fully justified in choosing that view which is more in consonance with his theological worldview.[26] This means that Peter Berger plays too much the role of scientific positivist when he writes,

> Questions raised within the frame of an empirical discipline (and I would emphatically consider sociological theory to be within such a frame of reference) are not susceptible to answers coming out of the frame of reference of a non-empirical and normative discipline [i.e., theology], just as the reverse procedure is inadmissible. As such, the argument of this book stands or falls as an enterprise of sociological theorizing and, as such, is not amenable to either theological support or theological critique.[27]

Such a claim to hermetically seal off the disciplines from each other is empirically false as a historical hypothesis and methodologically unsound as a philosophy of science. There is some truth to Berger's pontification: theology, philosophy, and ethics do not pretend to tell the scientist what he must believe in terms of his own discipline. The truth must be discovered in each science by the canons of acceptability found within each discipline. Dogmatics does not want to be dogmatic in the negative sense! All I am suggesting is that the results of a more fundamental discipline can be called into question by a higher-level explanatory scheme, and that this can then send us back to the other dis-

---

26. This position is pressed by advocates of "Christian scholarship" in the university, such as Nicholas Wolterstorff, *Reason within the Bounds of Religion*, second ed. (Grand Rapids: Eerdmans, 1984) See further Chapter Four of this book.

27. Peter Berger, *The Sacred Canopy* (Garden City: Anchor, 1990 [1967]), p. 179.

cipline to argue — *on the basis of accepted scientific evidence and methods within that discipline* — for a different conclusion. This is in fact what happens in sciences from time to time in any case.

Theological, philosophical, and scientific evidence are all relevant to answering important worldview questions, and any attempt to hermetically seal-off these disciplines will lead to incoherence. Neither reality nor human reason can be so neatly sliced into pieces. Determinism, for example, is either true or false, and cannot be true "for science" but false "for religion." As realists (even as dialectical realists) we are committed to the unity of reality and therefore to the fruitfulness of seeking harmony among many voices and perspectives. There may well be times in which we cannot decide, given the complexity of a problem, what the truth is in a particular case. Scientific evidence and theological conclusions may lead in different directions, at least for the moment. Yet the conviction that they must be in harmony is grounded in the fact, long advocated by Christian tradition, that God is the Creator of the universe and the author of revelation. There is one God (or religious Reality) and one world, which we are all struggling to discover more fully.

Apart from specific conclusions and questions in which theology and science can reinforce each other, or (temporarily) conflict, what can science learn from theology? I will limit myself here to the theology I know best, Christianity. There are several theological conclusions that are important to the disciplines of the sciences: that God is the creator of the world and both rational and good, for example. This has been an important theological datum in the history of Western science. Other conclusions include that we can trust our senses, as well as the general view found throughout science that the world is understandable by human reasoning and experience. Science itself is good because knowledge is good, when it is used properly and in the service of God.

We cannot, however, live by science alone. The natural and social sciences are limited. They are unable to answer our deepest needs for meaning, values, and purpose, needs which are theological or philosophical in nature. So science is important but not all important. Science cannot save us. It is itself based upon important assumptions and values that it cannot justify in its own terms but must assume from other disciplines. There are fundamental presuppositions in science which the disciplines *own* but cannot *ground.* At the same time, very of-

ten in history science has caused theology to rethink its own conclusions and presuppositions. Hence, I believe the collegial model is the
one we should be aiming toward in the religion and science dialogue.
Each religious tradition and worldview can learn from, and in turn influence and inform, the special sciences. Our mutuality model, then, is
of theology and the sciences having a mutual dialogue, each discipline
learning from the other and both working together as colleagues. We
seek a philosophy of life that is intellectually adequate yet also satisfies
our ethical and existential needs. In such a quest all the disciplines
should work together.

In the following chapters, we will explore areas in philosophy,
theological method, social science, and natural science. Our overall
purpose is to spell out, and defend against misunderstanding, my proposal for a collegial metaphor and mutuality model in the religion-
science dialogue.

2 Dialectical Realism in Theology and Science

This chapter presents and defends the broad philosophical basis for the mutuality model developed in the rest of the book. The religion and science dialogue has important issues on its agenda that are constructive and substantial and not part of philosophy, but philosophy (along with the disciplines themselves) provides a framework or environment in which the debate takes place.[1] Some of the differences between various voices in this debate are at bottom philosophical differences rather than religious or scientific ones. I certainly do not think that philosophy should dominate this dialogue, but it can provide some useful clarifications and questions, especially given the current interest in postmodernity from all sectors of the academy. I agree with Wentzel van Huyssteen and Nancey Murphy, who in recent lectures have called for a postfoundational or postmodern epistemology, which should help create a philosophical space in which a fruitful dialogue and exchange between theology and the special sciences can continue.[2] Thus in this chapter we will explore my preferred framework for the mutuality model, which I call "dialectical realism." This exploration will include a look at the various kinds of realism and nonrealism, as well as the concept of dialectic important for the mutuality model. As

---

1. I stress the interdisciplinary ground for this discussion simply because no one academic discipline provides the common ground for the religion and science dialogue (not even philosophy!). "Turf wars" among specialists are odious, but alas all too common.

2. See Wentzel van Huyssteen, *Duet or Duel?* (London: SCM, 1998); Nancey Murphy, *Reconciling Theology and Science* (Kitchener, Ont.: Pandora, 1997). Both books represent lectures given in Canada.

part of a general defense of dialectical realism, I also summarize my view on the validity of informal reasoning.

In the previous chapter we developed a proposed collegial metaphor for the relationship between theology and the sciences, and philosophical issues have already raised their head. This should be expected. The current growth of literature on the dialogue between religion and science demonstrates the needs for a sound philosophical framework for this dialogue. Different models of the proper relationship between religion and science are often based upon different philosophies. In this chapter, I hope to set forth the philosophical frame within which a mutuality model for theology and science can best be pursued. Other philosophical frameworks are possible, of course, but this one is a particular proposal for grounding the mutuality model in epistemology, philosophy of science, and metaphysics.

Perhaps we should begin with, of all things, a defense of definitions. Some recent philosophical thinking would call into question any attempt at definition. All terms are fragmented and all reference is at best partial, the followers of such thinking assert. The word "essentialism" is sometimes invoked as a kind of rhetorical slam on the attempt to arrive at a working definition. We need to state at the outset, then, that definitions of theology, natural science, worldview, and the like in this book are not meant to cover every use these terms have had in all Western discourse since the time of Socrates! Rather, my use of definitions is meant to create a working handle, a pointer to an aspect of reality, a sign that for the sake of convenience we will call by this name, in this text. The terms "religion" and "science" are contested, and their use varies from time to time, author to author, place to place. I am not suggesting that my own working definitions are the only ones possible, nor have we reached into the "essence of reality" by putting forth a definition. But anyone who studies a subject, even a postmodern thinker, works with an implied definition of that subject matter. Otherwise any and all things — and therefore nothing at all! — would be the subject of their analysis. Someone writing a history of science brings some things and not others to the table, for example, however much they may put science into a broad cultural framework, and even if they refuse to give a definition of science. Avoiding definitions is no way to make progress in philosophy, and so we will continue the practice, perhaps with some sobering reflections on the abuse and misuse of the practice of giving definitions to temper our judgment.

The problem of definitions recapitulates epistemology in a nut-shell. It makes a good entrée into the issues surrounding human knowledge. How do we know anything about anything? Is not all of our so-called "knowledge" and "science" a mere human construct, or worse, simply words about words? What proof do we have of any connection between mind and thing or between word and object? A dialectical realism seeks to mediate and reply to these ancient disputes. These questions reach back to the very roots of Western philosophy.

Why Dialectic?

I believe a dialectical approach is the most fruitful epistemology for the current religion-science dialogue. One reason a dialectical approach is needed in both religion and science is because of the problem of perspective. All our knowing arises from our location, from our point of view and cultural context. Even the natural sciences are located in culture, language, and history. None of us has a God's-eye view, a "view from nowhere." Any approach that hopes to grasp the object of our studies will need a host of contrasting, alternative points of view on that object. A single flower can be studied from the perspective of *every* discipline in the natural sciences, and even such an exhaustive analysis will only begin to grasp the full nature of that single bloom of living matter. The world is an amazing and astounding place — we need as much and as many insights as possible. This point was in fact made long ago by Plato, who also (in the *Republic*) called this process "dialectics."[3]

Plato is in fact the father of dialectical thinking. The key to dialectics is the notion that important insights can be gained from contrasting perspectives. Voices in conflict may each grasp a partial truth. When Abelard wrote his famous *Sic et Non,* he used contrasting opinions to search more fully toward the truth.[4] In modern times, Kant,

---

3. *Republic,* bk. 7, 530d-e. Aristotle's definition of "dialectical reasoning" in the *Topics* is quite different, and does not affect current usage.

4. See the critical edition of *Sic et Non,* ed. B. B. Boyer and R. McKeon (Chicago: University of Chicago Press, 1977). Abelard also wrote a book with the title *Dialectica,* trans. L. M. de Rijk (Assen, Netherlands: Van Gorcum, H. J. Prakke & H. M. G. Prakke, 1956), which was an introduction to logic.

Hegel, Marx, and even Kierkegaard were all masters of dialectical thinking. The problem with these great masters of dialectic (excepting
Kierkegaard) was their attachment to grand metanarratives. Plato,
Hegel, and Marx placed dialectics into a grand synthetic system, and
they had an over-attachment to philosophical speculation, especially
their own conclusions and philosophies. Whether under the name of
the Realm of Forms, Absolute Spirit, or dialectical materialism, these
philosophers were too enamored of speculative systems, which tended
to obliterate in a synthesis the original tensions between thesis and an-
tithesis. This drowning of difference has come under severe attack by
postmodern critics, and I find these criticisms very much on target. In
fact, the critique of a System (capital S) that obliterates the individual
can be found powerfully in Kierkegaard already in the nineteenth century.[5] Thus the dialectical realism I am defending is not a complete
"system" of thought, but rather a proposed approach to epistemology
in science and theology. At this point I will focus on philosophy; later
in the chapter we will look at the dialectical theology of Greek Orthodoxy, which is my preferred approach in theology.

In his brilliant book *Negative Dialectics* (1966), Theodor Adorno
draws upon the work of Kierkegaard and others to develop a
postmodern dialectic that avoids the excesses of Plato, Hegel, and
Marx.[6] Adorno rightly notes that "matters of true philosophical interest at this point in history" are the very ones that Hegel scorned,
namely "nonconceptuality, individuality, and particularity" (p. 8). We
need to pay attention to detail, to the concrete, to difference. Adorno
was a philosopher of art, and the artist in any medium pays particular
attention to details. Negative dialectics pays attention first of all to the
limitations of any philosophical concept. "A matter of urgency to the
concept would be what it fails to cover, what its abstractionist mecha-
nism eliminates, what is not already a case of the concept" (p. 8). Reality greatly exceeds any and all philosophical concepts. For this reason,
negative dialectics begins with the criticism of current theories, concepts, and accepted systems of thought. But for Adorno, unlike some

5. See, among many examples, Søren Kierkegaard, *The Sickness unto Death,* trans.
W. Lowrie (Princeton, N.J.: Princeton University Press, 1941).

6. T. W. Adorno, *Negative Dialectics,* trans. E. B. Ashton (New York: Seabury, 1973).
Page references will appear parenthetically in the text.

postmodern critics, criticism is not the whole story. "In criticism we do not simply liquidate systems" (p. 24). The purpose of dialectical thinking, which seeks tensions, contradictions, and differences, is to open philosophy and science up to the reality of particularity. Adorno was a critic of both Enlightenment absolutes and the easy relativism of the contemporary culture (pp. 35-37).

Attention to detail and to particularity, to the concreteness of reality, leads us to value different voices and perspectives on the object. Dialectics begins with the difference between word and object, with Derrida's *différance*. No word, no definition, is fully adequate (working definitions may be adequate for a limited purpose, of course). A variety of languages and definitions, therefore, a variety of attempts to capture experience in words, is more than welcome. This will no doubt lead to contrasting, even conflicting, points of view about the object. Contemporary orchestral music often finds beauty in contrasting tones, even in clashing notes, rather than in the harmonies of classical music. This attitude is one that Adorno brings to philosophy. Synthesis is suspect.

Nevertheless, science is synthesis. Many great breakthroughs in science have been a combination of saturation in the details of the subject, and insightful, imaginative new models, laws, and theories. One of the best examples of this is the neo-Darwinian synthesis of genetics and classical Darwinism. The point is that science does advance through synthesis, at least in part. A new theory in a particular discipline contains a synthesis of older material and older problems, into which the new theory gives better insight (even while it creates new problems and avenues of research). If synthesis is suspect, then is not also science suspect?

The answer to this important question comes, I find, both in our attitude toward scientific knowledge and in Adorno's proposed corrections to dialectical method: attention to the particular, and an "ensemble of analyses." Not all systems of thought, nor all dialectics, are alike. Adorno rightly rejects a "closed system" (p. 27), which pretends to be absolute and in this pretense distorts the particular. The antidote to this is a healthy grasp of the limitations of concepts, systems, and philosophical reflection, attached to a new objectivity that pays greater attention to the objects themselves. "What is waiting in the objects themselves needs such intervention [from philosophy] to come to speak, with the perspective that the forces mobilized outside, and ultimately every theory that is brought to bear on the phenomena, should come to rest in the phenomena" (p. 29). A new kind of objectivity is called for — not a supposedly neutral or value-free science, which is impossible (as we shall argue in another chapter), but an objectivity that takes the particularity of things seriously. There is nothing here that is contrary to a genuinely scientific attitude, which is always self-critical, always paying attention to the facts. When we invest too much in scientific knowledge, however, we can easily lose this critical scientific attitude. As Adorno rightly argues, a scientific perspective or "objectification" upon things is a powerful but limited abstraction (p. 43). Reason itself must not be identified with this mathematical and measurable abstract reasoning, and there is more to truth than scientific truth. But these insights need not inhibit science. On the contrary, they liberate it from false demands and pseudo-religious attitudes, which one sees all too often in the popular mind-set and mass media.[7]

In addition to a new objectivity that respects difference and particularity, Adorno recognizes the philosophical need for something like a "system" of ideas. "The call for binding statements without a system is a call for thought models, and these are not merely monadological in kind. . . . Negative dialectics is an ensemble of analyses of models" (p. 29). This metaphor of an ensemble, or elsewhere a "constellation," suggests the need to see models and concepts in their interrelatedness. But the metaphor is also put forward as a way of avoiding the totalizing tendencies of synthesis and conceptual systems. A constellation or an ensemble may have tension, even contradiction, within it. There need not be a commitment, such as we find in Hegel, to a "true light" that sees everything in a completed whole, that is, in a finished system.[8] Nevertheless, things still are connected and related, around a general theme or subject, in an ensemble. Scientific knowledge is not in fact a great system of ideas, in any case. The actual body of scientific knowledge in any age ends up being an ensemble of models, meta-

7. See further on this point Mary Midgley, *Science As Salvation* (London: Routledge, 1992).

8. Hegel's definition of dialectical reasoning is "the indwelling tendency outwards by which the one-sidedness and limitation of the predicates of understanding is seen in its true light, and shown to be the negation of them. For anything to be finite is just to suppress itself and puts itself aside" (*Encyclopedia of the Philosophical Sciences*, §81, trans. T. F. Geraets as *The Encyclopedia Logic* [Indianapolis: Hackett, 1991]).

phors, and ideas, rather than some tightly connected logical system of propositions. If we return to our example of a single flower, what the various sciences can tell us about this flower is much closer to an ensemble than a system. In this particular case, there is no tension or paradox — but there might be in more complex phenomena.

Dialectics begins with difference, and with the epistemological fact that all knowing is a kind of interpretation and takes place from a particular perspective. It likewise begins with the gap between word and thing and with the inherent limitation of all concepts, definitions, and formulae. The resulting epistemology is dialogical, communal, and historical. Like good diplomacy, knowledge takes time, and improves with serious debate and attention to differences.

Why Realism?

The second aspect of epistemology that I commend to those interested in the religion and science dialogue is realism.[9] Attention to differences demands that we notice that not all "realism" is alike. There are at least naive realism and critical realism, and to that list I should like to add dialectical realism. We should also notice that realism is not a global concept. Rather, we are most often realist or nonrealist with respect to some domain of inquiry, such as numbers or beauty. Most criticism of realism in philosophy is an attack upon naive realism, a viewpoint I am not interested in defending here. No one who begins with dialectics is

9. For some other defenses of realism in theology, see Ian Barbour, *Issues in Science and Religion* (London: SCM, 1966); T. F. Torrance, *Reality and Scientific Theology* (Edinburgh: Scottish Academic Press, 1985); Arthur Peacocke, *Intimations of Reality* (Notre Dame: University of Notre Dame Press, 1984); Janet M. Soskice, "Theological Realism," in *The Rationality of Religious Belief,* ed. W. J. Abraham and S. W. Holtzer (Oxford: Oxford University Press, 1987); John Polkinghorne, *One World* (London: SPCK, 1987), and his *Belief in God in an Age of Science* (New Haven: Yale University Press, 1998); Roger Trigg, *Rationality and Religion* (Oxford: Blackwell, 1998); J. Wentzel van Huyssteen, *Essays in Postfoundationalist Theology* (Grand Rapids: Eerdmans, 1997); John Cobb, "In Defense of Realism," in *Theology at the End of Modernity,* ed. Sheila Davaney (Philadelphia: Trinity, 1991); K. V. Niekerk, "A Critical Realist Pespective," in *Rethinking Theology and Science,* ed. Niels Gregersen and J. W. van Huyssteen (Grand Rapids: Eerdmans, 1998); and Sue Patterson, *Realist Christian Theology in a Postmodern Age* (Cambridge: Cambridge University Press, 1999).

going to support a naive or direct realism in epistemology. On the other hand, I accept many of the arguments and positions of critical realism, but want to supplement and extend these insights with a dialectical approach.[10]

Critical realism in the United States arose as a critique of idealism among a group of American philosophers, starting with Roy Sellars in 1916. These philosophers were responding to the then-dominant school of Anglo-American idealism, and published a book of essays critical of that movement.[11] Realism historically arose as a rejection of idealist overemphasis on human consciousness and experience. Put in terms of Bishop Berkeley's philosophy, realism at its core insists upon a rejection of the notion that *esse est percipi* (to exist is to be perceived). It is possible to exist, to be real, without being experienced or perceived in any way: or at least this is the bedrock commitment of "realism" as they understood it, and as I wish to defend it in this work. Scientific realism, then, is the view that *the subjects studied in the special sciences exist independently of the investigator's experience of them*. Theological realism, likewise, is committed to the view that the true object of religious experience exists independently of human experience, if it exists at all. Both of these positions are quite controversial in today's philosophical context, yet both are important for the collegial metaphor and mutuality model we are here developing.

If some form of radical empiricism is taken in philosophy, for example, there is no reason to expect coherence between various realms of reality (or "experience," as we had better say) and the various special sciences that study them. This is because, if there is no underlying reality behind our experiences then, given the assumption-laden character of all experience and perception, why should we expect any coherence at all? Different domains of our experience, such as nature and religion, need have no coherence between them: reason will demand only

10. Roy Bhaskar, in his book *Dialectics: The Pulse of Freedom* (London: Verso, 1993), also sets forth a "dialectical critical realism" for both philosophy of science and social philosophy, sharing some of the goals of my own work. His approach and general position, however, are quite different from the one adopted here.

11. The origin of the term is a book by Roy Sellars, *Critical Realism* (Chicago: Rand, McNally, 1916). The collected volume is Durant Drake et al., *Essays in Critical Realism* (London: Macmillan, 1920), which includes essays by Sellars, A. O. Lovejoy, and George Santayana.

an internal coherence. As Ernan McMullin notes, "Take, for example, the desideratum that a theory should be consonant with well-established theories elsewhere in science. . . . From the non-realist standpoint, there is no reason why such a requirement should be enforced."[12] This is because, on a nonrealist account, a theory is merely a formalism for generating accurate predictions. As long as it does its job as a predictor, we cannot worry about any conflict with other theories, since we don't actually believe in the invisible parts of the theory.

Why is (dialectical) realism so important for the mutuality model? The answer has to do with the basis for the mutual influence of science and religion and with the notion of developing a coherent worldview. If there exists a real world, independent of human experience, then our worldview should be aimed at understanding that world as fully as possible. For this fuller understanding we need all the disciplines of the university, including the human sciences and theology. We will expect greater coherence in our worldview because we believe that at bottom there is one reality, which is whole and connected. On the other hand, given some kind of nonrealism, we have no reason to expect coherence among the many and diverse areas of academia. Various disciplines, with their quite distinct methods, aims, and histories, are so different that we have no rational basis for expecting coherence between them. The collegial metaphor and mutuality model for religion and science dialogue likewise assume that truth in one area rightly affects our grasp of truth in another area, because there is one real, independent world we study in the various disciplines. Without some kind of sophisticated realist metaphysics, these epistemological commitments and goals are difficult to justify.

What motivates realism? One answer might be humility. Human experience is not the sole determinant of reality, according to the realist. Nonrealism may be rather too epistemologically anthropocentric for a humble approach to the world that does not place human beings at the center of value. Another motivation is the underlying intuition that we are dealing with reality both in our interaction with the world and in our spiritual life. We may not have a perfect grasp of that reality,

---

12. Ernan McMullin, "Epistemic Virtue and Theory Appraisal," in *Realism in Science,* ed. I. Douven and L. Horsten (Leuven: Leuven University Press, 1996), pp. 13-34, quoting p. 30.

but we know it is there. We exist in and with the world, and yet reality also exists independent of us: we neither create nor control it (except in a rather small way). Yet fundamental to my realism, at least, is the conviction that there is a God who is the utmost Real Being. God is the creator of all reality. God has created me and you and all other things. Thus reality (God and the world) exists independent of me. If theism is true, then there is one God, one world, and one complete system of truth (God's own knowledge). In fact, Kant at one point defines God as the one who alone has perfect intuition of the thing-in-itself (noumena).[13] Of course, as humans we don't have God's knowledge; we know phenomena, not noumena. But we would be foolish to deny the existence of the noumenal world just because we humans are limited to phenomena. In Kantian terms, this would be to deny the existence of God.

In his *Method in Theology*, Bernard Lonergan noted that the term "object" can have two meanings.[14] There is the "object" as socially constructed, which is "mediated by a world of meaning." He was not a realist about this, and neither are we, except in the sense in which human social constructs are the real objects of social scientific research. They are "given" and "exist" as social institutions but reduce ontologically to persons and peoples. The second sense of "object," however, is that of the "world of immediacy," which existed before we did and in the midst of which we first came to consciousness. These objects are prior to our conscious interaction with them. They should not be reduced to persons and peoples (and their consciousness), and in fact they resist such reduction. Maurice Merleau-Ponty makes much the same point in his phenomenological study of perception. Our embodiment, he argues, creates the conditions for the possibility of perceptual interaction with the pre-theoretical world in which we come to consciousness.[15]

Most definitions of realism have focused on epistemology. Beginning there is, I would stress, a mistake. It distracts us from the real force of critical or dialogical realism, which is ontological. Human beings do not create reality, nor do they determine what counts as real. It

---

13. Immanuel Kant, *Critique of Pure Reason*, B70-72.

14. Bernard Lonergan, *Method in Theology* (London: Darton, Longman, and Todd, 1972), p. 263.

15. Maurice Merleau-Ponty, *Phenomenology of Perception* (London: Routledge, 1962).

is another matter entirely, however, when we talk about our grasp of reality. In this arena, namely in epistemology, much of what the antirealist has to say can be granted. We do not have a perfectly clear understanding or experience of either the world or God; all our perception and description is already assumption-laden; there are always, already, gaps between word and object; and so forth. But on the level of ontological commitment, there is very little reason to follow nonrealism, and excellent reasons not to do so. Most nonrealists are attacking a simplified and naive epistemology which they label "realism" for their own rhetorical purposes. After attacking this simple viewpoint, they announce their own, superior form of nonrealism.

Let us take Hilary Putnam as an example. He develops his own brand of nonrealism, fetchingly called "internal realism" just to confuse the unwary! His opponent is "metaphysical realism" or "externalism," which he identifies in this way:

> [According to this view] the world consists of some fixed totality of mind-independent objects. There is exactly one true and complete description of "the way the world is." Truth involves some sort of correspondence relation between words or thought-signs and external things and sets of things. I shall call this perspective the *externalist* perspective, because its favorite point of view is a God's Eye point of view.[16]

Let us examine this straw man definition critically. First of all, why is the realist (or externalist) committed to a *fixed* totality of objects? Yes, reality is mind-independent in its fundamental existence, but why "fixed"? Don't we believe in the process of becoming? This word is just a rhetorical flourish. Second, a dialectical realism does not affirm that there is exactly one true description of the world; a description, after all, is given in a language. Rather, assuming the existence of God, the realist is committed to there being one exactly true *knowledge* of the way the world is. But God's knowledge of the world is direct and internal, knowledge held by the omnipresent Creator and Sustainer of all that exists. As such, God's basic knowledge of things is neither linguistic nor propositional nor symbolic; it is direct and ontological. Realists

16. Hilary Putnam, *Reason, Truth and History* (Cambridge: Cambridge University Press, 1981), p. 49.

take it as a given that human beings are not God and that the way humans see things does not determine reality. Finally, realism is not committed to a picture-theory of meaning nor to a simplistic correspondence theory of truth. By saddling "external realism" with all of these epistemological burdens, Putnam finds it easy to knock down his opponent and make way for his brand of nonrealism ("internal").[17]

Alas, Putnam is not the only one to resort to such Aunt Sally definitions. A recent essay by a young evangelical scholar, Brad Kallenberg, defines a "realist" as (1) one who holds to a "representational theory of language," is therefore (2) committed to "some version of the correspondence theory of truth," and (3) "believes that reality divides neatly into subject and objects (or into language and world; or ideas and things)."[18] All three of these assertions are false as far as I can tell, at least among sophisticated realists. The representational or "picture" theory of meaning has been out of fashion among realists since the work of the early Wittgenstein was rejected by Wittgenstein himself. The correspondence theory of truth is not a very common commitment, although it still has a few defenders. I prefer what William Alston has recently called a "minimal realist" theory of truth for propositions, and later we shall discuss the notion of truth a little more.[19] But realism per se does not imply one specific theory of truth (one could be a pragmatic realist like John Dewey, for example). And why must the realist hold that subject and object divide "neatly"? Is Kallenberg denying the difference between subject and object? That is just another form of idealism, of course. While a realist does believe there is a difference, in philosophical analysis, between subject and object (or word and thing), it does not follow that this is a "division" or "separation" except in thought. What we have here is yet another example of caricature rather than analysis.

What epistemology is "realism" committed to? There is no right

---

17. We should note in fairness to Putnam that in a recent book, *The Threefold Cord: Mind, Body, World* (New York: Columbia University Press, 1999), he has abandoned his earlier nonrealism ("internal realism") for realism in the tradition of John Dewey and William James.

18. Brad Kallenberg, "The Gospel Truth of Relativism," *Scottish Journal of Theology* 53 (2000): 173-210, quoting p. 183 n.12.

19. William P. Alston, *A Realist Theory of Truth* (Ithaca, N.Y.: Cornell University Press, 1996).

answer to this question, because there are many types of realism. I prefer dialectical to critical realism because of the reasons already given in favor of dialectics. Critical realists usually take an individualistic and synchronic view of epistemology. I believe that knowledge and perception are diachronic, dialogical, communal, and traditional. It is this epistemology within which a mutuality model finds its home most naturally.

Informal Inference

We are handed our worldview and our language by our earliest communities, in which we first discover ourselves as selves. But as we develop intellectually, we want a better grasp of truth about the world, humanity, values, and deity. In short, as soon as we are able, we want to improve our worldview. In both science and theology, knowledge is very infrequently given through demonstrative, formal reasoning. Both the sciences and theology are based upon informal reasoning in their arguments and conclusions. Some philosophers, dating back to classical times, have called this type of "inductive" or informal reasoning into question. I cannot here give a full defense of informal reason, but I think this topic is so important to the religion and science dialogue that I will summarize an argument I give more fully later in this work.[20]

We use informal or inductive reasoning all of the time, as even Hume and other skeptics were well aware. The best reply given to Hume (who challenged us to find justification for such reasoning) in his own day was by Thomas Reid. Reid argued that we stand justified in our commonsense modes of reasoning for everyday life, even if we cannot give an abstract, propositional argument as to why we rely upon them rationally. A universal program of doubt, à la Descartes, is a dead end in epistemology. Taking Reid's position as a starting point, I argue that in a few cases, when a *particular* principle comes to be doubted for particular reasons, in a concrete and real situation, we are called to seek some further warrant for our principles beyond common sense. We may not be able to find it, but I think it is rational to look. The princi-

20. See "Induction after Foundationalism" (Appendix).

ples of informal reasoning are, first of all, fallible. We can be wrong about the way we state some principle, or in holding it at all, perhaps. Second, some of these principles may be justifiable on the basis of rational insight (what I call "noetic judgment"). This would provide further justification beyond common sense. Third, the principles of informal reasoning within the various academic disciplines are handed on within the tradition of that discipline. What counts as a good argument in law is different from what counts as a good argument in biology, for example. But these principles have been successful over a long time and so are justified within that discipline. Fourth, there is no simple set of principles that justifies informal reasons: rather, there are a great many! And they may be different in different contexts. So, finally, I argue that the principles of informal reasoning must be contextualized within the disciplines in order to function there. There may be some similarities between "simplicity" (as a virtue for theories) in math and biology, but in fact the meaning and use of this criterion is quite different in the two disciplines.

The reasonableness of informal or "inductive" arguments is important for both science and theology. The various disciplines use informal reasoning a great deal in coming to know reality. If this kind of argument is suspect, then the "knowledge" claimed in science or theology becomes suspect. Recently Alvin Plantinga has argued that believers have a special form of knowledge, a spiritual insight or *sensus divinitatus* that is the basis for their theological claims.[21] Even if that is true for the individual (and I doubt that it is very often!), Plantinga forgets the communal and traditional character of theological knowledge, especially with complex doctrines like the Trinity. In a debate between two sincere, humble, spirit-filled believers, both of whom claim this kind of direct knowledge (yet they contradict one another), only a public and informal argument in the church can settle the matter properly, if it is going to be settled at all. Such an informal argument will be based upon criteria of good argument and evidence in Christian theology. We will look further into the nature of theological reasoning in a later chapter.

This brief summary of the basis for informal reasoning will

21. Alvin Plantinga, *Warranted Christian Belief* (New York: Oxford University Press, 2000).

hardly deter a skeptical reader. Yet some attention to this type of reasoning is essential to a program of dialectical realism, and to the dialogue between theology and science. In an interdisciplinary setting, attention to good argument and sound reasoning of a general sort becomes particularly acute. We can no longer rely upon the traditional modes of argument in our specialty, which our particular discipline has made second nature to us. In these settings, attention to the form of good, general informal argument would very much assist the dialogue (which all too often devolves into two monologues).

Realism and Theological Knowledge

Even if we can begin to make a decent argument for realism in science, it seems well nigh impossible, in today's intellectual context, to argue for realism in religion. Nevertheless, I believe there are good arguments for realism even in religion. The first is that this is the viewpoint of almost all religious believers. The Ultimate Reality that they worship and live for must be real in order for it to be worshiped and for prayer to make sense. Even religions such as Taoism or some forms of Buddhism that have no gods assert some religious truths and believe them to be true independent of what other people may think or experience. But perhaps religious believers (who after all disagree so much among themselves) may all be deluded about this.

The second reason has to do with knowledge and explanation. For the purposes of religion and science dialogue, the notion of realism in religion is manifested in two areas: theological explanation and theological knowledge (or better, claims to knowledge). If both of these are allowed as legitimate and possible, then this is all the "realism" in religion that our mutuality model demands. In the last chapter, I made a plea for theological explanation. This clearly will be accepted only if God (for theistic religions) is real and causes things to happen (creates the world, for example, or meets Moses at the burning bush). Other than denying the existence of the true object of religious faith, I can see no reason in principle to deny the possibility of theological explanation. Obviously, an atheist will deny it, but that argument will take place in another area of philosophy; I can find no reason why religious believers should deny theological explanation, unless they think their

God is just a symbol for human aspirations. But that is another way of saying that God does not exist. So we now turn to the question of theological knowledge-claims. Against some philosophers who would question the very idea of theological knowledge, I argue that such knowledge is possible for human beings in this world. My main targets are Heidegger and Wittgenstein, but just for fun I have added the Chinese philosopher Lao Tzu.

My favorite classical Chinese text is the *Tao Te Ching*. This beautiful work begins with these famous lines:

> The Tao which can be uttered is not the eternal Tao;
> The name which can be named is not the eternal Name;
> The Nameless was the beginning of heaven and earth.

Here we find Lao Tzu denying even the possibility of what I am going to call "theological knowledge." We simply cannot know the truth about Ultimate Reality (the Tao). The Tao transcends any and all attempts to express it in propositions. For this section of our argument, let us agree to use the term "Tao" to stand for Ultimate Reality as various religions understand it (God, Nothingness, Brahman, etc.).

What counts, then, as knowledge of the Tao? What then is theological knowledge? It is, first of all, not knowledge about a religion. Knowledge about religions is certainly possible, since religion is a human institution with history, texts, and artifacts. No one should deny that we can have knowledge *about* religion — otherwise teachers in religious studies would be out a job. What I mean by theological knowledge, however, is knowledge of the Tao, which religious faith is about. Theology, as I use the term, is the conceptual, abstract dimension of a religious tradition. In this sense there is Muslim, Hindu, Christian, and even Taoist "theology." In Western religious terms, theological knowledge is knowledge about God, and not about religion, human religious experience, or religious faith. Theological knowledge may come *through* a religious tradition, religious experience, or religious faith, but these items are not what theological knowledge is *about*. Theology, after all, is the study of the Tao. Theology therefore should not be confused with religious studies, even though it often is. Religious studies is the study of religion; theology is the study of the Tao.

In his excellent volume on religion and revelation, Keith Ward sets forth a program of "comparative theology" that is not part of any religious tradition.[22] Ward wants to study God from the perspective of any and all religious traditions, scriptures, and experiences. Given this project, what then is theological knowledge? Ward wants to move us away from the older concept of theological knowledge as doctrine, that is, as assured propositional knowledge. "The propositions of theology are concerned to articulate and express, always provisionally and indirectly, such disclosures and forms of commitment [within a religion], rather than to define a set of truths which are directly and precisely descriptive of suprasensory reality."[23] Ward rightly insists that the communal and tradition-constituted project of knowing God is best understood as modest, provisional, dialectical, and open to revision. His perspective is very much in line with the proposal I am making concerning the mutuality model. Even conceived in such modest terms, however, is theology possible? Can we have conceptual, propositional knowledge of the Tao? My thesis is yes, theological knowledge is possible.

"One who speaks does not know; one who knows does not speak"; thus speaks Lao Tzu.[24] Like Lao Tzu, I must risk speaking about the Great Ultimate, thus showing myself to be one who does not know! But then theology is always paradoxical. I have no quarrel with those who think that theological knowledge is paradoxical, difficult, or can never arrive at the full truth. My complaint here is against those who argue that theology per se is impossible, or who misrepresent the object of theological study.

The two most important Western philosophers of the last century were Martin Heidegger and Ludwig Wittgenstein. Both were very interested in religion and passed through periods of genuine Christian faith. Both respected religion, religious faith, and the religious way of life. But alas for my project here, both were dead set against theological knowledge! I can only briefly respond here to their criticisms of the theological enterprise, giving some indications of where a fuller response might be headed.

Heidegger began his academic studies in theology, and tells us that theological studies brought him to an interest in hermeneutics

---

22. Keith Ward, *Religion and Revelation* (Oxford: Oxford University Press, 1994). This is the first book in a four-volume work in comparative theology.

23. Ward, *Religion and Revelation,* pp. 29f.

24. *Tao Te Ching,* chap. 56, line 128.

and phenomenology.[25] He published two essays on the relationship between theology and philosophy, both of which have become famous.[26] In these essays, Heidegger correctly sees that theology is a "positive science," that is, an area of knowledge with an object of study. So far we are in agreement. But Heidegger wrongly attributes to theology the study of *faith* (that is, *die Christlichkeit* or Christianness) rather than the study of God. Heidegger claims that the "given" or basic data of theological science is Christian faith and practice. "Thus we maintain that what is given for theology (its *positum*) is Christianness. . . . What does 'Christianness' mean? We call faith Christian. The essence of faith can formally be sketched as a mode of human existence" (p. 9). Christianness, then, is the life of faith. And this faith is the basis of theology as a positive science.

Heidegger is mistaken in his understanding of the purpose of theology as a positive science. I do believe that theology is a positive science (in the German sense of *Wissenschaft*), but with a different purpose. The purpose of theology is to understand the Tao. In this quest, of course, theology can and should make sense of the way of life within a particular religion. But this is not the only, nor the chief, purpose of theology. Rather, theology is, in part, the rigorous academic study of God, or the Tao, within a particular religious tradition. In making this mistake, of course, Heidegger is in good company! The problem with this common view is that in the end it collapses theology into religious studies (a collapse I am trying to avoid). This is so even when Heidegger allows that theology must also study "that which is revealed in faith" (p. 9), for such a study can also be merely descriptive (for example, "Christians believe that God is so-and-so"). This is clear when, in another essay, Heidegger states, "Above all else one must determine what theology, as a mode of thinking and speaking, is to place in discussion. That is the Christian faith, and what is believed therein" (p. 22). On the contrary, if theology is a discipline at all (a "positive science"), it must

25. This is disclosed in a dialogue Heidegger had with a Japanese philosopher, published in *On the Way to Language,* trans. P. D. Hertz (New York: Harper and Row, 1971), pp. 9-10.

26. These are collected in his book *Phänomenologie und Theologie* (Frankfurt am Main: Klostermann, 1970), and published in English in *The Piety of Thinking,* trans. J. G. Hart and J. C. Maraldo (Bloomington: Indiana University Press, 1976). My references, which will be cited parenthetically in the text, are to the English translation.

have the Tao as its object of study. What theology "places into discussion" is God, therefore, and not faith.

The other great philosopher of the last century, Ludwig Wittgenstein, had very different problems with theological knowledge. He believed that a religious way of life was a noble one and should be pursued with the utmost seriousness. His questions had to do with the validity of religious language. Religious language is legitimate, for Wittgenstein, when this "language game" is grounded in a genuine religious form of life. Both Wittgenstein and Heidegger, then, see theology as grounded in the way of life of a particular religion. And this is a valid insight. "*Practise* gives [theological] words their sense," Wittgenstein tells us in an illuminating passage from *Culture and Value*.[27] What is key to a right understanding of religious language, then, is the way of life — and of suffering — that it flows from. Wittgenstein rejected any notion of theology that would make it similar to an explanation of something, or like a scientific hypothesis.

There is clearly something right in Wittgenstein's remarks. People do not often come to religious faith because of some academic exercise proving the existence of God. Religious faith does not normally come about because of data, evidence, and argument of a scientific or empirical sort. Religious belief is not a scientific hypothesis. I also agree with Wittgenstein's insight that we must take particular care to examine the form of life that gives religious language its sense. But against Wittgenstein and some of his followers, on the other hand, religious beliefs and thoughts — *once entered into* — can and do provide some blocks for building an explanation. I have already argued for this position in the previous chapter, against Wittgenstein and at least some of his followers. The total separation of religious belief from explanation and propositional knowledge is a confusion and a misrepresentation. Of course, the meaning of some religious language just is the way of life it engenders. But to absolutize this — to insist that this is true of *all* religious language and belief — is a blunder in the philosophy of religion.[28]

---

27. Ed. G. H. von Wright with Heikki Nyman (Oxford: Blackwell, 1980), p. 85.

28. For a similar response to Wittgenstein and his followers (accepting basic insights, but rejecting extreme positions, as I seek to do here), see Anthony C. Thiselton, *The Two Horizons* (Grand Rapids: Eerdmans, 1980); Roger Trigg, *Rationality and Religion* (Oxford: Blackwell, 1998); and Vincent Brümmer, *Speaking of a Personal God* (Cambridge: Cambridge University Press, 1992).

The most natural and faithful understanding of religious faith (at least in the religions I have studied) is to allow that religion does have an explanatory dimension. You can explain things in the world using theological doctrines. Such explanations are put forward in all of the world religions I am aware of, within the history of their own theological developments. Wittgenstein is surely right, however, to distinguish such "explanations" from natural science.

Finally (to return to the *Tao Te Ching*), critics in East and West have insisted that theological knowledge is not possible because of the mystery of the Tao. God cannot be grasped in human words, both Lao Tzu and Dionysius the Areopagite (Greek theologian, ca. 500 AD) would agree.[29] I agree also, with the main point. The Tao cannot be *fully* grasped in language, for words are imperfect instruments. Nevertheless, they are the only instrument we have. While the meaning of ordinary words comes from ordinary life, language can be stretched to describe extraordinary things. A good example of this is the language of modern physics. In contemporary physics, the matter and energy of the physical universe are understood to be made up of very small, subatomic particles. Light, for example, is made up of photons, and electricity of electrons. While scientists call these things "particles," they are not like particles we know in the normal world of our human environment. These particles also behave like waves of energy, but a particle and a wave are very different things in our normal, everyday world! To describe the strange and fascinating subatomic world of quantum mechanics a stretching and bending of our ordinary words and concepts is required. The same thing is true in theology. The Tao is so far beyond our ordinary world that everyday terms and concepts must be stretched beyond their literal use. But surely we can refer to the Tao with metaphor and figurative language, even if our descriptions of it will always be less than fully adequate.[30] The *Tao Te Ching*, after all, is filled with just such metaphoric and poetic descriptions of the Tao. While a naive realism for religious language must be rejected, at the same time we can affirm that metaphor, sim-

29. See *Pseudo-Dionysius: The Complete Works,* trans. Colm Luibheid (New York: Paulist, 1988).

30. This point has been made particularly well by Janet M. Soskice, *Metaphor and Religious Language* (Oxford: Oxford University Press, 1985), chap. 6.

ile, figure (and sometime even literal language) can and do refer to the Tao.[31]

Dialectical Realism in Theology

This defense of "positive theology" must be put into a broader context. I have argued for "theological realism," understood as the affirmation of theological explanation combined with the acceptance of the possibility of theological knowledge. But this knowledge and realism should not be accepted without qualification. Once again, we can turn for help to dialectics, this time the dialectical theology of Greek Orthodoxy.

Although I greatly admire the twentieth-century German-speaking founders of "dialectical theology," for my own model of dialectical realism in theology I am indebted to the Greeks.[32] Pseudo-Dionysius, in particular, developed the language and method of a negative theology (apophatic) and a positive or affirmative theology (cataphatic), both of which are important. This tradition of dialectical theology has roots in the Cappadocian theologians of the fourth century, and is developed in such great Greek theologians as Maximus the Confessor and Gregory Palamas. In this tradition, God's own existence is affirmed, but God's infinite Being is understood to be beyond all thought and all language. The highest theology, then, is mystical theology, or the life of prayer and worship. Dionysius puts it this way in the beginning of his *Mystical Theology:*

> Timothy, my friend, my advice to you as you look for a sight of the mysterious [or mystical, *mystikos*] things, is to leave behind you everything perceived and understood, everything perceptible and understandable, all that is not and all that is, and, with your under-

31. See the studies by Ian T. Ramsey, *Models and Mystery* (London: Oxford University Press, 1964); Ian G. Barbour, *Myths, Models and Paradigms* (New York: Harper and Row, 1974); Richard Swinburne, *The Coherence of Theism* (Oxford: Clarendon, 1977); and Soskice, *Metaphor.*

32. Bernard Lonergan also finds a place for dialectics, as one among several "functional specialties," in his *Method in Theology* (London: Darton, Longman, and Todd, 1972).

standing laid aside, to strive upward as much as you can toward union with him who is beyond all being and knowledge.[33]

We should understand that this is a realist theology, but it is not a naive realism. The highest and best form of theology is mystical union with God. This God is not just a symbol (although Dionysius would agree that the word "God" is a limited human symbol). It is hard to understand how Gordon Kaufman, in his influential *An Essay in Theological Method,* can characterize traditional theology as holding that "God exists independently of the perceiver or knower and has a definite character which can be described."[34] Dionysius was quite influential in Latin theology (after being translated into Latin by Robert Grosseteste in the thirteenth century), and the basic point is common in Platonic-Christian thought as a whole, including the Latin tradition. It is hard to see how "God has a definite character which can be described" is anything like this traditional understanding of theological language. Kaufman goes on to insist that Kant "first [!] pointed out the root difficulties with this view, but his revolutionary insights remain unappreciated in much theological work." Kant is important because he "saw that ideas like 'God' and 'world' performed a different kind of function in our thinking than concepts like 'tree' or 'man'," writes Kaufman.[35] Such an exposition completely ignores the tradition of dialectical theology I am seeking here to recover.

The practice of Dionysius and other Greek theologians of the past ends up being something like Adorno's "cluster of metaphors." Dionysius' famous book *The Divine Names* is a series of models and metaphors within which positive theology seeks to know something about God.[36] His book *The Mystical Theology* then provides a kind of "critique of models" (by means of negative theology) that Adorno was also interested in developing. T. F. Torrance once put this Greek theological position in three points:[37]

---

33. *Pseudo-Dionysius: Complete Works,* p. 135.

34. Gordon Kaufman, *An Essay in Theological Method,* third ed. (Atlanta: Scholars Press, 1995), p. 26.

35. Kaufman, *Essay in Theological Method,* p. 29.

36. In *Pseudo-Dionysius: Complete Works,* pp. 47-132.

37. T. F. Torrance, *Theology in Reconstruction* (Grand Rapids: Eerdmans, 1965), p. 30. See also his *Divine Meaning: Studies in Patristic Hermeneutics* (Edinburgh: T&T Clark, 1995).

(i) One must recognize the unapproachableness of God, which calls forth from us the attitude of worship and reverence.

(ii) Only by God is God known, and only through God is God revealed.

(iii) The application of our ordinary language to speech about God involves a fundamental shift in its meaning.

In my own terms, seeking to know the One who loves us and yet is beyond our comprehension leads to a theology with two moments. A positive theology, based on the Word of God (the Second Person of the Trinity) as true revelation, is balanced with a negative theology, which negates the finite and worldly language we are forced to use concerning the One who is beyond all being and all thought and all language. In the seventh century, Maximus the Confessor put the point this way in his *Two Hundred Chapters on Knowledge:* On the one hand, "Every concept involves those who think and what is thought, as subject and object. But God is neither of those who think nor of what is thought for he is beyond them." At the same time, there is a positive knowledge of God through his Word, the Son. "In Christ who is God and the Word of the Father there dwells in bodily form the complete fullness of deity by essence"; being the full Word and Mind of God, he is able to "reveal the Father whom he knows."[38] Finally, both the apophatic and the cataphatic theologies are best combined in the life of prayer and spiritual discipline (mystical union), and in the worship of the community of faith (liturgy). This is the kind of dialectical realism in theology which I believe is most fruitful for the religion-science dialogue, for it pays attention both to the need to develop a metaphorical theology grounded in the Word of God and to our ecclesial life of the Spirit. At the same time, it continues a critique of any and all language about God, and of confident claims to know the truth about God. The Eastern tradition has kept alive the important point that theology is not done fully in academic seminars but in the life and worship of the church and the disciples of Jesus in the world today.

This brief essay into philosophy has sought to explain and defend a dialectical realist approach to science and theology. I believe such an

---

38. Maximus the Confessor, *Selected Writings,* trans. G. C. Berthold (New York: Paulist, 1985), Second Century on Knowledge, §2 (p. 148) and §21 (p. 152).

approach will prove to be most fruitful as we seek to develop a worldview that is both fully scientific and fully Christian. Both the realist and the dialectical elements of my proposal assist us in taking seriously the need for theology and science to mutually inform and modify each other. Therefore I find a sophisticated, dialectical realism the best philosophical framework for continued dialogue between theology and the sciences. A formal philosophical presentation of these ideas, on the other hand, would require an entire volume in itself. I must be satisfied here with an outline of a philosophical position, rather than a fully developed argument set forth in historical detail and reasoned debate with contemporary philosophers. We need to press on to a fuller understanding of what theology is about. And that will take us from the groves of Plato's Academy into the city of Jerusalem and the arms of the worshiping community within the City of God.

3 The Myth of a Purely
Historical Jesus

In the previous chapters, we developed a model of the relationship between science and theology in which each discipline can influence the other by means of large-scale interpretations of the universe. Our worldviews, if we are rational, will influence our theory choices, *all other things being equal.* Worldviews should influence theory choice in a rigorous discipline only after lower-level criteria (such as fit with data) have eliminated other rival theories. They ought not to overpower the facts and standards for theory choice within our established traditions of inquiry.[1] But religion can and should influence science, and our science can and should influence our theology. These influences are not direct, as we have seen in the last chapter, but work through the establishment of an overall view of the world that is both religious and scientific.

One area of great historical conflict between religion and academic studies has been in the rise of historical criticism of the Bible. In this chapter I will examine the claim of historical scholars to have a "purely historical" approach to Jesus, one that does not draw upon worldviews and religious faiths. One criticism of the mutuality model might be that science should be "value free" and operate independent

---

1. Paul Feyerabend, "Quantum Theory and Our View of the World," in his *Conquest of Abundance* (Chicago: University of Chicago Press, 1999), reprinted from Jan Hilgevoord, ed., *Physics and Our View of the World* (Cambridge: Cambridge University Press, 1994). Feyerabend does discuss the influence of worldviews on science but goes too far in defining a worldview as something that "imposes itself with a power far greater than the power of facts and fact-related theories" (p. 164). This ignores the ability of facts, well-grounded theories, and experience to modify and even overturn our worldviews. See further Chapter Four in this volume on "Science and Worldview."

of any faith or other subjective commitment. In this chapter I criticize and reject this kind of independence for religion and science. This should further establish the claims of our mutuality model.

Recently a very large body of literature on the "historical Jesus" has appeared, both in the popular media and in the many academic volumes speeding from the presses. A "third quest" for the historical Jesus has begun, and the so-called Jesus Seminar has produced a new version of the Gospels, the "Scholars Version" of *The Five Gospels,* dedicated to Galileo (among others).[2] Such general interest in historical scholarship provides us an opportunity to reflect on the legitimacy of this enterprise, and indeed, to reflect on the character of our academic approach to religious studies. In this chapter I will pursue two goals at once. First, I wish to debunk a powerful and influential myth, arising from the Enlightenment divorce of religion and science, which assumes that a purely neutral, value-free "scientific" approach to the historical Jesus is desirable and possible.[3] Second, I hope to provide an alternative, postmodern approach that integrates faith and science, as indeed the real Galileo did.[4]

---

2. Robert Funk et al., eds., *The Five Gospels* (New York: Macmillan, 1993). By the "Jesus Seminar" I will always mean the corporate authors of this book and its introduction. I am not talking about the scholars as individuals, many of whom I know and respect. For a good introduction to the work of the Jesus Seminar and the "third quest" for the historical Jesus, see Marcus Borg, *Jesus in Contemporary Scholarship* (Valley Forge, Pa.: Trinity Press International, 1993).

3. In this book I use "science" in a very broad sense, as it is used in Latin *(scientia),* Greek *(episteme),* and German *(Wissenschaft).* This refers to any academic, rigorous, and empirical inquiry that is based on evidence, reason, and argument. I do not reduce "science" to mean the natural sciences, as many Americans do.

4. Mine is a mild sort of postmodernism. By "postmodern" I mean only a view that is critical of the Enlightenment. Relativism is not implied in this term as I use it. After completing this chapter, I discovered that much the same thesis is advocated by Robert Morgan in the G. B. Caird memorial volume; see "The Historical Jesus and the Theology of the New Testament," in *The Glory of Christ in the New Testament,* ed. L. D. Hurst and N. T. Wright (Oxford: Clarendon, 1987). Morgan's elegant argument pertains, however, only to New Testament theology. I believe the thesis applies *(mutatis mutandis)* to any historical approach to Jesus from any faith perspective. Morgan in turn points us to Adolf Schlatter, who anticipated many of the points I make in this essay. See Robert Morgan, ed., *The Nature of New Testament Theology,* Studies in Biblical Theology second series, vol. 25 (London: SCM, 1973), which contains Schlatter's 1909 essay, "The Theology of the New Testament and Dogmatics."

Like earlier theologians reflecting on the problem of faith and history (such as Wolfhart Pannenberg, Alan Richardson, and Richard R. Niebuhr), I have found that reflection upon the early Christian claim that Jesus rose from the dead is a powerful place from which to consider the relationship between faith and historical research.[5] I will propose no new interpretation of the data but rather reflect on the very practice of historiography in the face of the historical claim that Jesus rose from the dead. I hope to show that reflection on the difference between historical and theological explanation clarifies the sense in which the resurrection is a "historical" event.

At one time in our Western universities we were certain of how history should proceed, as a rigorous, value-free, scientific discipline. But now that that modern era is over, how shall we proceed? Does "anything go" in historical research now that modernity is over? How shall we understand the discipline of religious history in a post-positivist, postmodern situation? — for modernity, with its faith in reason and its myth of neutral, scientific scholarship, is well and truly dead. *Requiescat in pace.*

We stand at the beginning of the twenty-first century asking much the same question as religious thinkers at the end of the nineteenth century in Europe: what is the right method by which to approach the history of religion? The answer given in particular by that brilliant German scholar, Ernst Troeltsch, is this: the proper method for the study of religion is a purely scientific historiography that is religiously neutral.[6] I have traced this answer and this method back to its

---

5. I am referring to Alan Richardson, *Christian Apologetics* (London: SCM, 1947), Richard R. Niebuhr, *Resurrection and Historical Reason* (New York: Scribner, 1957); and Wolfhart Pannenberg, "Redemptive Event and History," trans. S. Guthrie, *Basic Questions in Theology,* vol. 1 (Philadelphia: Westminster, 1983), also found in C. Westermann, ed., *Essays on Old Testament Hermeneutics* (Richmond, Va.: John Knox, 1963). See also Pannenberg's later work, *Jesus — God and Man,* trans. L. L. Wilkins and D. A. Priebe (Philadelphia: Westminster, 1968). Each of these works was published independently of the others in the 1940s or '50s, each in its own way responding to Barth and Bultmann on this topic.

6. See his essay "Historiography" in J. Hastings, ed., *Encyclopedia of Religion and Ethics* (Edinburgh: T&T Clark, 1913), vol. 6, pp. 716-23. Troeltsch's philosophy of history is in fact very nuanced. He rejected the certainty of historical judgment, arguing that worldviews and historical science are sometimes in tension. Nevertheless, for Troeltsch (as I read him), scientific historiography is an absolute value, arising within a particular

sources in Western intellectual history and have discovered that this "purely historical" approach to religion was first applied specifically to Jesus. The argument of scholars like H. S. Reimarus, David Strauss, and William Wrede was that the only proper, scholarly approach to Jesus was a purely historical, purely scientific one that rejected all religious belief as distorting and unscientific.[7] Because the Enlightenment was a Western movement, and because Christianity is the dominant religion of the West, the Enlightenment was forced to answer the question of what a proper, scholarly, "enlightened" approach to Jesus was. Their answer, which is the approach followed by the Jesus Seminar, I am going to label "the myth of a purely historical Jesus." I will use the specific issue of the resurrection of Jesus as a basis for examining the myth of a purely historical approach to religious studies. The resurrection is a fascinating claim made by early Christians, for it is at once both a claim about history and a claim about religious truth. How then shall we academics, we "scientific" investigators of religion, approach such a claim?

One easy and common answer is quite simple: dismiss the claim at once as impossible, and perhaps begin a historical and sociological investigation of why early Christians would create such a mythological tale. After all, we all know — don't we? — that dead people stay dead and that resurrections are in fact scientifically impossible. This is the approach of Rudolf Bultmann and his followers, along with most academics in religious studies today. This easy and common response to the claim that Jesus actually rose from the dead points to something important: the role of presuppositions and bias in historiography.[8]

---

context, that all academics should adopt *qua* academic. See further his *Reason in History*, trans. J. L. Adams and W. F. Bense (Minneapolis: Fortress, 1991). So even when he is striving "to recognize an influence of faith on science" Troeltsch can't help but write that "the empirical sciences in themselves are wholly independent of faith and follow their own laws" (*Reason in History*, p. 130).

7. See H. S. Reimarus, *Fragments*, ed. C. H. Talbert (London: SCM, 1971 [ca. 1775]); David F. Strauss, *The Life of Jesus Critically Examined*, trans. George Eliot (London: SCM, 1973 [1846]). For Wrede, see Morgan, *Nature of New Testament Theology*.

8. Numerous scholars have noticed this before, including Schlatter and Richardson (cited above). More recently is, among others, G. N. Stanton, "Presuppositions in New Testament Criticism," in *New Testament Interpretation*, ed. I. H. Marshall (Exeter: Paternoster, 1977). See also the next note on Bultmann. On worldviews and belief in miracles see Richard G. Swinburne, *The Concept of Miracles* (London:

This influence of worldviews upon academic and scientific investigation has many names and is widely accepted today. Any quest for knowledge, and considerations of argument and evidence, will be biased by the investigator's worldview. For want of a better name, I will call this "the prejudice of perspective." Bultmann himself would agree with us, of course. In a famous paper he asked, "Is Exegesis without Presuppositions Possible?"[9] The right answer, of course, is "No," and this was indeed Bultmann's answer, much to his credit. My problem with Bultmann is that he imports presuppositions that are antithetical to Christian faith, especially those that lie behind the myth of a purely historical Jesus.[10]

The Myth Exposed

Behind the myth is a basic assumption we need to examine: that religious faith corrupts scientific research. This powerful and attractive ideology in Western culture is still responsible for much of the rhetoric in biblical and religious studies about "scholarly" approaches to our topic. For example, the Jesus Seminar shows its arrogance and prejudice in this false claim: "The Christ of creed and dogma, who had been firmly in place in the Middle Ages, can no longer command the assent of those who have seen the heavens through Galileo's telescope."[11] My analysis of this myth reveals three underlying assumptions:

1. That religious faith distorts scientific, critical scholarship.
2. That because this is true, the only proper, academic, scientific methodology in religious studies is one that rejects religious faith itself.
3. That a purely historical, scientific, faith-free, and value-neutral

Macmillan, 1970), who argues that background beliefs influence our judgments of historical probability.

9. The English translation of this paper is found in Bultmann, *Existence and Faith*, ed. Schubert M. Ogden (Cleveland: Meridian, 1960), pp. 289-98.

10. For a careful critique of Bultmann, see R. C. Roberts, *Rudolf Bultmann's Theology* (Grand Rapids: Eerdmans, 1976).

11. Funk et al., *The Five Gospels*, p. 2.

methodology is available to us in what we might broadly call the social scientific disciplines.

I will argue that each of these ideas is false, and even more that this ideology as a whole is deluding and distorts the quest for truth about religion. Finally, I will demonstrate that the myth of a purely historical and faith-free approach to religion is part of an ideology that is destructive of human flourishing because it seeks to separate faith and values from science and reason.

Troeltsch, Wrede, and their many followers were working against an earlier approach to religious history called the dogmatic method or "apologetics" in the negative sense of these terms. In this method, one assumes the truth of a religion and then finds this truth in the historical sources (surprise!). This kind of circular reasoning can in fact prove anything to be true, and I therefore completely agree with modernity's rejection of that earlier, dogmatic approach to religious history. Furthermore, I do believe that we must continue to study religions in an academic, scholarly way that accepts criticism and argument as necessary correctives to our biases and prejudices. I do not want to be understood as suggesting that we throw out rigorous, scientific research; the canons of historical criticism are a lasting contribution to our civilization. My concern with biblical studies is not with our methods but rather with our attitudes toward them and toward religious faith. I want to examine the myth of a purely historical Jesus and consider its shortcomings. I will suggest that we must replace this attractive and powerful ideology (the "myth") with one that is more humble, holistic, and accepting of religious belief.

Such a claim obviously needs substantiation, so we will look at the basic assumptions of the myth. First of all, according to the myth, Christian faith distorts scientific research. The Jesus Seminar participants, and many others, intend to "liberate" Jesus research from the "oppression" of dogmatism. For example, Ed Sanders in his book *Jesus and Judaism* writes that "I have been engaged for some years in the effort to free history and exegesis from the control of theology" and "I aim only [!] to be a historian and an exegete."[12] Both aims are, alas, impossible, for we simply substitute one "theology" (or "mythology," as Burton

12. *Jesus and Judaism* (Philadelphia: Fortress, 1985), pp. 333f.

Mack calls it) for another. The myth of a purely historical Jesus helps the exegete fool herself about this substitution. (This is particularly obvious in the work of the Jesus Seminar.)[13]

Because of the prejudice of perspective there is no such thing as a purely historical, value-free, neutral scientific approach to the historical Jesus. Indeed, I would argue that there is no purely historical, value-free, neutral scientific approach to any great religious figure or controversial person from the past. The truth of this point is made clear by a controversial (but hardly religious) figure known to all of us: Richard Nixon. If you watch the Oliver Stone film *Nixon* and follow it with a visit to the Nixon Library, you find yourself asking, "Will the real Richard Nixon please stand up?" And it is obvious that the political biases of both the Nixon Library and Oliver Stone have influenced their quite distinct interpretations of the real Nixon of history. If the prejudice of perspective is true for our interpretation of Nixon — a famous leader in our own country and our own time about whom many, many facts are known — imagine how much more it must influence our treatment of Jesus or, for that matter, of Buddha or Confucius.

The myth of a purely historical Jesus, of course, has had tremendous cultural appeal, especially among academics, for some time now. For almost two hundred years academics have followed after this El Dorado, this powerful but ultimately elusive and deluding mythology, and like De Soto have often lost their way. I am not suggesting that no important advances have been made in the quest for the historical Jesus; they have. Rather, my point is that this mythology of a purely neutral, faith-free approach has deluded scholars about the importance, character, and meaning of their results.

I will examine two versions of this myth and criticize each one. In the first version, which I call "the neutrality two-step," the prejudice of perspective is recognized, but then we try and step around it back into scientific neutrality. For the "neutrality two-step" version of the myth, the problem of perspective is a problem only for faith — not for the sci-

---

13. For a good critique of the work of the Seminar, see Luke T. Johnson, *The Real Jesus* (San Francisco: Harper, 1995). I agree with much of what Johnson has to say, but in the end his own view still divides faith and science. Our spiritual knowledge of the real, risen Jesus must be subject to critical, scientific reflection and historical examination. (I do not say historical "verification" — I agree with Johnson that such a verification is impossible for historical science.) See further Chapter Eight in this volume.

entific, rational scholar who of course has no faith! A second version of the myth is one I call "the consensus Jesus," in which a consensus theory of truth is supposed to lead us to the real Jesus of history.

I will start with the most important version of the myth, the neutrality two-step. Many scholars today are sophisticated enough to realize that hermeneutic theory, epistemology, and the philosophy of science all converge at one point, namely, what I have called the prejudice of perspective. A purely neutral science is both undesirable and not possible in the first place.[14] Having recognized the prejudice of perspective, however, scholars still seem to hope that our biases and prejudices can be overcome through religious neutrality and scientific method. Let's pay attention to the facts and hope that all this interpretation stuff goes away, they seem to be saying. As long as we focus on the right methodology, are rigorously skeptical of the sources, and are as neutral and scientific as possible, excluding religious presuppositions, then the prejudice of perspective will not affect our results. This, of course, is simply self-delusion on the part of scholars.

Examples of the neutrality two-step include the work of both Ed Sanders and Burton Mack.[15] For both men, "theology" is a bad word and theological commitments tend to distort and warp neutral, scientific research. That their own worldviews distort and warp their own work is, of course, equally obvious, at least to us, for all of us approach our work with some sort of faith stance. Mack and Sanders have their own agendas, which distort their interpretations of Jesus, as does the Jesus Seminar. Another example of the neutrality two-step is the work of Gary Habermas, a conservative Christian apologist. He writes: "The

---

14. The separation of faith from science is the major problem I have with Peter Carnley's otherwise excellent book, *The Structure of Resurrection Belief* (Oxford: Oxford University Press, 1987). Carnley wants to add to pure scientific facts about Jesus a mythopoetic appropriation of the Spirit of Christ by faith (see pp. 352-58). The fusion of faith and science I have in mind presumes Christian faith *in the midst of* careful scientific work.

15. E. P. Sanders, *Jesus and Judaism*; Burton Mack, *A Myth of Innocence: Mark and Christian Origins* (Philadelphia: Fortress, 1988), and *The Lost Gospel: The Book of Q and Christian Origins* (San Francisco: Harper, 1993). For Mack it is not so much theology as "mythology" that is the problem (these words denote, for him, pretty much the same thing). A balanced reply to Mack is found in Pheme Perkins, "Jesus before Christianity: Cynic or Sage?" *Christian Century* 110 (July 28-August 4, 1993): 749-51; and in Paul Eddy, "Jesus as Diogenes?" *Journal of Biblical Literature* 115 (1996): 425-45.

best approach to take towards history is one of caution, as we should try and recognize this subjective bias and then make the proper allowance for it."[16] This sentence is, in fact, an almost perfect example of what I mean by the neutrality two-step. Of course Habermas and other apologists have their agenda, too, and want history to be neutral so they can use it to prove that Christianity is true. Allow me one more example: Willi Marxsen, a follower of Bultmann and a well-known New Testament scholar, defines "the historical Jesus" as "Jesus before anyone has ventured an interpretation of him."[17] That might be the true Jesus, but it is hardly the historical Jesus. Of course no such Jesus can be known, for the knowing process is itself an interpretation.

The neutrality two-step is close to being right. I agree that religious and historical claims must be subject to critical, scientific examination. The fundamental flaw in the neutrality two-step is this: all methods are already infected by theory. Worldviews don't just give us the questions we ask but also affect our understanding of the evidence and our historical judgment. There just is no such thing as data apart from some interpretation. The question of what counts as "evidence" or "data" is already biased by our prior interests, theories, and worldviews. So the neutrality two-step just trips us up as we reflect upon the relationship between faith and science. The neutrality two-step is also self-deluding. It leads to a bias against theological commitments in historical science, without recognizing the distorting elements in the researcher's own worldview. The rhetoric of the Jesus Seminar is a good example of what I mean by the self-deluding character of the myth.

The best-known and most sophisticated version of the neutrality two-step, which perhaps can illuminate the problems this outlook poses, comes from a book dedicated to Bultmann, Van Harvey's *The Historian and the Believer*.[18] Harvey develops a "morality of knowledge"

16. Gary Habermas, *Ancient Evidence for the Life of Jesus* (Nashville: Nelson, 1984), p. 18.

17. Willi Marxsen, *Jesus and Easter*, trans. V. P. Furnish (Nashville: Abingdon, 1990), p. 16. Of course Marxsen is not a slavish follower of Bultmann and disagrees with him on several points (these are helpfully outlined in G. O'Collins, *Jesus Risen* [Mahwah, N.J.: Paulist, 1987], pp. 65f.).

18. Van Austin Harvey, *The Historian and the Believer: The Morality of Historical Knowledge and Christian Belief* (New York: Macmillan, 1966). References will be to this edition. There is a reprint, with a new introduction (Urbana: University of Illinois Press, 1996).

in which the religious faith of the believing historian so distorts and warps her judgment that the validity of her reasoning process is called into question. Harvey's book downplays two important factors. First, the secular unbeliever is just as distorted and warped by his prejudice and worldview as the believer is. Second, who is to say that Christian faith does not give us better insight into the data than unbelief does? Why should unbelief, rather than faith, lead to the best explanation of the evidence? Would it be so strange if the followers of Jesus have an inside track in the understanding of Jesus? Why is faith so damaging to reason, anyway?

Granted that faith is a kind of prejudice, perhaps it is a helpful prejudice. Helpful prejudices can give us insight into the data and clear the way for understanding. The planet Neptune, for example, was discovered because of prejudice on the part of astronomers in favor of classical mechanics, and the Marxist prejudice of liberation theologians has helped us see what the Bible really does say about poverty and liberation. As Hans-Georg Gadamer has argued, we all stand in some tradition, and have some prejudice, when we approach the task of interpretation.[19] Not all tradition and prejudice is bad: some can be helpful. All reasoning is based on some prejudice, all insight and research takes place from a particular position and in the light of a particular worldview and tradition of inquiry. There is no "view from nowhere," to borrow a phrase from Thomas Nagel.[20]

The question of whether a certain prejudice is helpful or harmful in the evaluation of evidence cannot be decided *a priori* as Harvey wants it to be.[21] It is only in the give and take of dialogue, and in the evaluation of reasons, arguments, and evidence, that our pre-understanding will be found to be helpful or harmful. I am not suggesting that we abandon rational inquiry or scientific historiography. Nor do I suggest that biblical scholarship return to the Christian dogmatism of a previ-

19. Hans-Georg Gadamer, *Truth and Method,* second English edition (New York: Continuum, 1991 [1960]).

20. Thomas Nagel, *The View from Nowhere* (Oxford: Oxford University Press, 1985).

21. See, e.g., Harvey, *The Historian and the Believer,* p. 213. All of Harvey's discussion of "hard and soft perspectivism" is interesting just because he misunderstands the point being made that there are no objective standards of historical reasoning. Note his prejudice in favor of "what any historian would accept as a legitimate claim" (p. 218), or again, "events that are otherwise known in the way any event can be known" (p. 242).

ous age. Rather, I suggest that the myth of a neutral, scientific history, which Harvey assumes throughout his book, distorts the relationship between faith (or the lack of it!) and historical research. The casual dismissal of the claim that Jesus rose from the dead is not a helpful prejudice, for it is founded upon a fallacious conception of natural science and the "laws" of nature (which are purely descriptive, not prescriptive). It is no accident that Harvey's book is dedicated to Bultmann, for it perpetuates the misunderstanding of faith and science that one finds in Bultmann and his school.

The implications of the myth of a purely historical Jesus are in fact a roadblock to historical knowledge of the real Jesus, for it is part of the myth that religious faith distorts our knowledge of reality. Since the New Testament is written, in part, from a faith perspective, it must be questioned at every turn. For example, in his book *The Future of the Historical Jesus,* Lelander Keck writes (correctly in my view) that "every believer and every theologian has central things at stake in the historical study of Jesus."[22] I applaud Keck's rejection of the attempt (characteristic of the Bultmann school) to divorce faith and science. But when Keck insists that "a skeptical attitude toward the sources is necessary," he has obviously bought into the myth of a purely historical Jesus.[23] Why is a skeptical attitude necessary? Only because, as a hidden premise, we must doubt any historical claim that could come from a faith perspective. But all historical writing comes from a faith perspective. We must, indeed, accept a critical attitude toward all historical sources and artifacts. A critical attitude that gives a careful examination of the evidence is not, however, the same thing as a *skeptical* attitude based upon a prejudice against religious faith in the sources. Such a skepticism, the "guilty until proven innocent" modern attitude toward the New Testament, actually blocks good historical research. Once again we can cite the Jesus Seminar: "methodological skepticism . . . was a working principle of the Seminar; when in sufficient doubt, leave it out."[24] In fact the Seminar seems to work on the principle, "when there is *any* doubt leave it out." There is much we can learn historically from

22. Lelander Keck, *The Future of the Historical Jesus* (Nashville: Abingdon, 1971), p. 38.

23. Keck, *The Future of the Historical Jesus,* p. 21.

24. Funk et al., *Five Gospels,* p. 37.

the New Testament, but not if we insist on doubting every line of it until we can prove it to be true. In logic, we would call this the fallacy of "poisoning the well." In the history of philosophy, it represents Descartes's approach to epistemology, and that is a dead end. So, ironically, the myth of a purely historical Jesus ends up distorting the very quest for the true Jesus that it was created to assist. Such is the human condition!

Another version of the myth of a purely historical Jesus is the "consensus Jesus." Once again, some scholars recognize the prejudice of perspective but then try to dance around it. In this version, they hope that a consensus of New Testament scholars will provide us with the "true" Jesus of history. A brilliant example of this method, and one I admire very much, is *A Marginal Jew,* the multivolume work of John Meier. While Meier's historical judgment is excellent, and his scholarship and knowledge are profound, his presentation of method is quite flawed. To see why this is so, let us first make some distinctions in our terminology. By "the true Jesus," "the real Jesus," or "the Jesus of history" I will mean Jesus of Nazareth as he really was in the past. By "the historical Jesus," however, I will follow common usage and understand this phrase to designate Jesus as we can know him through historical research. Finally, I will understand "the consensus Jesus" to refer to that Jesus who is known to us through a consensus of current New Testament scholarship.

There is little hope that the consensus Jesus will yield to us the real Jesus. This is so for both theoretical and practical reasons. As any first-year philosophy student knows, the consensus theory of truth is bogus. Just because a group of humans think something is true does not make it true. On the practical end, we always have to ask the critical or Marxist question: who defines the consensus? The so-called "consensus" of the Jesus Seminar is obviously based upon personalities and *a priori* ideology, as anyone who is aware of the history and personalities behind the group knows. Or again, in his interesting book *The Quest for a Post-Historical Jesus,* William Hamilton tells us that it is a consensus among current scholars that no historical knowledge of the real Jesus is possible.[25] As a factual statement about the academy of biblical

---

25. William Hamilton, *The Quest for a Post-Historical Jesus* (New York: Continuum, 1994), p. 19.

scholarship, this "consensus" is obviously false. I am afraid that the consensus Jesus will yield us nothing and cannot lead to any sound, scientific results about history or, indeed, about any scientific topic.

Now consensus is important, of course, in many areas of life. We are wise to rely on a consensus of experts, when there is such, for topics in which we are not well versed ourselves. But in their own areas of expertise, scientific investigators must ignore the "consensus" in favor of the evidence and arguments themselves. At best a consensus might provide a beginning for our own careful examination of the issues. Unlike the Jesus Seminar, which is "pop" scholarship, Meier is better than the methodology he espouses. Like so many other scholars, he is aware of the prejudice of perspective but does not realize the implications of this prejudice for his own work. He writes, "we abstract from Christian faith because we are involved in the hypothetical reconstruction of a past figure *by purely scientific means.*"[26] In another place he indicates that, "To be sure, *A Marginal Jew* works with presuppositions, but they are the general presuppositions of historiography."[27]

The point that must be made, against the "consensus Jesus" version of the myth of a purely historical Jesus, is that the presuppositions of biblical scholars are diverse and conflicting. These diverse presuppositions inevitably influence our gathering of the data, our grasp of what counts as "evidence," and our interpretation of that evidence. None of the natural or historical sciences has as a criterion or index of truth a consensus among investigators, and for good reason. We may try to be as reasonable and rational as possible, but we cannot escape our own prejudices. And since our perspectives are so pluralistic, the consensus Jesus becomes a minimalist Jesus. If we were really to base a book on Jesus just on what all New Testament scholars agreed upon — or on 90 percent or 75 percent (how shall we define "consensus"?) of what they agreed upon — the resulting book would be a lot shorter than *A Marginal Jew*! And, honestly, of what scientific value would such a purely sociological study be? At best it might give us a starting point for our own investigations based upon our own faith and our own methods, but we would still have to re-investigate each point for our-

26. John P. Meier, *A Marginal Jew,* 2 vols. (Garden City: Doubleday, 1991, 1994), vol. 1, pp. 30f., my italics.
27. Meier, *A Marginal Jew,* vol. 2, p. 14 n. 6.

selves. And this consensus Jesus would a jaundiced, emaciated Jesus, for there are so few facts we can all agree on. The consensus Jesus is not even the historical Jesus, much less the real Jesus of history.

I hope I have said enough to indicate that the myth of the purely historical Jesus is a false ideology imposed upon religious studies by the Enlightenment. It is self-deluding, and it also distorts the attempt to come to know the real Jesus. The myth "poisons the well" with respect to the only significant sources we have to study the historical Jesus. Now, it is certainly true that a dogmatic method, which presumes the results of critical inquiry before the give and take of evidence, argument, and reasoning takes place, is destructive of true critical scholarship. But religious faith does not have to lead to dogmatism of this kind, and it often does not. I have met many dogmatic atheists who arrogantly assume that scientific materialism is the only rational worldview and that Christian theology is just another kind of ancient myth. Belief that all truth is God's truth, that God is the maker of heaven, earth, and of my neighbor, can and does lead to open enquiry, toleration, understanding, and careful scholarship. Adolf Schlatter would be a good example of this in New Testament studies. Moreover, have we forgotten that the founders of natural science were people of faith? For Copernicus, Kepler, Galileo, and Newton, belief in a rational Creator was a fundamental assumption for the scientific quest. So the first assumption of the myth, that religious faith corrupts scientific research, is both false as an idea and self-deluding as an ideology. It allows researchers to believe about themselves — falsely, of course — that their own faith stance and their own worldview does not corrupt their research.

The assumption, left over from Enlightenment prejudice, that religious faith corrupts science is self-deluding, and it distorts the quest for religious truth; but most importantly, perhaps, it is part of the divorce between science and faith. The idea that the only proper approach to religion is one that ignores or brackets religious faith is part of an overall attempt to "free" science from the "biases" of religion and morality, an idea we can trace to the French encyclopedists. And this divorce has been destructive in our own century, to our own people. It leads to bad religion, and to bad science and technology. Who wants a religion divorced from reason, or scientific experiments and applications that ignore moral truth? We know now that science and technology are not autonomous realms, free from such biases as respect for life and love for people of other cultures and classes. In short, the myth of a purely historical Jesus is part of the overall attempt to separate faith and moral values from science, and this attempt has been destructive to the human race, to religious faith, to good scientific methods, and to the environment. Science and technology, divorced from religious wisdom and moral values, is not only a myth but the nightmare of the twentieth century.

Toward a Dialogue between Faith and Science

I have indicated several reasons for dropping the self-deluding myth of a purely historical approach to religious studies. But if we drop this ideology, what shall replace it? This question is, I think, the major reason so many scholars continue to have faith in the myth. They feel that if they drop the idea of a purely neutral, value-free approach, then history will be left in a quagmire of subjectivity. To quote from Meier again,

> Whether we call it a bias, a *Tendenz,* a worldview, or a faith stance, everyone who writes on the historical Jesus writes from some ideological vantage point; no critic is exempt. The solution to this dilemma is neither to pretend to an absolute objectivity that is not to be had nor to wallow in total relativism.[28]

Notice two things in this quotation: first, that a faith stance creates a dilemma for the historian, and second, the fear of relativism if we drop the myth of a purely historical Jesus. In fact, Meier accepts here some version of the neutrality two-step: let's admit our bias, follow a rigorous methodology, and try to be as objective and religion-neutral as possible. But this assumes, all along, that faith is some problem for scientific objectivity. There is, as Ben Meyer puts it, a fear of subjectivity here. We are afraid, as scholars, that a postmodern perspective will lead to "anything goes." Any view of Jesus will be just as good as any other. We will, in fact, be out of a job, no longer needed to guide young minds

28. Meier, *A Marginal Jew,* vol. 1, pp. 5f.

to the truth about religious history. Ben Meyer also points us to the proper way out of this fear in his review of criteria or indices of authenticity: we should not shun subjectivity but embrace it as a moment on the way toward objectivity.[29]

Let us put this point in the broad terms of philosophy of science. First of all, let us recognize the prejudice of perspective. This means that I, as a scientist (social or natural) recognize that my worldview is bound to influence what I choose to call data and how I weigh the evidence in reaching toward the best explanation. Second, we recognize pluralism in worldviews: there are many different ways of understanding reality. Pluralism and the prejudice of perspective should not, however, lead us to despair or relativism, but rather to intellectual humility. As argued in the previous chapter of this book, cognitive relativism does not follow from plurality nor from the prejudice of perspective;[30] there is a real world out there to know, and a real past as well. It does, however, lead to humility. Our results are not certain. They are not purely neutral. They may be "scientific," but that does not grant them certainty, as Troeltsch himself knew. What I am proposing, again, is a form of dialectical realism.

Let us embrace our faith, therefore, and recognize it for what it is. And of course by "faith" I do not mean only religious faith but would include all worldviews, such as Marxism or scientific materialism. They, too, operate on faith or trust. We accept that faith may distort our judgment, but at the same time, it may give us deeper understanding. There just is no *a priori* way to tell, except in the give and take of pluralistic and public dialogue, whether our faith is distorting or helpful to our understanding of the object of study. So, in the end, we subject our conclusions to public scrutiny and careful scientific examination, then revise them in the light of what we learn in that process.

I am not, therefore, abandoning the quest for truth and reality.

29. Ben Meyer, "Objectivity and Subjectivity in Historical Criticism of the Gospels," in *The Interrelations of the Gospels,* ed. D. L. Dungan, Bibliotheca Ephemeridum theologicarum Lovaniensium 95 (Macon, Ga.: Mercer University Press, 1990). Also found in his volume *Critical Realism and the New Testament* (Allison Park, Pa.: Pickwick, 1989).

30. See also Gadamer *(Truth and Method)* on hermeneutics, Alasdair MacIntyre *(First Principles, Final Ends and Contemporary Philosophical Issues* [Milwaukee: Marquette University Press, 1990]) on ethical principles, and Larry Laudan *(Beyond Positivism and Relativism* [Boulder, Col.: Westview, 1996]) on the philosophy of science.

Relativism is just as destructive of true historical and scientific research as the myth of a purely historical Jesus. I affirm objective truth;
it is the claim to objective knowledge that I find problematic. Nor am I
suggesting a return to the old dogmatic method of presuming the
truth of our faith and refusing to change in the light of evidence. But
let us face the facts. The evidence about Jesus is slight, and capable of
many equally reasonable interpretations. The social sciences do not
have the same objective status as the natural sciences, for they cannot
do experiments (except in a few cases) to test which theory or interpretation is true. Measurements and mathematical theories are few and
far between in history, so the social sciences draw more fully on subjective judgment. But that does not mean they are unscientific. Moreover,
the fact that our faith stance is bound to have a tremendous influence
on our reconstruction of the historical Jesus does not mean that the
quest is in vain, or that faith is not at risk. It is: Christianity has made
certain historical claims, and must demonstrate to a public, pluralistic
audience that it has reasons, arguments, and evidence for them. We can
prove that Christianity is reasonable — even if we cannot prove it is true
— in the open marketplace of ideas.[31]

We are pressing once again toward a collegial metaphor for faith
and science. In other words, each scholar should integrate faith and science, reason and religion, in an overall coherent and rational worldview.
Each aspect of our worldview, both faith and science, has its place. Each
is open to modification in the light of the other. Faith and science must
be in dialogue and mutual modification, as we seek an overall worldview
that is rationally satisfactory and existentially meaningful.

There is one point at which the myth of a purely historical Jesus is
correct. This has to do with the distinction between history and the
other sciences. While history does investigate the past, its explanations
are in terms of psycho-social understanding. History is limited to the

---

31. This position represents what Stephen T. Davis calls "soft apologetics." See his
debate on the resurrection with Gary Habermas and James Keller in the pages of *Faith and
Philosophy:* Davis, "Is It Possible to Know That Jesus Was Raised from the Dead?" 1 (1984):
147-59; Habermas, "Knowing That Jesus' Resurrection Occurred: A Response to Davis" 2
(1985): 295-302; Davis, "Naturalism and Resurrection: A Reply to Habermas" 2 (1985): 303-
8; Keller, "Contemporary Christian Doubts about the Resurrection" 5 (1988): 40-60; and
Davis, "Doubting the Resurrection: A Reply to James A. Keller" 7 (1990): 99-111. See also
Davis, *Risen Indeed* (Grand Rapids: Eerdmans, 1993).

human, to human events and artifacts, and to explanations in terms of psycho-social forces, symbolic meanings, and social institutions. There is in fact a precise parallel here with natural science. Take as an example the initial expansion of the universe at the Big Bang. This is clearly a past event, but it is not a historical event (in the sense of history as an academic discipline). In fact, I believe the term "historical event" is a misleading one, since it can mean either a past event or an event subject to historical explanation. More precision can be had if we stick to natural scientific explanations versus historical explanations. The Big Bang is subject to natural scientific explanations but not to historical explanations. The American Revolution, on the other hand, is an event that cannot be adequately explained by natural science. We need historical explanations, based on psycho-social causal factors and meanings, to understand it fully.

The myth of a purely historical Jesus insisted on a distinction between theology and history. And this distinction is a valid one. But it is best understood along the model of levels of explanation in the sciences.[32] When teaching about Jesus in an academic and pluralistic context, therefore, we should say this: our teaching is limited to the events in the life of Jesus that are subject to historical explanation or verification. We focus on normal historical explanations for the life of Jesus and exclude from consideration any theological explanations. In fact this is what we do in any case, but let us be open and up-front about it. It is important to distinguish history from theology, in terms of the goals and methods of each discipline, but we can separate history and theology without the arrogance of the myth of a purely historical Jesus. In terms of scholarly publications let us return to John Meier. His conclusions are better than the methodology he espouses. His results are not based on a mythological consensus among scholars. What he should say about his methodology is this: it is limited to the events in the life of Jesus that are subject to historical explanation, focusing on normal historical explanations for Jesus' life and excluding from consideration any theological explanations. In fact this is what he does in any case.

With this difference between history and theology in mind, let us return to the resurrection of Jesus. If this event happened at all it is a past event. Some have suggested that it did not take place in space and

---

32. For more on levels of explanation in the sciences, see Chapter One in this volume.

time, yet if it took place at all it surely did so in space and time. If Jesus rose from the dead, this event has a date and it took place at a certain location in space, just outside Jerusalem. If it did happen, however, it is not subject to natural scientific explanation. Likewise, it is not subject to historical explanation. Historical science is incapable of making a theological judgment about whether or not God could or did raise Jesus (at the same time, historical scientific judgment is important to the theological issue, of course). Rather, if the resurrection did take place, only a theological explanation, based upon the causal powers of God, will be fully satisfactory to human reason. Social science cannot explain how someone rose from the dead. So we can and should accept the difference between natural scientific, social scientific (including historical), and theological explanations. When John Meier writes about the resurrection, he will no doubt limit himself to natural and historical explanations of the event. That will be helpful and important. But we can separate history and theology without the myth of a purely historical Jesus and all of its arrogant and self-deluding properties. We must insist that theology and science respect and learn from each other, while recognizing that they are not the same thing. That is, after all, the main thesis of this book.

This leads us to a final issue, which again can only be touched upon briefly. I have been arguing that we should recognize and publicly admit our faith during scientific investigations. Christian historians, then, should openly acknowledge their belief in the resurrection even while seeking careful historical and public evidence for this claim. Such a position avoids "dogmatic" circular reasoning, however, only if our faith is open to revision in the light of evidence. One objection to the view I am arguing for might come from a misunderstanding of "faith."

A major error in Western thought has been committed in the analysis of faith. Because of the deep effect faith has upon life, some thinkers have insisted that faith must have existential certainty.[33] Therefore, faith cannot be based upon the probable arguments of history, philosophy, and science. This error in analysis is at the root of the division between faith and science.

---

33. For example, Søren Kierkegaard, *Concluding Unscientific Postscript*, trans. D. F. Swenson and W. Lowrie (Princeton, N.J.: Princeton University Press, 1941), pp. 28-33. Kierkegaard wrote this under a pseudonym; his actual views could be different.

We must not separate faith and science in our culture, for this leads to terrible destruction. But what then is the right understanding of the relationship between faith and reason? As a Christian I have faith in Christ, a faith I would, under God's care, be willing to die for (though I hope I will not be put to the test!). But this strong existential certainty does not translate into a need for epistemic certainty. That's the category mistake that John Knox, Willi Marxsen, and so many others have made.[34] Rather, my interpretation of the meaning of my faith in God must be open to rational reflection and revision in the light of reason, evidence, and argument. Of course, this rational reflection does not happen at the same moment, or in the same mood, as the experience of faith itself. My rational reflection and interpretation of faith is a different, critical moment, quite distinct from the personal and existential moment of faith. Few people hold to their deepest faith because of arguments, and religious faith is certainly quite different in its logic and "grammar" from a scientific hypothesis. Nevertheless, our faith itself, and especially our interpretation of the meaning of that faith, must be open to revision in more critical and reflective moments. In the face of objections to faith, or in the face of terrible experiences such as suffering or oppression, I may come to doubt. At that point my continued faith may well depend upon arguments, reasons, and evidence, as well as the private and personal grounds on which faith originally rose and continues to well-up in my soul. I may also encounter difficult questions or rational problems with the implications of my faith. In such instances, I have a duty to myself and to the truth to investigate the reasonableness of my beliefs. Fideism is in the long run unsatisfactory.

Let us take up the example of the resurrection of Jesus once again. Imagine that after careful historical research I concluded not only that there is limited evidence for a resurrection (which is compatible with belief in the resurrection) but that all the best evidence was against the resurrection. What then? Would that change my faith? I think that if I were rational, it would have to. It would certainly change my interpretation of Christianity. Gone would be any hope of my own real resurrection after death, for example. My understanding of biblical authority would no doubt weaken if this central historical claim turned out to be false. But I hope that my faith in God, and in Jesus, would still re-

---

34. For John Knox, see his *The Church and the Reality of Christ* (London: Collins, 1963), pp. 16f.

main. I might become a liberal United Methodist theologian, but I would not cease to be a Christian.

Our interpretation of both faith and science must be open to revision in the light of reason, evidence, and argument. Of course there is no one right understanding of reasoning or logic, nor of what counts as evidence and a good argument. Here we have to do the best we can, with the tools and methods that are most appropriate to our quest for truth. But there can be no guarantees to truth, not in the area of faith and not in the area of science.

Let us therefore embrace our faith, and recognize it for what it is, but be willing to admit that others' faiths have insight we need. Let us use our best methodologies and scientific, critical thinking, but not assume that we must also be skeptical of the religion we are studying or of its texts and sources. Let us, instead, seek to understand, sympathize with, and appreciate the religious faiths we study. In terms of education, this means that the job of religion and Bible teachers is *not* to destroy the faiths of our students. We should not, as teachers, use our position to undermine and shock students' religious faiths, however naive or closed-minded they may be. Instead, let us help each student to integrate his or her own faith (not ours, theirs) with the methods, scholarship, and results that vigorous academic training has provided us. I suggest that it is bad pedagogy to seek to "blow away the fundamentalists," however tempting it may be! Rather, college and university students need help in the integration of faith and science, whatever faith they may have.

The myth of a purely historical Jesus has distorted scholarship long enough. It has served as a mask to shield us from criticism, to delude ourselves and others, to confuse us as to the character of the historical method and the certainty of our historical results. In our postmodern situation, progress will be made only when we each embrace and understand our own faith stance, stake our claim in the public and pluralistic marketplace of ideas, and give what reasons, evidence, and arguments we can for our conclusions. My plea, then, is this: let us take off the mask of pure objectivity and speak to each other face to face.[35]

---

35. The author is grateful for his kind reception by the American Academy of Religion, Western Region, and the Society of Biblical Literature, Pacific Coast Region, where he read an earlier version of this chapter as a Presidential Address for 1996. A very early version of this chapter was also read to the Joseph Butler Society at Oxford, in 1987.

4 Science and Worldview

We have argued that there is no neutral and value-free approach to the social sciences that provides a purely scientific approach to the study of religion. But whatever the troubles of these "soft" sciences may be, surely the "hard" (what a question-begging metaphor!) natural sciences are not subject to such fuzzy thinking, are they? In this chapter, we answer this question. Our thesis is a rather common one these days among philosophers of science, namely, that our paradigms influence our scientific practice (and thus the body of scientific knowledge). One possible way to establish this thesis would be to tell a story, specifically the story of the development of the philosophy of science in the twentieth century, from logical positivism to postmodernity. This has in fact been done well by other writers, including those interested in the religion and science dialogue.[1] So I will here just give a brief outline of some of the reasons for this significant shift in the philosophy of science.

Science and Human Interest

The word "science" can be used in at least two senses. We might refer to science as an activity or practice. This is the turn that Ludwig Wittgenstein made in his later philosophy, and he was followed by

---

1. See Del Ratzsch, *Science and Its Limits* (Downers Grove, Ill.: InterVarsity, 1999), or J. Wentzel van Huyssteen, *Theology and the Justification of Faith* (Grand Rapids: Eerdmans, 1989).

N. R. Hanson, Stephen Toulmin, and Thomas Kuhn. Such an understanding of "science" lies at the foundation of the developing field of "science studies." On the other hand, another sense of "science" is a body of received knowledge. In both senses, I will argue, value commitments play a role in the criticism and growth of knowledge. Worldview commitments, therefore, likewise play a (limited) role. But this relationship must not be seen as one-sided. Rather, science and our worldviews are most healthy when there is an ongoing relationship between them, with no member a dominant partner.

There are a number of points that lead us to this conclusion. Karl Popper, reacting to the work of the Vienna Circle, already in 1934 argued that there is no neutral observation. It is simply not possible to "observe" without some interest, and some assumptions about what we are looking for.[2] Pierre Duhem had made the same observation some decades earlier,[3] and in his volume *Personal Knowledge,* Michael Polanyi also makes a good case for all observation, and all scientific practice, being guided by personal interest.[4] All our perception is "assumption-laden" and guided by our human concerns.

At the same time, we should note (as Polanyi does) that science contains rigorous methods of testing and communal criticism, which means that scientific proposals must stand up to high standards before they are accepted by others. Nevertheless, the point remains: science is guided by values, which cannot be justified by science itself. For this science turns to philosophy and to the worldviews and traditions that ground our quest for truth and meaning. And just as science is guided by values, so too the growth of scientific knowledge and the actual practice of science can and should give shape to our epistemology and metaphysics, that is, to our worldviews. This is a key part of my proposal in the present work: science, philosophy, and theology are colleagues. One partner should not dominate the others.

Not only is observation guided by assumptions and values, so also is the rationality of science within the disciplines. Thomas Kuhn

2. Karl R. Popper, *The Logic of Scientific Discovery,* tenth ed. (London: Hutchinson, 1980).

3. Pierre Duhem, *The Aim and Structure of Physical Theory* (Princeton, N.J.: Princeton University Press, 1954 [1906]), part 2, chaps. 4 and 6.

4. Michael Polanyi, *Personal Knowledge* (Chicago: University of Chicago Press, 1962).

wrote one of the most popular and influential academic books of the last century, *The Structure of Scientific Revolutions*. Arguing that the sciences are based on "paradigms," he noted that there are no pure rational rules for deciding between paradigms when "revolutions" happen in the history of science. We can define a "paradigm" as "a set of scientific and metaphysical beliefs that make up a theoretical framework within which scientific theories can be tested, evaluated, and if necessary, revised."[5] Note that a paradigm includes metaphysical as well as scientific beliefs. And our paradigms also include values that guide us in theory choice, and perhaps even in paradigm evaluation. Kuhn wrote in this regard that "the premises and values shared by the two parties to a debate over paradigms are not sufficiently extensive for [a purely rational choice to be made]."[6] Nevertheless, he notes that such shared epistemic values are "the permanent attributes of science."[7] What are some of these shared values? Kuhn mentions accuracy, consistency, scope, simplicity, and fruitfulness. Other lists could be made. For example, that great defender of Darwinism, Michael Ruse, writes:

> There is a set or body of norms or values or constraints that guides scientists in their theorizing and observing: predictive accuracy, internal coherence, external consistency with the rest of science, unificatory power (consilience), predictive fertility, and to some degree simplicity or elegance.[8]

These values are not arbitrary, but have been found over time to yield fruitful, well-established theories. My point is that such metaphysical commitments and shared values are part of larger philosophies and worldviews, which place them within a broader epistemology in which they can be spelled out more fully, and grounded more carefully, than

---

5. B. Enç, "Paradigm," *Cambridge Dictionary of Philosophy* (Cambridge: Cambridge University Press, 1999), p. 557.

6. Thomas Kuhn, *The Structure of Scientific Revolutions,* second ed. (Chicago: University of Chicago Press, 1970), p. 94.

7. Thomas Kuhn, *The Essential Tension* (Chicago: University of Chicago Press, 1977), p. 335.

8. Michael Ruse, *Mystery of Mysteries: Is Evolution a Social Construction?* (Cambridge, Mass.: Harvard University Press, 1999). Ruse goes on to argue that "good science" should not have any "cultural-value components" (p. 238), but I do not think he can make such a neat division stick in practice.

the sciences themselves can accomplish (given their limited aims and methods).[9] As Ernan McMullin concluded in his presidential address to the American Philosophical Association:

> The rationality of science can be philosophically justified. Here I disagree with Kuhn. What philosophers of science have labored so long to show is that such values as fertility are an appropriate criterion of theory. Their arguments are in a broad sense logical or epistemological.[10]

Science and philosophy can work together, then, to increase our knowledge. One cannot be substituted for another, nor do the work of the other. The same is also true, I shall argue later, for theology.

I would argue, then, that science takes place within a shared community of values, practices, and traditions, which account (in part) for the amazing coherence of that community of inquiry. These shared values can in turn be developed and defended within philosophies and worldviews, which seek to be in accordance with the best science (i.e., they seek to be "scientific" in character). The large degree of long-term consensus in natural science also depends upon the natural sciences' empirical and mathematical methods and their focus on physical objects. When we move to social science, there is less stability in the subject of inquiry and much more complex systems which do not obey (so it seems) any social "laws of nature" or simple mathematical constants. There are also far fewer shared methods and values in the social sciences. But what about this rather abstract and vague notion of a "worldview"? Can we possibly know anything about that, or make any rational decisions about our worldviews? Are we not leaving the realm of solid scientific knowledge when we move into values and philosophy?

Perhaps more pragmatic readers will be thinking something like this: while it is true that science draws on cultural factors in its histori-

---

9. See also Stephen Wykstra, "Have Worldviews Shaped Science?", in *Facets of Faith and Science,* ed. Jiste van der Meer, 4 vols. (Lanham, Md.: University Press of America, 1996), vol. 1, pp. 91-113. Wykstra needs a more mutual conception of the relationship between worldviews and science than he allows in this paper, in which the relationship seems rather one-way.

10. Ernan McMullin, "The Goals of Natural Science," *Proceedings of the American Philosophical Association* 58 (1984): 37-64, quoting 57.

cal origins, the long-range success of science, and its rational practice over time, means that the values of science are eventually refined. They are justified by the practice of science itself, and therefore we lose the need for some kind of "first philosophy" that will pretend to save science from epistemic uncertainty. For example, W. V. Quine writes that "naturalism" (what I will call "scientism") entails "the abandonment of the goal of a first philosophy." Natural science is not, he thinks, "answerable to any suprascientific tribunal, and not in need of any justification beyond observation and the hypothetical-deductive method."[11] Setting aside Quine's rather too simple view of scientific justification, it must be noted that the main point of such a view is that science does not need philosophy; science itself justifies its own values in the long run.

There are two models that stand opposed to a mutuality model for worldviews and science. One, like Quine's, sees science as being all-powerful and foundational. Philosophy must take its cue from science, and for Quine that means physics. On the other hand, there are those who think worldviews dominate scientific practice, and thus set up another one-way street, this time from worldviews to science. Paul Feyerabend takes this strong view, for his own relativistic and anarchistic purposes.[12] If natural science were indeed to allow this kind of dictation from worldviews (which despite Feyerabend does not seem very likely), it could not keep its own integrity, its explanatory focus on physical things and their powers and structure, and its goal of explaining phenomena on natural grounds (more on this below). This division of labor was important for the focus, growth, and development of natural philosophy in the high Middle Ages, and it has continued to be fruitful for natural science up to our own day.

The most likely alternative to the mutuality model developed here is scientism. I will define "scientism" as the combination of naturalism in ontology with the view in epistemology that science is the best, or only reliable, vehicle for knowledge of the real world. A good example of this comes from the philosopher Patricia Churchland: "In the

11. W. V. Quine, *Theories and Things* (Cambridge, Mass.: Harvard University Press, 1981), p. 72.

12. Paul Feyerabend, *The Conquest of Abundance* (Chicago: University of Chicago Press, 1999), p. 164.

idealized long run, the completed science is a true description of reality, there is no other Truth and no other Reality."[13] Scientists themselves, however, are divided on just this issue. For example, Francisco Ayala, a biologist and philosopher, writes,

> My purpose in this essay [on evolution and human nature] has been to provide what I see as a necessary dimension, the biological one, of any view of human nature that seeks to be relevant and complete. But I do not pretend that biology provides now, or will ever provide, a complete understanding of what we humans are and our place in the universe.[14]

Is the difference here between two distinguished professors, both members of the University of California faculty, simply a matter of taste?

A full and complete refutation of naturalism is beyond our purpose in this work,[15] but I will pause to argue briefly that science itself does not present us with a complete worldview. In other words, *scientism is a philosophical position, not a science.* The shortest path to this conclusion is to ask, why should I take science as a guide to knowledge? The easy answer is that science has proven in the past to give us truth about the world. But I must now assume, in order for science to guide my future actions, that *the world will continue to be like it was in the past.* And this is an assumption that science itself presupposes, but cannot and does not ground (any more than our common human experience does). Another way of putting this would be that science cannot solve the problem of induction. In fact, science cannot even solve the larger question of the rationality of the world: it simply assumes it, and gets about its task of discovering new truths about that world. There is another telling criticism of scientism that is rather easy to see: scientism is not a scientific proposition.[16] Consider the following proposal, P: "Believe all and only things demonstrated by the methods and results

13. Patricia Churchland, *Neurophilosophy* (Cambridge, Mass.: MIT Press, 1986), p. 249.

14. F. J. Ayala, "So Human an Animal," in *Science and Theology: The New Consonance,* ed. Ted Peters (Boulder, Col.: Westview, 1998), p. 135.

15. See the collection of essays in *Naturalism: A Critical Appraisal,* ed. Stephen J. Warner and Richard Wagner (Notre Dame: University of Notre Dame Press, 1993).

16. See George Myro, "Aspects of Acceptability," in *Naturalism,* ed. Warner and Wagner, pp. 197-210.

of the natural sciences." Is P itself a result of the methods and doc-trines of natural science? Of course not. But then, when we apply P to itself, we cannot believe P! So scientism is self-refuting (often consid-ered a bad thing by philosophers), and we are better off looking else-where for epistemological advice. The values and assumptions of the sciences are not self-grounding. For this reason, there cannot be a sim-ple one-way model of science always and everywhere dictating to episte-mology.

"All people by nature desire to know." So Aristotle begins his clas-sic *Metaphysics.* Human beings possess an innate desire to know the truth. Philosophy, science, and theology, each in their own way, seek to satisfy this desire. Philosophy is a quest for understanding. It does not seek to explain the world so much as to understand it. The task of phi-losophy is to analyze the broadest categories of human thought and seek conceptual clarity and analysis. Philosophy is rational reflection upon experience and reason, seeking to answer qualitative questions about life, meaning, and reality. Philosophy begins with experience but as a discipline is not fully empirical. So philosophy turns to rationality, another source of knowledge for humans. Rationality is based on ideas, experiences, and arguments that are, in principle, open to any human being. Philosophy asks, and seeks to answer, the larger questions of life and knowledge, including those surrounding God, goodness, beauty, meaning, and truth. As such, then, philosophy is capable of evaluating worldviews. Naturally, all the disciplines of the university contribute to (and criticize) aspects of our belief systems, but only philosophy takes up the task of criticizing systems of belief as a whole.

But are there any rational methods in philosophy as an academic practice, which can guide our evaluation of worldviews? Alas, philoso-phy lacks the kind of coherent and unified community of practice we find in the natural sciences. Nevertheless, philosophy as an academic discipline is useful and can help us in the evaluation of worldviews. This is particularly true because philosophy seeks clarity and precision in the most important tool we have as humans in our common quest for life and thought together: language. It also studies various forms of argument and various claims to knowledge, in formal and informal logic. Philosophy seeks to guide our lives through reason and reflec-tion, especially reflection upon our most basic commitments and val-ues. It can help to clarify our beliefs and expose our prejudices. Most people — including scientists — have philosophical beliefs and tacit philosophies, which they often do not develop academically.

To say that science is itself grounded in values and metaphysical beliefs, therefore, is not to leap from the secure home of scientific certainty into the dark night of obscurity and irrationality. Rather, it implies that a naive scientism, which sees science as the only legitimate form of reason and truth-seeking, is contrary to the very practices of science.[17] It also means that a full evaluation of science as a rational practice requires philosophical as well as scientific thinking and argument. But such reasoning can be done without passing into relativism or arbitrary ideologies.

What Are Worldviews?

We have argued, then, that the practice of science, and the rationality of scientific theory-evaluation, is based on shared values. These values, in turn, are grounded in worldviews and traditions of inquiry. But what is a worldview, and what role does it play in human life? There is no standard definition of worldview, but a general working definition is possible.

The notion of a "worldview" became popular in German thought after Kant. Kant himself was the first to use the term *Weltanschauung* in German literature,[18] and soon after it became rather common. In fact, James Orr could write in 1893, "Within the last two or three decades the word has become exceedingly common in all kinds of books dealing with the higher questions of religion and philosophy."[19] Among those German philosophers and theologians Orr was speaking of, Wilhelm Dilthey used the concept more than anyone else. It formed part of his "Critique of Historical Reasoning" and his attempt to give a solid grounding to the social sciences. For Dilthey, worldviews come in his-

---

17. For a further critique of scientism, see Mary Midgley's Gifford lectures, *Science As Salvation* (London: Routledge, 1992).

18. Immanuel Kant, *Critique of Judgement,* trans. James Creed Meredith (Oxford: Oxford University Press, 1952), §26; *Gesammelte Schriften,* ed. Akademie der Wissenschaften, 29 vols. (Berlin: de Gruyter, 1902-1997), vol. 5, p. 255.

19. James Orr, *A Christian View of God and the World* (Edinburgh: A. Elliot, 1893), p. 365. In this book Orr is attempting to set forth a Christian worldview.

torical contexts and traditional packages. They are often not so much reflected upon as acted upon, and they give us a basic understanding of ourselves, the world around us, and our place in it. Dilthey analyzed worldviews chiefly in terms of values.

> All worldviews, if they seek a complete solution to the enigma of life, invariably contain the same structure . . . [in which] questions about the meaning and significance of the world are answered in terms of a conception of the world. From this ideal, a highest good and supreme principle of conduct are deduced.[20]

Dilthey focused on basic moral concepts, historical context, and experience as giving rise to our worldview. In the twentieth century, Wittgenstein gave a more practical and action-oriented image of "world-pictures" (he used the term *Weltbild*). According to Wittgenstein, our picture of the world is grounded in a form of life and in a language. In a famous phrase, he argued that "to imagine a language is to imagine a form of life."[21] Instead of Dilthey's "experience," Wittgenstein focused more on language and on the practical framework of our lives, out of which language has its meaning and purpose. But this means, too, that our values and world-pictures are grounded in the practices of our lives and make overall sense in that context.

Combining Dilthey and Wittgenstein, we can understand a worldview to be a basic framework for life, which orients us in the world and guides our practice. It is given to us in history, in a community, but is capable of being altered with experience and reflection. Worldviews contain basic commitments, which give them a deep structure, along with surface beliefs and values that are more easily changed in the light of reason or experience. For most people, their worldview remains unexamined. One of the great values of true education is the beginning of reflection upon our deepest intellectual, moral, and spiritual commitments. In other words, we begin to develop a more satisfactory worldview or philosophy of life.

A worldview, then, can be classified by the religious and/or philo-

---

20. Wilhelm Dilthey, "Types of Worldviews and Their Development," in *Selected Writings,* ed. H. P. Rickman (Cambridge: Cambridge University Press, 1976), p. 137.

21. Ludwig Wittgenstein, *Philosophical Investigations* (Oxford: Blackwell, 1967), part I, §19.

sophical tradition it exemplifies. Different people share common worldviews, even in the midst of important differences. This allows us to speak of a Christian, Buddhist, or materialist worldview, for purposes of analysis, while still allowing that individuals and subgroups within these broader traditions will often vary in their own particular version. Like Imre Lakatos's notion of a "research program" in the philosophy of science, worldviews will have certain "core commitments" that are difficult to give up, along with more loosely held auxiliary hypotheses and ordinary beliefs, which are more easily revisable.

Worldviews and the Unity of Reality

I have argued that philosophy, theology, and the sciences should be colleagues. They can and should work together, to help us develop and improve our worldviews. The end goal of this collaboration is a worldview that is both religiously meaningful and scientifically sound. The joining of religious wisdom and scientific rigor is a vital task for our generation of intellectuals because the division of science and technology from religion and ethics has created a scenario in which the extinction of homo sapiens from the planet is a genuine possibility. If these areas of academia worked together they could supplement one another in the quest to discover the meaning of our lives and our place in the universe.

There is a unity to reality. It is true, however, that we all experience that reality in different ways, and this means we need to hear and learn from each other and always be open to correction and insight from other persons of goodwill, who are fellow pilgrims with us in the journey to deeper knowledge. The natural and social sciences provide important foundations, both in terms of truth and knowledge and in terms of important epistemic values and practices, but philosophy and theology seek knowledge of a different type, and must do so in their own way. Science seeks factual and theoretical knowledge built upon empirical data and mathematical and informal reasoning. Theology and philosophy, too, use informal reasoning, but their database is quite different. All of these disciplines seek truth, but in very different ways.[22]

22. This position has long been defended by Ian Barbour, among others. See his work, *Issues in Science and Religion* (Englewood Cliffs, N.J.: Prentice-Hall, 1966).

There are many so-called "definitions" of truth, and we cannot here evaluate them. I will simply state that "truth" as I use it in this work will mean *the mediated disclosure of being* (or reality).[23] Sometimes that truth will be mediated through everyday experience or common sense, sometimes through the specifics of propositions. It is also possible to find truth in art and poetry, in spiritual experience, and in religious worship. We need an expansive conception of truth, and this one will do for our present purposes. The reason we need such an expansive conception of truth is that theology and science seek very different kinds of truth in very different ways. Nevertheless, the mutuality model is based upon a bedrock commitment to the unity of reality.

That theology should be allowed to influence scientific theory choice can make sense only if we believe that science aims at the truth, and further that theology makes legitimate claims to truth. Of course theology cannot use the methods of the sciences, since it is seeking an altogether different aspect of reality, namely, the divine. Theology makes use of spiritual insight, revelation, religious traditions, and communal worship and praise. These are not scientific methods! But I would argue that they are well fitted to their task, which is to come to understand the deeper things of God. If there is a God, we can expect to know something about him only through new avenues of insight that take us beyond the empirical truths of science. Science may help us some, of course. We may marvel at the creation and reflect upon its Creator. But deeper unveiling of being (truth) in the realm of religion requires affective and spiritual mediation. The unity of reality implies that science and theology must work together. Their very different aims and methods demand that they keep distinct their own disciplines and paths. These two truths taken together generate the mutuality model.

---

23. See, among others, Augustine, *On True Religion (De vera religione)*, par. 36 (§66): truth is *"quae ostendit id quod est,"* "that which points to what is" (Corpus Christianorum Series Latina 32:230). Cf. *Augustine: Early Writings*, ed. J. H. S. Burleigh (Library of Christian Classics; Philadelphia: Westminster, 1953), p. 258. See also Martin Heidegger, "On the Essence of Truth," in *Existence and Being*, trans. W. Brock (Chicago: Regnery, 1949).

Naturalism, Secondary Causation, and Intelligent Design

Even if science does not and cannot generate its own worldview, some philosophers have argued that science acts as if naturalism were true. This view often goes under the name of "methodological naturalism." The term "naturalism" is used in a variety of ways in art, science, and philosophy,[24] but for the most part, naturalism in philosophy and science is a kind of physicalism and atheism, identical with materialism. In this book, then, I will use "naturalism" to indicate philosophical positions in which nothing exists other than physical objects and their properties, powers, and relationships. What epistemologists sometime call "naturalism" I will name "scientism" for the sake of clarity.

Naturalism is a philosophical position, and as such deserves to be discussed with respect in philosophy. My problem is this: sometimes naturalism is *assumed,* without a properly critical and reflective analysis, to be the only worldview consistent with science. I will not try here to defeat naturalism as a philosophy. Rather, I wish to argue for the more modest proposal that naturalism must be defended philosophically and cannot be "read off" of the natural sciences without further metaphysical argument. I will argue, therefore, that *there is no such thing as a merely methodological naturalism* in the sciences.

First of all, what is this "methodological naturalism"? One definition might be that in the sciences we *act as if* naturalism were true, in our quest to explain the world.[25] No thoughtful Christian would want this, upon reflection. For do we not wish to glorify God in all our activities, including our scientific ones? Perhaps a less tendentious defini-

---

24. See Ted Benton, "Naturalism in Social Science," *Routledge Encyclopedia of Philosophy* (London: Routledge, 1998), 6:717-20. I share with David Griffin the desire to bring religion and science into harmony, in a worldview; see his *Religion and Scientific Naturalism: Overcoming the Conflicts* (Albany: State University of New York Press, 2000). I part company with him, however, in his suggestion that the religious community should accept naturalism, or even "minimal" naturalism. Furthermore, I cannot share his definitions of naturalism, which are at odds with the common and accepted meaning. For this reason, Griffin's proposal for a "theistic naturalism" looks like an oxymoron. I will continue common philosophical practice by equating "naturalism" in philosophy with "scientific materialism," which is a form of atheism.

25. This is the definition given by Del Ratzsch, *Science and Its Limits,* p. 122.

tion might be this: in science, explain physical phenomena only on the basis of physical laws and properties. This, however, will not do. The social sciences explain things in terms of human agency and intention, and not in a purely physical manner. The hope of some reductionists to reduce social to natural science without remainder is just that: hope, not achievement. In fact, as both natural and social sciences become more complex, this kind of reductionism seems less and less plausible. But in any case, such a physicalism is a leap of faith, not a scientific fact. So we need to modify our definition: in *natural* science, explain physical phenomena only on the basis of physical laws, principles, and properties. In the words of Paul De Vries, natural science seeks "to place events in the explanatory context of physical principles, laws, fields."[26] This seems a good working definition.

But is it naturalism? (De Vries, for one, thinks that it is, or at least that it is methodological naturalism.) In other words, given this definition of how natural science works, does this have anything to do with *naturalism?* My thesis is a simple one: No. In historical terms, natural science arose from (and was once called) natural philosophy. This notion was based on the works of Aristotle, whose natural philosophy books entered into the newly founded universities in Europe in the thirteenth century. Robert Grosseteste (ca. 1170-1253) is one famous example of someone who helped to bring Greco-Arabic science into the Latin culture of Europe. Not long after that some of the Aristotelian-Arabic results were rejected by the church, especially in a famous condemnation in Paris in 1277. Following this condemnation, *natural philosophy* developed its own special focus, over against sacred doctrine (theology). Natural philosophers like Roger Bacon (ca. 1220-1292) and Jean Buridan (ca. 1292-1358) examined the secondary causes by which God upheld the common course of nature. Buridan wrote, for example, that "in natural philosophy we ought to accept actions and dependencies as if they always proceed in a natural way."[27] This division between science and theology, then, is not a product of the Renaissance (which of course did much to enlarge the division!). Buridan in particular made significant

---

26. Paul de Vries, "Naturalism in the Natural Sciences," *Christian Scholar's Review* 15 (1986): 388-96, quoting 388.

27. Quest. de caelo, bk. 2, q.9, in Benoit Patar, ed., *Ioannis Buridani Expositio et Quaestiones in Aristotelis De Caelo* (Louvain: Peeters, 1996), pp. 423f.

headway in setting forth scientific methodology, which was distinct from theological methods and conclusions. We should note, however, that Buridan was devoutly Christian and that his natural philosophy was framed within a Christian worldview. After the quotation just given, for example, Buridan goes on to state, "Nevertheless God is the cause of this world." He argues in the same Question that the motion of the heavens, and other effects, depend upon God as their Primary Cause.

This view of the difference between natural philosophy and theology became the standard Western notion of what "natural philosophy" was about, from the time of Buridan until about 1800. We find this view in René Descartes's natural philosophy, for example. In his *Principles of Philosophy,* he wrote: "From God's immutability we can also know certain rules or laws of nature, which are the secondary or particular causes of the various motions we see in nature."[28] Much the same view can be found in the Christian philosophers and scientists of the seventeenth and eighteenth centuries.[29] Due in part to this useful division of labor, natural philosophy (science) was able to make great gains in the period from roughly 1350 to 1800. Later natural philosophy was to divide into natural and social science. But the study of human and animal intelligence is still a study of secondary, created causes. It is still a part of "natural philosophy" in the proper sense.[30] We should notice, then, that the focus of natural philosophy upon secondary causes *has*

28. *Principles of Philosophy,* II, §37; in *Philosophical Writings of Descartes,* trans. J. Cottingham et al., 3 vols. (Cambridge: Cambridge University Press, 1984-1991), vol. 1, p. 240.

29. Del Ratzsch cites the views of Dugald Stewart (as found in his 1792 work, *Elements of the Philosophy of the Human Mind,* vol. 1, p. 52) to pretty much this same effect: "In the investigation of physical laws, it is well-known that our inquiries must always terminate in some general fact, of which no account can be given, but that such is the constitution of nature. After we have established, for example, from the astronomical phenomena, the universality of the law of gravitation, it may still be asked whether this law implies the constant agency of mind; and (upon supposition that it does) whether it be probable that the Deity always operates immediately, or by means of subordinate instruments? But these questions, however curious, do not fall under the province of the natural philosopher. It is sufficient for his purpose, if the universality of the fact be admitted" (*Science and Its Limits,* p. 180 n.12). Ratzsch goes on to critique this perspective, as we shall see.

30. For a historical overview of these points, with citations, see A. G. Padgett, "The Roots of the Concept 'Law of Nature': From the Greeks to Newton," *Perspectives on Science and Christian Faith* 55 (2003): 212-221.

nothing to do with naturalism.[31] The scientists who developed this careful division of labor were not philosophical naturalists, nor were they atheists. They believed in a Primary Cause (God) who could work miracles, and thus were supernaturalists. At the same time scientists like Roger Bacon were interested in the investigation of the world of secondary causes, through empirical and mathematical methods (hence the title of Newton's classic, *Mathematical Principles of Natural Philosophy*). Yet the study of these secondary causes is never fully complete, in a metaphysical sense. Even if there were no gaps in the causal chain of events from the Big Bang until now, secondary causation cannot explain everything in reality. As William Stoeger (a contemporary advocate of this traditional distinction) explains:

> It is essential to conceive primary causality very differently from the causes — secondary causes — we discuss and deal with every day. The primary cause is not just another one of these — it completely transcends them and provides their ultimate basis in reality. There are no gaps in the secondary causal chain, but the whole chain demands a primary cause to support and sustain it.[32]

While I am not as sure there are no gaps in the causal chain (what of the resurrection of Jesus?), the main point is well taken. The laws of nature, and objects and events we study in science, all require a larger explanation which theism provides. But the differences between primary and secondary causes allow for the integrity of both theology and the sciences. One does not reduce to the other. The sciences are in principle complete in the domain they study, and in the manner in which they explain it. But they are not complete from a theological perspective.

---

31. Even a sophisticated philosopher like Griffin can simply assert that "Science, it is widely agreed in scientific, philosophical, and liberal religious circles, necessarily presupposes naturalism" (*Religion and Scientific Naturalism,* p. 11). This is yet one more refutation of the consensus theory of truth! He goes on to equate "scientific naturalism" with the view that there are no divine interruptions in the causal flow of events. This sleight-of-hand definition confuses a mere symptom (no miracles) with the logical cause of that position (naturalism implies atheism, therefore no divine interruptions).

32. William Stoeger, "Describing God's Action in the World in the Light of Scientific Knowledge of Reality," in *Chaos and Complexity: Scientific Perspectives on Divine Action,* ed. R. J. Russell, N. Murphy, and A. Peacocke, second ed. (Vatican City: Vatican Observatory, 2000), p. 247.

Given the great success of this division of labor in Western universities for many centuries, what problems might result from its contemporary retrieval? First, we must be careful not to confuse it with (atheistic) naturalism. It has nothing to do with naturalism, it never was naturalism, and only those interested in promoting atheism should continue to call it naturalism. Actually, they too should stop, to be fair to others; yet I predict that they find the association of science with atheism so useful they will not give it up easily. But *theists* should stop using the term "methodological naturalism" and replace it with a better one. Second, Ian Barbour has complained that the traditional viewpoint of primary and secondary causation was based in a kind of theological determinism, in which God directly willed every event.[33] While historically accurate, this is not a necessary part of the proposal. God may well grant some creatures freedom, and others randomness, in the overall structure of natural order. Humans would still owe their freedom to God, just as the quantum world owes its properties and capacities to the First Cause.

I find, then, this traditional notion to be much more helpful in the religion-science discussion than the term "methodological naturalism." Both the critics and the proponents of a merely "methodological naturalism" almost never stick to the merely methodological level. Opponents of methodological naturalism end up attacking naturalism, plain and simple. Advocates of methodological naturalism often defend naturalism, plain and simple.[34] Therefore I find that the word "methodological" in this phrase is too often a front for full-blown naturalism. Some theists, like Paul De Vries and Ernan McMullin, defend methodological naturalism,[35] but nevertheless I think we are better off without this terminology. I propose this traditional alternative: *science is the rigorous and empirical investigation of secondary causes.* The sciences focus on what Howard Van Till helpfully calls "the creaturely world" of atoms, stars, ants, and people, seeking to discover their creaturely properties and capabilities, given to

33. Ian Barbour, *When Science Meets Religion* (San Francisco: Harper, 2000), pp. 159-61.

34. For advocates see, e.g., A. C. Dorno, "Naturalism," *Encyclopedia of Philosophy* 5:488-550; Willem B. Drees, *Religion, Science and Naturalism* (Cambridge: Cambridge University Press, 1996), pp. 11-24; Michael Ruse, *Darwinism Defended* (Reading, Mass.: Addison-Wesley, 1982); Kai Nielsen, *Naturalism without Foundations* (Buffalo: Prometheus, 1996). For opponents, see note 37 below.

35. See De Vries, "Naturalism in the Natural Sciences"; and Ernan McMullin, "Plantinga's Defense of Special Creation," *Christian Scholar's Review* 21 (1991): 55-79.

them by the Creator.[36] In the terms I propose we adopt, natural and social science seek to expand our knowledge of the world of secondary causes, rather than looking at the world in terms of the Primary Cause. It is the task of theology and philosophy of religion to evaluate our knowledge of the First Cause or Ultimate Reality. Scientific materialists can even adopt this terminology: their Ultimate Reality or Primary Cause will be the universe itself (including all the laws of nature).

Recent theistic philosophers, under the umbrella of the "intelligent design movement," have criticized the practice of "methodological naturalism" in science.[37] They wish to bring "intelligent design" back into science, as a possible explanation for phenomena. The first thing to notice is that social science already investigates *created intelligence*. So science thus understood (the investigation of secondary causes "as if they always proceed in a natural way") already includes some "intelligent design." Examples would include anthropology, archeology, economics, and primatology. Once this point is made clear, however, the debate turns to *natural* science. I happen to think that the differences between disciplines is not just an arbitrary matter but turns on the aims of an academic discipline, its tradition of inquiry (paradigm), and its standards of what counts as good evidence and good argument. The natural sciences have taken as their task the study of the world in physical terms and explain the events they focus on in terms of physical explanations. Their tradition of explanation focuses on just these items, and no other. Created intelligence is passed over to social sciences or to interdisciplinary work. The reason for this is obvious. Physics, chemistry, geology, biology, and the like know nothing about intelligent agency in terms of their explanatory schemes and traditions of inquiry. So they must rely upon interdisciplinary work to investigate, say, animal intelligence or human behavior.

36. See, for example, his chapter, "The Fully Gifted Creation," in *Three Views on Creation and Evolution*, ed. J. P. Moreland and J. M. Reynolds (Grand Rapids: Zondervan, 1999), pp. 171, 174.

37. For some representative criticisms, see Ratzsch, *Science and Its Limits*, pp. 110-32; Alvin Plantinga, "Methodological Naturalism," in *Facets of Faith and Science*, ed. Jitse van der Meer, 4 vols. (Lanham, Md.: University Press of America, 1996), vol. 1, pp. 177-221; J. P. Moreland, ed., *The Creation Hypothesis* (Downers Grove, Ill.: InterVarsity, 1994); Phillip Johnson, *Reason in the Balance* (Downers Grove, Ill.: InterVarsity, 1995); and William Dembski, *Intelligent Design* (Downers Grove, Ill.: InterVarsity, 1999).

I would advocate this same move when the natural sciences encounter aspects of empirical phenomena that a given scientist may suspect are the result of intelligent design. We need empirical criteria, true. But we need an *interdisciplinary* study of the phenomena, to draw upon traditions of inquiry that focus their study upon that area of reality. When and if we discover good evidence for extraterrestrial intelligence, I can almost guarantee that such interdisciplinary examination will occur. Why? Because astronomy, as a discipline and an explanatory scheme, does not and cannot study intelligent activity. It is beyond the explanatory scope of that discipline. Astronomy will need the help of other disciplines, including the social sciences, when and if we stumble upon evidence for intelligent life from other planets. I don't consider this a radical suggestion; on the contrary, it conforms to current practice. One thinks, for example, of the many disciplines involved in a well-funded, large archeological dig. Despite the complaints of some critics, the hypothesis of intelligent design is not ruled out in such a community of scientists.

I would advocate the same approach when and if the natural sciences, in the view of competent experts in those disciplines, come across evidence suggesting a direct effect of the Primary Cause. Theologians, philosophers and scientists will need to work together (collegial metaphor!) in an interdisciplinary way to make a reasoned judgment about this evidence. Is it true that an act of God is the best explanation of this evidence? We will likely discover that "best explanation" arguments in that context will take us beyond the confines of the sciences into metaphysical and theological argument. Such arguments can, of course, still be rigorous and rational — science is not the only rational discipline! — and these arguments will of course be made based on scientific evidence. But the overall argument to the activity of the Primary Cause as the "best explanation" will take place within many disciplines, including metaphysics and theology. In fact, when we take a look beyond the narrow confines of science, we can find some people making such an argument already. Richard Swinburne and Paul Davies are two good examples, and there are others.[38]

38. See Richard G. Swinburne, *The Existence of God*, rev. ed. (Oxford: Oxford University Press, 1991); Paul Davies, *The Mind of God: The Scientific Basis for a Rational World* (New York: Simon and Schuster, 1992).

Del Ratzsch, in his recent book *Science and Its Limits,* has put forward some arguments against the position I have just outlined.[39] A brief reply seems called for, given our agreement on so many other issues. First, he notes that there is no clear, accepted definition of science.[40] I agree. But that does not mean that just anything will count as scientific. I have tried to outline what I take to be a fruitful, historic, and important division of labor between natural philosophy (the sciences) and theology. I do not claim to have reached into the true essence of science, nor to give a delineation that must hold true in all possible worlds.[41] But as a matter of historical and practical division of labor, theology takes as its task the focused study of the Primary Cause, while science studies secondary causes. True, I do not think this gives us a pure and essential definition. But it does point to some important differences between *traditions of inquiry,* into which experts are *inducted and trained.* Second, Ratzsch argues that scientists should pursue the truth, wherever they find it, and not bow to artificial disciplinary divisions. The kind of division of labor I am advocating, he writes, "commits science to either having to deliberately ignore major (possibly even *observable*) features of the material realm or having to refrain from even considering the obvious and only workable explanation, should it turn out that those features clearly resulted from supernatural activity."[42] This criticism ignores the difference between a person and a discipline. Scientists, as persons, can and should pursue truth as they see it. But this may well lead them outside the discipline in which they are experts, and in which their turn of mind most naturally finds its habits of thought, due to years of careful and patient training. All I am suggesting is that in such a case as the one Ratzsch is considering, the natural scientist will need to move outside the narrow confines of natural science. She will, in fact, need to call upon social science, philosophy, and theology. And being finite, she may be well advised to find helpful colleagues who are open to this investigation and who are ex-

---

39. Some of these points are developed more fully in Del Ratzsch, *Nature, Design and Science: The Status of Design in Natural Science* (Albany: State University of New York Press, 2001).

40. Ratzsch, *Science and Its Limits,* p. 121.

41. This point is in response to J. P. Moreland's criticism of methodological naturalism in his edited volume *The Creation Hypothesis,* pp. 45-49.

42. Ratzsch, *Science and Its Limits,* p. 122, his emphasis.

perts in these fields. Again, my point is not about ignoring evidence or halting the quest for truth; rather, my point is that the disciplines have a purposeful narrowing of scope in their explanatory schemes. This gives them the power to continue the growth of scientific learning in their respective domains, but also creates limits on what a given *discipline* is capable of studying with care.

My purpose throughout this chapter has been to promote the mutuality model, and the collegial metaphor, for the relationship between theology and science. The idea of mutuality depends upon disciplinary integrity and distinctions (I do not say "separation") such as those I have insisted upon in my debate with Del Ratzsch. But I also do not want to fall into a rigid division between the academic disciplines. When they operate through an overarching worldview, it is fully rational for one discipline to influence theory evaluation in another discipline. This influence must, however, take place within the accepted standards and explanatory schemes of the science (or discipline) in question. And such a "fit with overall worldview" criterion comes at the very bottom of the list of shared scientific values. Most of the time, theories will be fully and finally evaluated within their own discipline.

In this chapter I gave some limited criticism of naturalism and scientism in the philosophy of science. Philosophy, theology, and science are distinct but collegial areas of inquiry, and as such one discipline should not dictate to the others. I have insisted, in fact, on the equal importance of philosophy and science, adopting the medieval distinction between the study of primary and secondary causes. In the next chapter, we will continue to insist on this egalitarian hypothesis, this time with respect to the relationship of philosophy and theology.

5 Putting Reason in Its Place: A Dialogue with Process Theology

In previous chapters I have developed at some length the rejection of a purely neutral, value-free science. Science is rightly influenced by our broad worldview, including key value commitments. This chapter continues in the rejection of rationalism and scientism, this time in theological method. Having argued that theological explanation and theological realism are at least possible, in this chapter (in true dialectical fashion!) we consider those who have taken too rationalistic an approach to theological knowledge. I believe these arguments are necessary, even in our postmodern times. Scientism and rationalism are still prominent in the writings of living American scholars. These voices should be attended to, with respect, since for many years they defined what counted as "good" academics both in the sciences and in theology. Respect in this case also includes a solid critique, but not, I hope, an unsympathetic one.

I am a United Methodist pastor and theologian. There has been a happy marriage between Methodist theology and process philosophy for the last several decades. Some of the most important work in the religion-science dialogue has been influenced by process theology, as well. We find, even today, a continuing vitality in this union of a particular Christian theological tradition and a specific metaphysical school. My purpose in this chapter is to raise a voice of caution. In the past, process theology has tended to privilege reason or metaphysics over Scripture and tradition. Here, I give some reasons why this has been a

---

I would like to dedicate this chapter to John Cobb Jr., a man of many virtues, intellectual and personal, and a model of Christian grace in scholarship.

problem and may indeed continue to be unless care is taken by process thinkers. The question here is not *whether* faith and reason, or theology and philosophy, belong together. The question is *how*. My entry into this question will be through Martin Heidegger's rejection of ontotheology, although in the end I will turn Heidegger on his head.

Recent work in process theology has moved in the direction of humility in metaphysics and rationality combined with a greater respect for tradition. Examples of this would include John Cobb Jr.'s recent book on Wesleyan theology, Charles Hartshorne's collection of essays on moderation in philosophy, and Marjorie Suchocki's book on sin, along with her recent essay on John Wesley's theology of prayer.[1] This is a salutary movement in process theology, one I would like to commend. In the past, however, process thought was not nearly so humble, nor so interested in valuing the sources of Christian thought in Scripture and tradition. My basic concern is that even in the current examination of Scripture and tradition, process theologians may continue to give explanatory priority to metaphysics and/or philosophical rationality. Process theologians have rightly complained that classical theism is too tied to Greek metaphysics; my complaint is that Wesleyan theology must not be too tied to process metaphysics.

This chapter is primarily about method: method in metaphysics and method in theology. A careful and thorough reply to process theology would include a detailed critique of process metaphysics, especially the work of Alfred North Whitehead, which we will address. I have chosen to focus, however, on the key problem with process theology, a problem in metaphysical and theological *method*, rather than with any particular doctrine. (I should note, in fact, that I have discovered a number of important doctrines in process theology, although there is neither time nor space to explicate them here; nevertheless, there is much of value in process thought.)

The problem of method can be stated very briefly. In the past, process theology has allowed philosophy to set the terms for the Christian theological quest to know God. Because Christian theology is

---

1. John B. Cobb Jr., *Grace and Responsibility* (Nashville: Abingdon, 1995); Charles Hartshorne, *Wisdom As Moderation: A Philosophy of the Middle Way* (Albany: State University of New York Press, 1987); and Marjorie Suchocki, *The Fall to Violence* (New York: Continuum, 1995), and "The Perfection of Prayer," in *Rethinking Wesley's Theology*, ed. Randy Maddox (Nashville: Kingswood, 1998).

based on revelation, however, it can and must resist this move. The path to truth about God is based upon faith and comes through revelation, especially that revelation in Jesus Christ that is made available to us in the witness of Scripture, as the Spirit gives us new eyes to see the truth.[2] Tradition, spiritual practices, reason, and experience are secondary to this primary witness. Philosophy may, indeed, teach us something about God. But for a theology dedicated to the truth about God in Jesus Christ, special revelation is the primary source of truth about God. Philosophical theology must accommodate itself to revelation, not the other way around, if indeed revelation is what it claims to be: knowledge of God beyond reason (but not contrary to reason).

This is an old debate, and process thinkers have, for example, already replied to Barth and his school. But the postmodern twist has put new bite into the criticism of the pretensions of philosophical systems, or metanarratives, that attempt to encompass all of reality — including God — into one vast regime of Truth with a capital T. Of course, we could have learned this lesson if we had listened carefully to John Dewey's Gifford Lectures of 1929, on the quest for certainty.[3] But Dewey was ahead of his time, and did not write in French! The philosophy of Whitehead represents the last great philosophical system in Anglo-American thought (at least so far) and is a primary example of what postmodern critics have argued against, that is, a totalizing metanarrative. But we anticipate ourselves. To grasp the power of the postmodern critique, we should begin with its expression in the works of Martin Heidegger, one of the greatest philosophers of the twentieth century.

Heidegger's own very early metaphysical speculations developed into his classic phenomenological study of human Being *(Dasein)* in *Being and Time* (1927).[4] In that text he begins his path toward the suspi-

---

2. "The necessary and fundamental form of all scriptural exegesis that is responsibly undertaken and practised in this sense must consist in all circumstances in the freely performed act of subordinating all human concepts, ideas and convictions to the witness of revelation supplied to us in Scripture" (Karl Barth, *Church Dogmatics* [Edinburgh: T&T Clark, 1956], I:2, §21.2.2, p. 715).

3. John Dewey, *The Quest for Certainty* (London: Allen and Unwin, 1930).

4. I will refer to the pages of *Sein und Zeit* (Tübingen: Max Niemeyer, 1953). The two English translations refer (in their margins) to this edition. See *Being and Time*, trans. J. Macquarrie and E. Robinson (London: SCM, 1962), and *Being and Time*, trans. Joan Stambaugh (Albany: State University of New York Press, 1996).

cion of metaphysics. Take, for example, his section on a "destruction of the history of ontology."[5] Heidegger famously takes Western, traditional metaphysics to task for forgetting Being in its focus on things. His main task in this book remains a positive one, attempting to explicate the "positive aspects" of Being.[6] After this work, Heidegger became more suspicious of metaphysics and eventually argued that we should "overcome" it. One text along this journey is his 1957 volume, *Identity and Difference*.[7] In this work, Heidegger sets forth the ontotheological constitution of metaphysics and is critical of it. We cannot do justice to the whole of Heidegger's text here, but seek only to outline his implicit argument against process metaphysics, and indeed against all metaphysical systems that claim a systematic, unitary knowledge of God and existence. While Heidegger's critique is couched in terms of Aristotelian philosophy, Whitehead's system is just as problematic and falls under the same ontotheological critique.[8]

The problem, Heidegger states, is how God comes into philosophy. Theology cannot be allowed to dictate answers to philosophy, according to Heidegger. "God [*der Gott*] can come into philosophy only insofar as philosophy, of its own accord and by its own nature, requires and determines that and how God enters into it," he claims.[9] And again, "We can properly think through the question, How does God enter into philosophy?, only when that *to which* God is to come has become sufficiently clear: that is, philosophy itself."[10] In my own language, Heidegger is concerned for the integrity of philosophy as a rational discipline of the university, and for the methodological focus and limits of philosophy. If any other science or discipline can dictate answers in advance for philosophy, he held, then philosophy loses its purpose. He states, "It would be rash to assert that metaphysics is the-

---

5. Heidegger, *Sein und Zeit*, introduction, §II.6.

6. Heidegger, *Sein und Zeit*, p. 44.

7. German with English translation, ed. Joan Stambaugh (New York: Harper and Row, 1969).

8. Process theologians wishing to reply to my critique should distinguish between *finality* and *totality*. I accuse Whitehead of advocating the latter, but not the former. He was aware of the need to abandon claims of "dogmatic certainty" (i.e., finality) in metaphysics.

9. Heidegger, *Identity and Difference*, p. 56, translation altered.

10. Heidegger, *Identity and Difference*, p. 55, his italics, translation altered.

ology because it is ontology,"[11] fully aware that Aristotle called part of his metaphysics "theology." He makes this clear in an earlier lecture, *Introduction to Metaphysics*:

> Anyone for whom the Bible is divine revelation and truth has the answer to the question "Why is there beings rather than nothing" even before it is asked: everything, that is, except God himself has been created by him. God himself, the Incarnate Creator, "is." One who holds to such faith can in a way participate in the asking of our questions but he cannot really question without ceasing to be a believer and taking all the consequences of such a step.[12]

Because Christian theology is based on Christian revelation and Christian faith, it cannot be philosophy and should never pretend to be. For Heidegger, the ontotheological problem of metaphysics is this: in assuming that it knows all about God, it short-circuits the due attention that Being deserves, and distorts both God and Being in the process.

I believe Heidegger makes some valid points here, but I want to defend the distinction between philosophy and theology from the other side, that is, from the side of theology. Just as the philosopher rightly defends the autonomy of her discipline against theological preemption, so the theologian can and must defend revelation, and the theology based on it, from philosophical preemption. In the past, the writings of process theologians accepted Scripture and tradition to the extent and degree they fit into a Whiteheadian metaphysical system or into an *a priori* conception of what counts as rational.[13]

What is wrong with this? If a system of metaphysics is true, do we not want to fit our theology to the truth it contains? Shall theology be irrational? The problem here has to do with, in Heidegger's words, how God enters into metaphysics. The God of metaphysics, as Pascal knew long ago, is not the God of religion, and philosophy is not concerned with the goals and modes of knowing found in religion, namely, salvation and

---

11. Heidegger, *Identity and Difference*, p. 55, translation altered.

12. Trans. R. Manheim (London: Oxford University Press, 1959), pp. 6-7, translation altered.

13. See, among many examples, Schubert M. Ogden, *The Point of Christology* (San Francisco: Harper, 1982). Ogden tends to privilege rationality more than Cobb and the Claremont school, which focuses on metaphysics or "philosophical theism."

revelation. Christianity is devoted, first and foremost, to Jesus Christ. The Bible, as the book of Christ, is the primary witness to the revelation of God in Christ, at least for Christians, and ecumenical, long-standing tradition provides us with a deeply Christian understanding of that book. By putting metaphysics or rationality on top, some process thinkers in the past tended to distort theology from the very start. The goal of Christian theology is a knowledge of God based on special revelation. The task of theology is not to develop an abstract notion of God, still less to construct systems of logical propositions. The true task of theology, grounded in religious practice and revelatory claims, is to know and enjoy God forever. As Suchocki recently wrote, "theologians work out the reasonableness of faith within a particular construal of reality that is already shaped by Christian faith. . . . Faith does not have to live from pretensions of universal truth, as if it were a God's-eye perspective."[14]

Why is theology necessarily grounded in revelation? To ask this question another way, why does Wesleyan theology rightly insist on the primacy of Scripture as source and norm of thinking about God? Contemporary American Wesleyan theologians are well aware of the so-called "Wesleyan Quadrilateral" (composed of Scripture and ecumenical tradition, followed by reason and experience).[15] This phrase, developed by Albert Outler, is inadequate in its expression, but the substance captures an important aspect of Wesley's thought: the primacy of Scripture and the importance of tradition. I call this ordering of theological sources the Wesleyan Norms. In my understanding, both the Spirit and the human community are at work in all of the norms. Wesley's belief in the importance of good and helpful theological traditions can be found in his discussions of "Christian antiquity," or the "analogy of faith," or the "Church of England."[16] Such tradition was a

---

14. Suchocki, *Fall to Violence,* pp. 49, 54.

15. See Donald Thorsen, *The Wesleyan Quadrilateral* (Grand Rapids: Zondervan, 1990), and W. Stephen Gunter, ed., *Wesley and the Quadrilateral* (Nashville: Abingdon, 1997).

16. Listing the "analogy of faith" (basically, some essential doctrines that guide our reading of the Bible) under tradition is contrary to Wesley's own practice. He would have put it under Scripture, because he thought he could read these doctrines directly out of the Bible. Such an old-fashioned view is hermeneutically naive and unacceptable in the light of current theory. Wesley in fact derived his version of the analogy of faith from the Bible, Christian antiquity, and the Church of England, so I list it under tradition. See further the books on the Quadrilateral in the previous note.

major factor in Wesley's own theological thinking and should remain a norm for us today, under the primacy of Scripture. The substance of the Wesleyan Norms does capture in a simple way the priority of norms in Wesley's own theology. He, along with the vast majority of Christian thinkers throughout the world and throughout the history of theology, would put Scripture ahead of reason and metaphysics as source and norm for deeply meaningful religious truth. But are they correct on this score?

Before continuing on with this theme of Scripture and revelation, I should like briefly to consider what role philosophy, in my view, rightly plays in theology. I do not want my process friends to think I am some kind of bibliomaniac, with no place for philosophical reflection in theology. In his contribution to the famous *Christian Century* series on "How My Mind Has Changed," John Cobb was critical of christocentric theology, stating, "the attempt to rest belief in God *solely* on Jesus Christ is, from the historical perspective, questionable and, from the perspective of systematic theology, illusory."[17] I agree here with Cobb. But the question, again, is about the role and priority of metaphysical theism. What role does philosophy play in theological reflection?

For one thing, philosophical training can bring clarity and logic to the reflective, systematic, and constructive tasks of Christian theology. Philosophy may also provide key ideas necessary to explicate revelation. More than this, philosophers may pose problems of internal coherence within the patterns of life and thought that are Christian tradition, religion, and theology. This is a valuable service, and one theologians have not ignored over the long history of engagement with philosophical partners. Philosophy can also pose other questions to the Christian religion, giving shape in sharp and poignant ways to the problems of our place and time. But the content of the concept of God, the Blessed Trinity, for and within the Christian religion cannot be determined by philosophy, even for its own place and time. The gospel is the center of Christianity and the focus of theological reflection. There is a unique reasonableness to the pattern of gospel truth, a deep grammar theology must attend to, which is logically prior to any and all

17. John B. Cobb Jr., "Christian Natural Theology and Christian Existence," reprinted in *Frontline Theology*, ed. Dean Peerman (London: SCM, 1967), p. 40, his italics.

claims from science, philosophy, and the world to set the universal standards of reason.[18] There may be some very vague notion of common sense among most people, but there is no developed, neutral system of standard truths and logics to which theology must conform upon peril of being irrational. Rather, theology can and must shape that inchoate, incipient common sense to fit the patterns of gospel truth before turning to other proposed logics. We should not say that gospel truth, and it alone, determines the content of the Christian doctrine of God. But Wesleyan theologians must say that revelation is the primary source of the knowledge of God. To help people outside the faith, we should not jettison our special revelation and our special way of life. On the contrary, to help people grapple with questions and minister to the suffering, we need the strengths of faith and revelation in Jesus Christ. In Christian theology as well as in Christian mission, the struggle for peace and justice, evangelism, and worship, Jesus Christ is Lord. Philosophy must return to its own domain and discipline if it seeks to rule.

But why is this so? Why does Christian theology strive for a knowledge of God that is first and foremost grounded in the revelation and person of Jesus? The first, simple reason is that philosophy has sometimes come to dominate the partnership, setting forth a supposed "rational" and universal picture of God that was then developed in theological terms. In such cases, theology has given up its true role in the church: to seek a saving knowledge of God in Jesus Christ and special revelation. The second reason is more profound. There is no universal, transcultural, and extra-perspectival ground upon which a human being can seek to know God. There are various systems of logic, various traditions of rationality. The various world religions have within them claims to special revelation, but these claims are conflicting and dissonant. Significant, saving knowledge of God, the sort that gives life meaning and purpose, is to be found neither in comparative philosophy of religion nor in metaphysics. We can and must seek deep religious truth in particular religious traditions and communities,

---

18. See William Placher, *Unapologetic Theology* (Philadelphia: Westminster, 1989); Basil Mitchell, *Faith and Criticism* (Oxford: Oxford University Press, 1994); and Trevor Hart, *Faith Thinking* (London: SPCK, 1995). Among many predecessors, see, for example, Augustine, *On Christian Doctrine*.

shaped by their particular vision of Ultimate Reality, the meaning of life, ethical practices, and religious worship. The theologian has no special place or pure, rational insight but shares this common human condition relative to a deeply meaningful knowledge of God. As Heidegger rightly wrote about the God of the philosophers, "Humanity can neither pray nor sacrifice to this god. Before the *causa sui* humanity can neither fall to its knees in awe nor can it play music and dance before this god."[19] Generic theology have we none, or at least none that is of any deeply religious significance.

Natural theology may have a place in Christian thought and mission, but it is a severely limited place, as handmaiden to evangelical faith. I cannot agree with Cobb's statement that to reflect on "the whole range of intellectual questions with which modern [humanity] is fated to struggle, natural theology . . . must eschew appeal to any authority not recognized outside the church, such as Scripture, revelation, tradition, or personal religious experience."[20] As a definition this is fine, but it has not been a happy project. In its own terms, natural theology *alone* has not found answers to our deepest questions and longings. This is not to say that natural theology has no place in the church. But my point is that we can and must return to the roots of Christian religion and call people into that deeper truth which is founded exactly and centrally upon Scripture, revelation, tradition, and personal religious experience.

In his 1965 volume *A Christian Natural Theology,* Cobb argued, against the popular "God is dead" movement, that we have good reasons to believe there is a God. The reasons Cobb gave are basically those of a Whiteheadean philosophy of religion. He recognized that all philosophy begins from some perspective but argued that a natural theology must not appeal to specifically Christian sources of truth. This seems correct. On the other hand, even those doing specifically Christian theology must accept some philosophical teachings. We always presuppose some philosophical doctrines in developing systematic theology. "The problem, then, is how the theologian should reach his conclusions on those broader questions of general reflection presupposed in his work. . . . What the theologian thus chooses functions for him as

---

19. Heidegger, *Identity and Difference,* p. 72, translation altered.
20. Cobb, "Christian Natural Theology," p. 41.

a natural theology."[21] Cobb argues that we must choose carefully the philosophical system that we, as Christian theologians, will then "adopt and adapt" into our systematic theology.

There is much of value in Cobb's arguments concerning theology and philosophy. My point in this chapter is to call into question the need for Christian theology to adopt and adapt a complete philosophical system or metaphysics. I would likewise reject Cobb's argument for the priority of natural theology in doctrinal development. It is true that in developing a systematic theology, we always must include some philosophical ideas. But it seems to me a very large jump from this truism to the claim that Christian theology must adopt and adapt a whole *system* of philosophy. I believe the theologian is better off accepting philosophical notions on a piecemeal basis, seeking the inner coherence of gospel truth and adapting those philosophical doctrines that may help us, in particular times and places, to advance that truth.

Theologies then find themselves in particular religious traditions, accepting the vision, worship, prayer, and practice that is most meaningful and that best makes sense of life. A Christian theology that knows what it is, that is conscious of these facts of particularity, will place Jesus Christ at the center of our quest to know God in a deeply personal way. The traditions and practices of the vast consensus of Christians before us, the saints, martyrs, and apostles, will all point us toward God. And in pointing us to God, they will also point to his book, the book of Christ, that is, the Scriptures. Wesley was one with this great witness in declaring himself to be a man of one book. Of course Wesley did not read only the Bible; he was very learned. But the Bible was central to his knowledge of Christ and his practice of Christianity. The Bible is not alone in bearing witness to the truth of God. Ecumenical, classical tradition also helps us to understand Scripture and guides us into deeper understanding of Christ (hence Wesley's "analogy of faith"). Our own encounter with Christ, in the power of the Spirit, is a massively important source for our knowledge of him. But these latter sources are subject to the normativity of the Bible, not the other way around.

---

21. John B. Cobb Jr., *A Christian Natural Theology* (Philadelphia: Westminster, 1965), pp. 262-63; see also pp. 11-12.

The meaning of the Bible as text is never fixed, of course, and this witness comes to us in human language and history. But these facts do not alter the primary claim of the principle that, of all the sources of our knowledge of God in the Christian religion, Scripture is primary. The primacy of metaphysics or generic rationality can lead to a distortion of genuine Christian theology and cannot be accepted by a Christian doctrinal method that understands itself. Such a method should and must reject all claims to supposed universal reason and experience that arise from philosophical systems. We cannot agree, therefore, with Cobb and Griffin when they state that the problem of philosophical distortion of theology lies in not finding the right philosophy![22] Instead, a Christian theology that understands its place and role in the world will always and everywhere give epistemic honor to our Savior, Jesus Christ. Philosophical systems per se do not enter into it.

Shall philosophy, then, have nothing to do with God? Such a view is too extreme, too contrary to history, to be accurate. Philosophers can and should discuss God. But metaphysics needs to be much more humble than it is in Whitehead's system and in some of his descendants' systems. My own view is that after the postmodern critique of Enlightenment pretensions to complete truth, metaphysics must remain close to a variety of experiences: close to life and the arts and sciences, close to human beings. Rather than seeking grand unified systems, metaphysics should humble itself before ordinary life and the multiplicities of our various experiences, contexts, and stories as human beings. Metaphysics can proceed, if at all, only in piecemeal fashion. The age of grand metaphysical systems is over, or at least it ought to be. But a humble, piecemeal metaphysics is doubly suspect when one uses it to set the terms for Christian theology.

Whitehead did indeed place too much confidence in his metaphysical system, as a few remarks in his lectures on science and the modern world make clear.[23] In *Science and the Modern World* he claimed, for example, that "these metaphysical chapters are purely descriptive."[24] Whatever else metaphysics may be, it is always very theoretical

22. John B. Cobb Jr. and David Ray Griffin, *Process Theology* (Philadelphia: Westminster, 1976), p. 159.

23. Alfred North Whitehead, *Science and the Modern World* (New York: Macmillan, 1925).

24. Whitehead, *Science and the Modern World*, p. 220.

and speculative. I have become convinced, through both philosophical hermeneutics and the philosophy of science, that all descriptions are already assumption-laden. Since metaphysics is an abstract, philosophical theory of what lies behind our everyday experience, and one that attempts to make sense of results from all the arts and sciences, it is the most assumption-laden of all. Whitehead fooled himself when he thought his metaphysics was purely descriptive, and later in his life he did not make such a mistake. Of course, this is only one example of the problem I am pointing to, not a systematic examination of Whitehead's complete writings.

Whitehead fell into the same trap, the Enlightenment ideal of pure access to truth, when he made more claims for metaphysics. This standpoint, he tells us, is "antecedent to any special investigation."[25] Within metaphysics we "put ourselves at the standpoint of a dispassionate consideration of the nature of things."[26] I believe that Whitehead's project of a critique of abstractions (and this chapter of *Science and the Modern World* is called "Abstractions") is a valuable one. But his ambition of perfectly clear, "purely descriptive," "dispassionate" metaphysics "antecedent to any special investigation" is simply unbelievable today, and for good reasons. Perspective and presupposition enter into all epistemic investigation, and, *a fortiori*, into metaphysics.

Whitehead developed his early speculations in metaphysics into a grand system of ideas in his Gifford Lectures, *Process and Reality* (1929).[27] In this text it is clear that Whitehead aims to construct a totalizing metanarrative, that is, a grand system of ideas that everything and everyone must fit into. He sets the task of speculative philosophy as nothing less than "the coherent, logical, necessary system of general ideas in terms of which every element of our experience can be interpreted."[28] The goal of metaphysics, he tells us, is to know the essence of the universe. "The doctrine of necessity in universality means that there is an essence to the universe which forbids relationships beyond itself, as a violation of its rationality. Speculative philosophy

25. Whitehead, *Science and the Modern World*, p. 220.
26. Whitehead, *Science and the Modern World*, pp. 219f.
27. Alfred North Whitehead, *Process and Reality* (New York: Macmillan, 1929). Page numbers from this edition are also found in the Corrected Edition, ed. D. Griffin and D. Sherburne (New York: Free Press, 1978).
28. Whitehead, *Process and Reality*, p. 4.

seeks that essence."[29] To be fair, Whitehead then goes on to note that this is an ideal, a goal that philosophers will never achieve. He recognizes that his understanding of metaphysics may seem "overambitious,"[30] but presses forward because rationality demands the attempt at a system of ideas that describes absolutely everything.[31]

I have come to believe that these goals for metaphysics are problematic. I do agree that philosophy should be *coherent,* but when ideas clash who gets to mediate the debate? There are no neutral, value-free, universal, and objective sets of criteria by which to mediate between all of the already partial, already assumption-laden experiences of all human beings. Even the attempt seeks to obliterate otherness, diversity, variety — the spice of life. Is it even possible to create a system of *necessary* ideas that will describe the world? Will the philosopher take a God's-eye view, knowing all necessary truths and the interlocking systems of the entire universe? The over-ambitious character of these goals, which Whitehead shares with Leibniz and a whole host of others, is clear at the beginning of the twenty-first century. Philosophy in general, and metaphysics in particular, must adopt more modest goals and be more realistic about its limitations. I do accept the idea that philosophy is based in part upon rational truth, or *a priori* judgments, which I call noetic concepts.[32] But noetic concepts must be subject to critical, ongoing, and communal testing. They may claim to be based on reason and intuition, but they are in fact always and everywhere open to revision. Here Kant's method in metaphysics must be openly repudiated.

Why? What is wrong with a set of *a priori* categories, analytic and synthetic, given as a provisional but total description of reality? One answer is inductive and historical: they have, so far, always proved inadequate. Another is the more general point that our access to reality is, at best, distorted. Experience does not give us pure sense data. Rather, experience is already and always my experience, rooted and grounded in my body, my worldview, which is limited to my place and time. It is thought, not experience, which reaches beyond these limitations, if anything does. Finally, such totalizing claims have obliterated other-

---

29. Whitehead, *Process and Reality,* p. 6.
30. Whitehead, *Process and Reality,* pp. 20-25.
31. Whitehead, *Process and Reality,* pp. 6, 23-24.
32. See the Appendix to this volume.

ness and distorted, at times even harmed, the ideas and bodies of our neighbors. One thinks here of the *a priori* attachment to "doing one's duty," a notion we can trace back to Kant, and which shows up in Adolf Eichmann's memoirs.

Metaphysics should be provisional, grounded in local knowledge, in one's limited understanding of the world we live in and in the things we can learn from the arts and sciences. Metaphysics is a descriptive philosophy, as Whitehead saw, but it is a humble, piecemeal task. Grand systems of logically necessary ideas do not, and cannot, describe the rich variety and diversity we discover in the world around us. The analysis of a single concept in metaphysics, done correctly, is an amazing achievement, and one with which we should rest happy. Done properly, the analysis of that single concept will need to be open to the experience of all humanity and the teachings of all the disciplines of the university. Even when this task is done, and it never will be fully, there is no reason at all to believe that a grand *system* of such concepts can ever be constructed or that there will be logical, necessary connections between these contingent, humble, and provisional analyses.

Most of my process friends are attracted to process theism not because it provides a grand metaphysical scheme but because of its theology, especially its understanding of God and the world. If you press them, they will refer to the metaphysics. If you criticize the metaphysics, they will appeal to the theology. It is time, I think, to end this philosophical shell game.

The justification of theological concepts, even after proposed revisions from philosophy, comes neither from appeal to metaphysical systems nor from alien notions of rationality. Rather, such Christian theological justification comes in the lengthy process of communal discussion and of comparing the idea to careful work in biblical, historical, practical, and moral theology. The pattern of Christian truth is found in Christianity, not in general revelation. Of course, we turn to culture, reason, science, and art to criticize, revise, and apply theology. We also turn to these areas for some of the questions and problems that prompt our quest for understanding God. But in this hermeneutical circle, Wesleyan theology gives priority to Scripture and the tradition of the church, and returns to these points again for guidance and insight.

In this chapter, I have tried to turn Heidegger on his head. He claimed that faith corrupts philosophy. Instead, I have argued in the other direction, that too strong or too early a commitment to philosophy distorts the development of truth and reason from Christian sources of insight, especially the whole Bible read in the light of Christ, and the unified, pre-European Christian tradition. I would now like to anticipate the criticisms that process theology might make of this position and respond to them.

In the 1960s, John Cobb and James Robinson edited a volume on the later Heidegger and theology.[33] Given Cobb's contribution to that volume, I believe I can anticipate some criticisms of my position. First, critics would argue that the text of Scripture is not unified but diverse and even conflicting. As Cobb wrote then, "Once we acknowledge diversity in the Christian witness, we are placed as theologians in a situation closely parallel to that of the philosophers."[34] Second, they would argue that tradition is at least as harmful and distorting as it is helpful. Again, to quote Cobb, "The history of Christian witness poses — it does not answer — the theological questions for our own day. . . . [O]nly by this same act of liberation [from tradition] can we attain a renewed openness to God such as that of primitive Christian witness."[35] Finally, critics might ask, what happens when those outside the Christian faith demand some proof for our beliefs? Shall we not appeal to philosophy at that point? Here we might cite Whitehead, who once wrote that "Religion collapses unless its main positions command immediacy of assent."[36] Even if these criticisms are not ones Cobb might make today, some response to them seems in order.

First of all, I do not believe the diversity of Scripture puts us in a place similar to that of the philosopher. We have a text that, despite its diversity, has an overall consonance and resonance, especially when read as a whole and with Christ at the center. We have a tradition of reading the text that can give shape to the task of biblical theology today without determining the outcome in advance. I would reject the notion that the authority of Scripture is based on the speculative re-

---

33. James Robinson and John B. Cobb Jr., eds., *The Later Heidegger and Theology* (New York: Harper and Row, 1963). Page numbers that follow refer to Cobb's chapter in this book.

34. Robinson and Cobb, *Later Heidegger,* p. 187.

35. Robinson and Cobb, *Later Heidegger,* p. 188.

36. Whitehead, *Science and the Modern World,* p. 274.

sults of historical critical scholarship. Biblical criticism helps us to understand the final form of the text, but criticism does not replace the text. Scriptural authority rests on the texts themselves. And I do not think these texts are a wax nose that may be shaped into any idea we like: there is a responsible hermeneutics that can guide a faithful reading of the Bible for the purpose of doctrine and life.[37]

Second, I do not accept Heidegger's radical rejection of tradition. Rather, with Hans-Georg Gadamer, I believe that traditions are both necessary and sometimes quite helpful. There is a common core to Christian tradition, especially in its pre-European, intercultural witness to the catholic faith. Of course, slavish attachment to the past is not something I have in mind, but rather a willingness to go with tradition when in doubt and to be guided and shaped by the living faith of classical Christianity.

Finally, the question of proof or grounds for belief is bound to come up in discussion with one of America's foremost natural theologians! Here I can only repeat my previous point that natural theology should have a very limited role. It has no place in the development of doctrine because it rejects from the start the very sources of insight upon which Christian truth is founded. At best, it can defend a few limited ideas drawn from Christian theological reflection. I believe we should give reasons for our faith when called upon. Perhaps we can show that other systems of belief and life have problems, or defend an idea or two in an ad hoc manner in discussion with a particular person or worldview. But natural theology, by definition, cannot determine the content of Christian doctrine. We may have to be satisfied with simply explaining genuine Christian faith as best we can and inviting others to participate in its life, thought, and worship.

The knowledge of God, I have argued in this chapter, depends neither upon philosophical systems nor upon supposedly universal concepts and logics. Rather, human reason must be cleansed and redeemed by faith for a meaningful knowledge of God to progress. We

37. See, for example, Roger Lundin et al., *The Responsibility of Hermeneutics* (Grand Rapids: Eerdmans, 1985); Anthony C. Thiselton, *New Horizons in Hermeneutics* (London: HarperCollins, 1992); John Goldingay, *Models for Interpretation of Scripture* (Grand Rapids: Eerdmans, 1995); Nicholas Wolterstorff, *Divine Discourse* (Cambridge: Cambridge University Press, 1995); and Kevin Vanhoozer, *Is There a Meaning in This Text?* (Grand Rapids: Zondervan, 1998).

should and can discover the deeper patterns of truth and insight in Scripture and tradition, to guide our minds' progress to God. In this manner, to truly know and enjoy God forever is the true goal of theology.[38]

38. My thanks to Sally Bruyneel, Randy Maddox, Sam Powell, Thomas Lindell, and Tom Oord for very helpful comments on an earlier version of this chapter.

6 Theology As Worship:
The Place of Theology
in a Postmodern University

If you are a theologian, you will pray truly. And if you pray truly, you are a theologian.

EVAGRIUS PONTICUS

Divine theology brings into harmony the voices of those who praise God's majesty.[1]

DIADOCHUS OF PHOTIKE

In the last chapter, we argued that theology must not lose itself to philosophy (or to science for that matter) in the academy. The purpose of theology is to understand God truly. In this chapter, I will develop this theme more fully and consider the common question of the place of theology in our universities today.

I studied theology at two universities, Oxford and Drew. Thomas Oden was my favorite teacher in systematic theology at Drew University, and I have learned much from him over the years. It was wonderful to be at Drew among his students just as he was publishing his *Agenda for Theology* and working out his new position in "postmodern orthodoxy."[2]

1. Both quotations are from the *Philokalia*, vol. I, ed. G. E. H. Palmer et al. (London: Faber and Faber, 1979): Evagrius, "On Prayer," §61, p. 62, and Diadochus, "On Spiritual Knowledge," §67, p. 275.

2. Thomas C. Oden, *Agenda for Theology* (San Francisco: Harper and Row, 1979). This was later revised as *After Modernity — What? Agenda for Theology* (Grand Rapids: Zondervan, 1990).

104

From Professors Oden and James Pain at Drew I first learned to honor and study the great mothers and fathers of the first ecumenical centuries of Christian thought, and this orientation has never left my theological reflection. My time at Oxford only deepened this commitment.

In this chapter I will take a page from Oden's "postmodern" orientation to classic Christian sources, asking the question, "What is the true nature of theology? Where is the true home of theological reflection?" This is not a question about geography, but a spatial metaphor for revisiting the "agenda of theology." In particular, I wish to explore theology's self-understanding of its nature and purpose. In brief, my answer will be that *theology is a form of worship.* Or, as perhaps I ought to say, good theology can and should be a form of worship, a form of giving glory to God. In developing this view of the nature of our theological task, I will also discuss the role theology thus understood can play in a postmodern university.

Theology As Worship

What is theology all about? I believe no reasonable answer to this question can be given until we settle what the aim, goal, or telos of theology is. Philosophy of science has taught us that our understanding of methods and principles in science is dependent to a great deal upon our grasp of the *aims* of that science. Our first question, then, is this: what is the aim of theology? I am going to defend a traditional answer: the goal of theology is to praise and worship God.[3]

Theology is concerned with knowing God and with the study of God. But that study has been isolated, for too long, from the spiritual and religious quest to know God in a personal way. The spiritual and religious quest, this hunger for God and for the truth of God, is the true root of theological reflection. One example of the divorce between knowing God in a spiritual and in a "scientific" way is the division between Protestant orthodoxy and Pietism in the seventeenth century.

---

3. See also Geoffrey Wainwright, *Doxology* (New York: Oxford University Press, 1980); Dan Hardy and David Ford, *Praising and Knowing God* (Philadelphia: Westminster, 1985); and Frans Josef van Beeck, *God Encountered,* vol. 1: *Understanding the Christian Faith* (Collegeville, Minn.: Liturgical Press, 1989), chap. 7.

The roots of this breach go back to the founding of university faculties of theology in Europe. But this is a story we cannot detail here.[4] After the end of the Enlightenment project, in our postmodern times, we have been given the opportunity to heal this breach in the heart of theology. Once again, we can seek to know God truly in both an existential and an academic way.[5] Only this holistic approach will, in the end, satisfy our spiritual and intellectual needs. I am in full agreement with the Westminster divines when, in their Shorter Catechism (Question One), they teach that the chief end of human Being is to know God and enjoy him forever. This point has deep roots, going back to Aquinas and Augustine. Both of them argued that the ultimate human happiness lies in the knowledge and love of God.[6] As Augustine states in *On Christian Doctrine,*

> For the divinely established rule of love says, "you shall love your neighbour as yourself" but God "with all your heart, and with all your soul, and with all your mind" so that you may devote [*confero*] all your thoughts and all your life and all your understanding to the one from whom you actually receive the things that you devote to him.[7]

I propose to follow Augustine and locate the proper home of theology in the greatest commandment, that is, in the commandment to love the Lord with all our mind (among other things). Even before Augustine, Clement of Alexandria taught that the true Christian theologian (gnostic) "is before all things a lover of God."[8] The purpose of the section of his unfinished *Stromateis* from which this quote is taken was "to prove that the gnostic alone is holy and pious, worshiping the true God

---

4. See one version of this story: Edward Farley, *Theologia* (Philadelphia: Fortress, 1983). Another version is found in David Kelsey, *Between Athens and Berlin* (Grand Rapids: Eerdmans, 1993).

5. See David Kelsey, *To Understand God Truly: What's Theological about a Theological School* (Louisville, Ky.: Westminster John Knox, 1992).

6. Aquinas, *Summa Theologiae* Ia-IIae, q.3; Augustine, *City of God* xix.26.

7. Augustine, *De Doctrina Christiana,* ed. R. P. H. Green (Oxford: Clarendon, 1995), I.xxii, p. 30.

8. Clement of Alexandria, *Stromateis,* vii.4, in *Alexandrian Christianity,* ed. J. E. L. Oulton and H. Chadwick, Library of Christian Classics vol. 2 (Philadelphia: Westminster, 1954), p. 95.

as befits him; and the worship which befits God includes both loving God and being loved by him."[9] I think we are within our rights to interpret Clement's "Christian Gnosis" as the discipline of Christian theology itself, for our day.

The thesis I am putting forth, then, has deep roots in the classical Christian tradition. This basic ecumenical understanding of the knowledge of God grounded in the love of God leads to my larger point: the knowledge of God comes best and first within the life of prayer, worship, praise, and obedience that is the spiritual life of the church, for these things are the way that the church loves God. Thus the knowledge of God, and so also theology, finds its proper home in the worship of God.[10]

The praise and worship of God, in both Scripture and our Christian liturgy, includes telling the wonderful deeds of the Lord and extolling his glorious divinity. The Psalms are filled with such theology, and we find it often in Paul and in the book of Revelation. Take Psalm 8, an early hymn of praise, as an example. Mixed together in this psalm are both the praise of God and a truth-telling about the majesty and glory of God. The name of the Lord is majestic in all the earth, and the psalmist praises God as creator of all: of the starry heavens, of the human race, and of all living things. This hymn ends as it began: O Lord, our Lord, how majestic is your name in all the earth! Notice that the praise of God is grounded in the truth about God, that is, in theology. To rightly worship God, we need to know the story of God. Right worship implies sound theology, and sound theology can and should be a kind of worship. The purpose of theology, I am pressing, is to know God, to tell the truth about God, and to give glory to God: in short, to worship God.

The English word "worship" is related to the word "worth." To worship someone is, etymologically, to tell of their worth, esteem, honor, and renown. In biblical language, the concept of worship is conveyed for the most part either in bodily terms, such as "bowing down before," or under words like "glorify" or "praise" (e.g., hallelujah). Like

---

9. Clement of Alexandria, *Stromateis* vii.3.

10. I am very much in sympathy with Ellen Charry's notion of the sapiential and salutary function of theology, in *By the Renewing of Your Minds* (New York: Oxford University Press, 1998).

the English word for worship, the biblical terms "to glorify" and "to praise" also suggest a telling of the wonderful honor, esteem, and magnificence of the one who is to be praised.[11]

This basic point is also clear in the history of Christian liturgy and hymnody. First-class hymns are also first-class theology! The best liturgy has always been grounded in, and expressed, the best theology. To take just one example from the service of Holy Communion: in the Great Thanksgiving, there is a long section on the mighty deeds of God in Jesus Christ, which form the foundation of the sacrament. My argument is that this giving of glory to God in Jesus Christ is the proper place of theology. Theology is best done, one might say, before the Word and Table, in the worshiping community of faith. This is, I am arguing, the true home of theology.

I have learned a great deal from Geoffrey Wainwright and accept his basic point in *Doxology* that "worship, doctrine and life," all three, intend the praise of God.[12] I cannot agree with him, however, when he makes liturgy itself the primary language of Christian worship, moving theological language to the role of a secondary reflection upon "the primary experience" of worship.[13] Theology, too, is an integral aspect of the liturgy, and of the worship and praise of God. *Prayer, sermons, hymns, worship, and liturgy are already theology.* I find a separation between them rather artificial.

The fact that theology is worship raises the issue of the truth about God. To worship someone is to tell of their worth, to ascribe glory to them, and to describe their worthiness. Unlike flattery or marketing, worship is interested in the *truth* about the one we worship. True worship can be grounded only in the truly wonderful things about the one we worship. True worship, then, is grounded in truth. Schubert Ogden correctly insists that the Christian witness of faith carries with it an implicit truth-claim: "Any act of Christian witness, just like any other act of human praxis, necessarily implies, even if it may not express, certain claims to validity."[14] Unfortunately, Ogden

---

11. I have in mind here the Hebrew roots *halel* (הלל) and *yadah* (ידה), as well as Greek verbs like *aineo* (αἰνέω) and *doxazo* (δοξάζω).

12. Wainwright, *Doxology*, p. 10.

13. Wainwright, *Doxology*, p. 21.

14. Schubert M. Ogden, "Process Theology and the Wesleyan Witness," in *Wesleyan Theology Today*, ed. Theodore Runyan (Nashville: Kingswood, 1985), p. 65; reprinted

goes on to find those claims to validity primarily in a pseudo-universal "common sense" rationality. Here I must disagree.[15] The truth as we know it in the story of God, and most of all in Jesus Christ, must be allowed the freedom to correct our common human reasonings. These are, after all, distorted by sin — as most of the Christian tradition has affirmed.

I am arguing, then, that theology is not merely a "critical reflection" upon some other kind of experience or language or rationality that is "primary." Theology is a reflection only in the sense that it is a response: a response to the love of God, to the priority of God's action in salvation and creation. Theology as I see it is fundamentally a participation in the worship of God by telling the truth about God. It is grounded in the quest to know God in a deeply personal way — to love and to be loved by God, to use the words of Clement. Theology, of course, does have many tasks and dimensions, including critical reflection. But theology should not be reduced to academics.

This understanding of theology is not far from what we find in Karl Barth, especially in the first part of his *Church Dogmatics*.[16] Barth explicitly begins by stating, "theology is a function of the Church. The Church confesses God as it talks about God" (p. 3). But Barth goes on to talk about theology as a science, which he sees as "the third, strictest, and proper sense of the word" (p. 3). Barth rightly sees that the church itself "puts to itself the question of truth" (p. 4). He then goes on to state, "Theology follows the talk of the Church to the extent that in its question as to the correctness of its utterance it does not measure it by an alien standard but by its own source and object," namely the Word of God. So Barth understood this latter, proper task of "dogmatics" to

---

from the *Perkins Journal* 37 (1984): 18-33, and newly reprinted in *Thy Nature and Thy Name Is Love: Process and Wesleyan Theologies in Dialogue*, ed. Bryan Stone and Thomas Oord (Nashville: Kingswood, 2001). See further, Schubert Ogden, *On Theology* (San Francisco: Harper and Row, 1986), esp. pp. 3-21. Note this telling remark in the latter book: "its [theology's] appeal in support of this claim [to truth] is to no other conditions than those universally established with existence as such" (p. 20). I would love for Ogden, or any philosopher, to spell out convincingly just exactly what those conditions are!

15. See further the previous chapter, "Putting Reason in Its Place: A Dialogue with Process Theology."

16. Karl Barth, *Church Dogmatics,* I/1, English translation (Edinburgh: T&T Clark, 1975 [1932]). Page references will be cited parenthetically in the text.

be "the task of testing, criticising and correcting the actual proclamation of the Church at a given time" (p. 288). The basis for this criticism,
of course, is the Word of God. And this Word, for Barth, is clearly established only in Jesus Christ, the Word made flesh. In a late essay on the
relationship between theology and philosophy, Barth wrote, "In Jesus
Christ the free grace of God summons the gratitude of the human being, and the free gratitude of the human being answers the grace of
God, not the reverse!"[17]

I agree fundamentally with Barth's notion of theology as a free response of gratitude toward the work of God, especially in Christ. I also
agree with Barth that revelation must, for the theologian, be the primary source of insight into the God whom we worship. But I do not
and cannot agree that the "third sense" of theology, the critical or "scientific" task, is the most proper sense of theology as an academic discipline. As Barth correctly argued, theology as an academic discipline
must take as its axiom the First Commandment, to worship the one
true God, and him alone.[18] But this implies that the critical moment
for theological reflection is secondary to the primary aim of telling the
truth about God, that is, praising the Lord.

I have been arguing that the proper and primary goal of theology
is worship: the praise of the one true God. If I am right, several serious
questions that come from our Enlightenment heritage raise their
heads, questions we cannot ignore: How can theology be a rigorous academic discipline? How can theology as an academic discipline ("science") legitimate its truth-claims? How does theology as a discipline relate to the other arts and sciences of the university? It is to these
questions we now turn.

---

17. Karl Barth, "Philosophy and Theology," in *The Way of Theology in Karl Barth,* ed.
and trans. H. M. Rumscheidt (Allison Park, Pa.: Pickwick, 1986), p. 90. Originally published as "Philosophie und Theologie" in the Festschrift for his brother, Heinrich Barth,
who was a philosopher: *Philosophie und christliche Existenz,* ed. Gerhard Huber (Basel:
Helbing und Lichtenhahn, 1960).

18. See his essay "The First Commandment as an Axiom of Theology," in
Rumscheidt, *The Way of Theology;* German original, "Das erste Gebot als theologisches
Axiom," in *Theologische Fragen und Antworten: Gesammelte Vorträge,* vol. 3 (Zürich: Theo-
logischer Verlag Zürich, 1957).

Three Publics for Theology

David Tracy has argued that theological literature has three "publics" or potential readers/hearers. These are the church, the academy, and the broader culture or society.[19] Tracy's question of the larger publics for theological work (written or spoken) is an important one for answering the question of the "scientific" character of theology. But my argument so far suggests a very different set of answers to the question, who is addressed in theological discourse? Of course, we assume as obvious the rhetorical skill of an author or speaker, which must focus on the primary audience for any text. This primary audience is uppermost in our mind and will determine the grammar, academic level, language, and topic of the text as one creates it. A sermon will thus be a very different text from a public and pluralistic academic lecture, even if the same speaker is talking on the same topic.

My concern here is not with "audience" in this rhetorical sense but rather with "publics," that is, with the potential audiences we keep in mind even when we are focused on our primary audience. The first public for theology, what we keep uppermost in the back of our minds as we write, should be neither the church nor society but God. This is because theological literature, like so much (but not all!) of our worship, is a linguistic form of the praise of God. The Blessed Trinity is the first public for our theological literature.

The second public, then, will be the community of all those who, alongside us, praise and worship the one true God. They will, as co-celebrants with us in the life of worship, be interested in the truth about God as we understand it. I, for one, do not believe this community is coextensive with the visible church; but that is a topic for another day.

In principle, the third public includes all of humanity, for it is all those interested in "the Christian thing." All people of reason and goodwill, interested in knowing about Christians and their God, compose this third public. And it may well be that the theologian, from time to time, needs to address this public directly, to explain the substance of gospel truth and Christian practice to the wider culture of our own time and place. This may be the very best kind of "apolo-

---

19. David Tracy, *The Analogical Imagination* (New York: Crossroad, 1981), p. 21.

getics." But nevertheless, even such apologetic or explanatory writings are written to the glory of God, and in fact have God as an important audience; we know that at least God will read what we write, even if no one else does!

What, then, about the so-called criteria for truth, meaning, and adequacy in theology? If God is our first public, we will want most of all to be true to God's own revelation. The majority of Christian theologians would affirm that God is revealed in history (and to a lesser extent in nature and reason), with the acme of this historical revelation being in Jesus of Nazareth. The Scriptures are the primary witness to this revelation, and embody it in textual form. They form, therefore, the first or primary source and norm for theological reflection. The Wesleyan Norms (or "Quadrilateral") would also include (as we noted in the previous chapter) ecumenical, orthodox tradition as a second norm, followed by reason and experience. These norms are also concerned to discover the truth about God, wherever it may be found. The theologian draws upon all of these sources, *in this order,* in order to speak the truth in praise of God. (To be clear: the order of the Wesleyan norms is a methodological, not a chronological, one.)

Tracy, along with many others, allows the terms of theological meaning to be dictated to by the third public, that is, by our broader society. "The theologian," he states, "should argue the case (pro and con) on strictly public grounds that are open to all rational persons."[20] There is a sense in which we can and should agree here. Theological works should be understandable and clear so that our second and third publics may grasp what it is we are saying. Yet our ultimate source of truth, meaning, and coherence comes from revelation, not a supposed "universal" human experience or rationality (*pace* Tracy and Ogden).

Theology and the Postmodern University

There is and must remain a critical moment, a self-searching, for theological literature, even when it is understood as a type of worship. We want to do the very best for God, and in the realm of the intellect this means searching out the truth with diligence, vigor, and clarity. Any-

20. Tracy, *Analogical Imagination,* p. 64.

thing less would not honor the One who is the Truth. Because theology is a kind of worship, we are interested in the truth about the One we worship. This truth can indeed come from many sources, including other academic disciplines. Despite this, many theologians go wrong in making the other arts and sciences of the university too independent of the truth as we know it in Christian revelation and faith. Barth argued as he did only because, for him, philosophy, science, and the rest could begin their work only apart from faith. On this specific point both Ogden and Barth follow Kant, Schleiermacher, and indeed most of the Enlightenment. Modernism insisted on the importance of independent faculties of arts and science: independent, that is, of church dogmas and regulations. Schleiermacher, ever the preacher, put it this way:

> Unless the Reformation from which our church first emerged endeavors to establish an eternal covenant between the living Christian faith and completely free, independent scientific inquiry, so that faith does not hinder science and science does not exclude faith, it fails to meet adequately the needs of our time.[21]

There is a sense in which we should agree with Schleiermacher, and a sense in which we cannot and should not follow him down this path. We can and should agree that all of the university, all the arts and sciences, should be free of political control by Christians. Indeed, they should be free of all merely political (as opposed to ethical) controls, from any ideology or faction. Science and art must be free to pursue the truth as they know it. This freedom is not and cannot, of course, be completely independent of all philosophical and religious issues. As we have already seen in this book, the modernist myth of a purely value-free science was the nightmare of the twentieth century. Scientific pursuit and technological innovation, apart from ethical concerns, are destructive to the planet and harmful to all living things, including human beings. Apart from these humanistic and ethical limitations, however, theology and the church should support the freedom of the arts and sciences to pursue and publish the truth as they see it.

No academic discipline is free of presuppositions, however, nor is

---

21. Friedrich Schleiermacher, *On the Glaubenslehre*, trans. J. Duke and F. S. Fiorenza (Chico, Calif.: Scholars Press, 1981), p. 64.

any discipline self-interpreting. That "freedom" we cannot allow the arts and sciences, since they in fact are dependent in exactly these areas. As we have argued in previous chapters, no science or academic discipline is value-free or neutral: all are based upon certain presuppositions, and all have results that can and should be more fully interpreted within a particular worldview (and its associated tradition). This implies that there is room for a faith-based approach to any academic discipline, including physics, art criticism, computer science, and the rest. What I am talking about here is Christian learning, or Christian scholarship.[22]

Enlightenment thinkers like Kant would argue that the very idea of a Christian approach to science or art would be a betrayal of the rigor and intellectual discipline of that subject. This understanding of the rigor of academic pursuit has been called into question, and rightly so, by philosophers as diverse as Søren Kierkegaard, Abraham Kuyper, and Wilhelm Dilthey. In the last century, thinkers as various as Heidegger, Polanyi, Kuhn, Gadamer, and Habermas all rejected a "value-free" or "neutral" understanding of what counts as good academics (*episteme, scientia,* or *Wissenschaft*), and rightly so. The distinction between science and theology is not found in the difference between reason and faith, or knowledge and myth, or some other muddle-headed confusion. Both the sciences and theology draw upon faith and reason. The *aim* of the arts and sciences on the one hand, and theology on the other, dictates differences in what counts as data and good methods in each. Here is where the true differences lie: in the goals of each discipline. All are rational in their own way, however, and all are grounded in certain basic commitments, which they cannot fully justify on their own. The Enlightenment ideal of a universal rationality has to be abandoned because it simply failed to achieve its goals, according to its own principles (whether those are empiricist, Hegelian, Cartesian, etc.).

A postmodern approach to science and higher education will avoid the errors of Enlightenment rationality; but I am likewise unwilling to abandon the pursuit of truth as the goal of science, and of the

22. See, among recent expositors, George Marsden, *The Outrageous Idea of Christian Scholarship* (New York: Oxford University Press, 1997), and Nicholas Wolterstorff, "Public Theology or Christian Learning?" in *A Passion for God's Reign,* ed. M. Volf (Grand Rapids: Eerdmans, 1998); cf. his earlier *Reason within the Bounds of Religion,* second ed. (Grand Rapids: Eerdmans, 1984).

university.[23] Academic disciplines pursue truth in the areas of their interest and focus, based upon certain value judgments they *own* but cannot *ground*. Such virtues as honesty, humility, attention to detail, and rigorous testing of theories are commitments that come to each discipline from the broader culture: we might say, from a worldview.[24] Yet at the same time, the postmodern academy should not be committed to any one religion, philosophy, or worldview. The Christian, too, is committed to "welcome the stranger" and appreciate the great variety of voices and perspectives within the academy and culture. While a postmodern university should allow diversity and embrace difference, the various disciplines are still committed to the pursuit of truth and scholarship, according to the epistemic practices of each discipline's tradition. To learn chemistry, for example, or film criticism, is to be tutored in particular epistemic practices and to be initiated into a particular tradition of inquiry. These various traditions of academic inquiry assume certain values and principles, which they cannot and do not pretend to justify. Furthermore, the results of these sciences and arts must still be interpreted and reflected upon, within the broader culture and within specific worldviews. Aspects of our worldviews, then, both make the academic disciplines possible and place them into a broader perspective in which they are interpreted and applied.

Christian theology, then, has two roles in the postmodern, public academy. First of all, Christian theology is a key part of the Christian worldview, which in turn informs Christian scholarship in the academy. Christian scholarship or Christian learning is thus scholarship informed by, grounded in, and interpreted within the Christian worldview (a worldview that arises out of Christian tradition, practice, and faith). Not only the theologian, but the economist, scientist, and poet should, if they are Christians, approach their work in a way that is

23. I am happy to see that J. Wentzel van Huyssteen has come to similar conclusions, independently, about the "postfoundational" rationality of theology in the midst of an important "interdisciplinarity" within the university. See his new book, *The Shaping of Rationality: Toward Interdisciplinarity in Theology and Science* (Grand Rapids: Eerdmans, 1999). Especially important is van Huyssteen's argument that in the universal "quest for intelligibility" in the academy, we need a "postfoundationalist notion of rationality" that leads us "to rediscover *the embeddedness of this process of rational reflection in the living context of our evolving, developing traditions*" (p. 174, my emphasis).

24. See my earlier chapter on "Science and Worldview."

informed by Christian commitments. This should not lead to shoddy scholarship. On the contrary, since this intellectual work, too, is done to the glory of God, only the best scholarship is admissible. What counts as good data, excellent methodology, and acceptable theory is determined by each discipline. The Christian enters into this method of inquiry with a specifically Christian grounding for the value judgments and presuppositions that make it possible. Christian scholars may well be guided by their ultimate concerns in choosing a topic for intellectual study. The Christian scholar, also, will interpret the results of this academic discipline within a broad Christian worldview. And, as I have argued elsewhere, Christian scholars are right to accept that theory which is most in consonance with their faith, when two or more theories are equally sound according to the standards of their discipline. In fact, the Christian scholar may wish to defend that theory as "best" — not on the basis of special revelation or faith but on the basis of what counts as good evidence and argument in that discipline. Of course, Christian scholarship is only one form of scholarship, but it should be allowed within a pluralistic, postmodern academy, along with the many other voices and perspectives. So this is the first role of Christian theology in a postmodern university: to be a key element in a Christian worldview that informs and interprets Christian learning in all the arts and sciences.

From this perspective, religious studies is just like any other academic discipline in a pluralistic university. Christians may be experts in Islam or Taoism, in Hebrew studies or early Christianity. The roles can also be reversed, with fine Jewish scholars in New Testament studies and the like. The many academic disciplines that make up "religious studies" will determine what counts as excellence in scholarship in any of these specializations. Professors in a religious studies department who are also Christians will do their best to explain the religion that they are academic specialists in, without advocating it (even if that religion is their own). A pluralistic and open academic context would not allow the advocacy of any one religion; the activity of Christian theology as the worship of the one true God, in proclamation and praise, can only be described in the classroom. It cannot be engaged in within the classroom and academy of a postmodern, pluralistic university.

This leads to the second role for Christian theology in a pluralistic university, and that is to address its third public. The primary audience in such a context will, after all, be the third public for Christian theology, that is, all people of reason and goodwill interested in Christianity. For this reason, if a Christian theologian is employed as an expert in Christian or biblical studies at such a university, she must focus primarily on the third public for theology, but without forgetting the first and second publics. Christian theology in all its variety can and must be described and evaluated, but not advocated, within this context. Even in this context, however, the Christian religious studies professor will seek to glorify God in the excellence with which she describes and evaluates Christianity. In other contexts, outside the pluralistic academy and classroom, such professors are free to worship God more openly in their academic work. They will not (if they are wise) lose sight of the true goal, and primary public, of their scholarly productions.

A corollary of my argument is this: Christian theology can be fully articulated and taught only within a faith-based institution of higher learning. This turns on my previous point that the true home of theology is at Word and Table, in the worshiping community. When seminaries understand their scholarly production to flow from preaching and liturgy, then some healing of the unfortunate state of our theological schools (at least the mainstream Protestant ones) may begin. *The full and complete teaching and learning* of Christian theology is not possible in a pluralistic context. This has to do, again, with the aim of theological work. Of course anyone, anywhere, can engage in Christian theology in the privacy of personal study. We should be allowed to write and publish as we see fit, as well. But these facts are irrelevant to my point, which is about corporate teaching and learning. Teaching and learning Christian theology as a worshipful activity can take place only in a fully Christian context, that is, in the context of the worship and praise of God within a Christian university, college, or seminary.

In a recent volume entitled *Taking Religion to School: Christian Theology and Secular Education,* Stephen Webb has argued that the teaching of religion is always itself a religious act.[25] I am in full agreement with this viewpoint. But he insists that, by way of empathetic engagement, the religion scholar can appreciate and present a variety of religions in

---

25. Stephen Webb, *Taking Religion to School: Christian Theology and Secular Education* (Grand Rapids: Brazos, 2000).

the classroom. Further, he argues that each religion teacher should come clean with respect to his or her own religious biases, which we are usually bad at hiding from bright students anyway. The classroom then becomes a safe place for a diversity of religious perspectives, including the teacher's own, without imposing any one religion as "the true" one. I find this book to be a refreshing look at its topic and agree with the main points, but unlike Webb, I would argue that teaching theology *as theology* requires advocating the truth of a particular religion, and this can be done only in a faith-based context. The pluralistic context Webb is discussing can and should embrace his proposals. But the advocacy of a particular religion as the true one in class — an advocacy he argues against — is what I find unique about theological education in the strict sense, and it is why a faith-based context is vital to it. Will such "confessionalism" lead to irrational, non-academic religious instruction, as some suggest? That is the next question we will explore.

The Academic Character of Theology

We are now in a better position to answer the question of the "critical moment" in theological reflection. In what way is theology "scientific" or academically sound? How can theology meet the needs of modern intellectuals without losing itself? In my work on the problem of induction, I argue that there are no univocal, universal standards of good informal argument.[26] Instead, there are "family resemblances" among the standards in various traditions of inquiry. The standards of argument, inference, and evidence must be contextualized by each discipline, given its aims and focus of study.[27] What counts as "good argument," or "evidence" or "coherence," differs slightly from discipline to discipline. These values and criteria do operate in a general way as part of any informal logic, but they are vague and need to be spelled out within each tradition of inquiry.

Theology is no different from the other academic disciplines in

26. See the Appendix, "Induction after Foundationalism."
27. Formal systems of reason, such as mathematics and symbolic logic, are more universal. But even they must be applied properly in each context.

this regard. What counts as clear, coherent, and sound argument will
need to be assessed, in part, by the criteria of intelligibility found in the
Christian religion, including its way of life, history, creeds, sacred texts,
religious practice, and worldview. On the other hand, there will be par-
allels and analogies in method and logic which theology will wish to
borrow from other disciplines. Textual criticism in biblical studies will
be pretty much the same as the textual criticism of other literature, for
example. What counts as coherent within theology may be similar to
what counts as coherent in a particular philosophy. The list can be ex-
tended. My major point is that theology must be true to its first source
and norm, that is, revelation. Theology must always remember its first
public. These commitments will very often alter and shape the methods, criteria, and data brought to theology from other disciplines. Theology should strive to honor reason, but not a supposed universal rationality. Rather, reason in theology is in the service of faith; our minds
seek to love the one true God. We are not interested in Mind in the abstract, but rather "the mind of Christ" (1 Cor. 2:16).

Because theology is about God, including the work of God in the
world, it will always be interested in the results of the other arts and sciences. Theology does not stand alone here, however, but depends upon
Christian scholarship. Christian theology will be done in cooperation
with Christian learning, that is, with the best Christian scholarship in
the other arts and sciences. The theologian will take on board truth as
it is known in other disciplines, but will depend upon Christian experts
in those disciplines to interpret this "truth" in a Christian manner. So I
would argue, against Barth, that theology is based on "revelation and
Christian scholarship" and not revelation alone. Barth himself seems
to allow for just this in his article on "The First Commandment As an
Axiom of Theology." He gives three cautions to those who would add
the little word "and" to revelation. First, we must speak of revelation
"with a notably heightened seriousness and interest, and by speaking
of that other criterion only secondarily and for the sake of revelation."[28] Second (and this sounds very much like what I am calling
Christian scholarship), theology expresses its commitment to the first
commandment by "interpreting those other things according to revela-

28. Barth, "First Commandment," in *The Way of Theology,* ed. and trans. Rumscheidt, p. 73.

tion and not the other way around."[29] Third, theology must permit "no possibility . . . of intermixing, exchanging, or identifying the two concepts in this relation."[30] I believe all these cautions are well taken, yet there is plenty of room here for theology to be based not simply on revelation but on any truth that bears upon our knowledge of God. The quest for truth about God demands that theology look also to Christian scholarship in all the disciplines as its guide and helper. This would include both philosophy and natural science, understood within the Christian worldview.

In a recent lecture on spiritual and practical theology, Randy Maddox argued that there are four "dimensions" or senses of the word theology.[31] First, there is theology in the life and thought of the individual believer, often tacit and undeveloped. This kind of theology is practical and living, including the mind of Christ and the fruit of the Spirit at work in the life of the believer. This is an important sense of "theology" which I admire and believe to be important, but which I have not emphasized here. A second sense is the Eastern Orthodox notion that liturgy is theology, that is, the theology of the worship of God in the community. Here is the emphasis of my chapter. The third sense of "theology" is a second-order kind of theology: academic, critical theological reflection. Although I have not emphasized this, I do accept it and value it. Finally, the fourth dimension of theology is theological method and apologetics, which Maddox calls third-order theology. This, too, is crucial. Put in terms of this expansive notion of what "theology" is, my thesis that "theology is worship" I understand to be true for all four dimensions, but especially for the second one.

There is clearly an important place for second- and third-order reflection upon the primary theological data (upon the individual and upon the worshiping community). Christian theology is an academic discipline because it seeks to know the truth about its focus of study in a rational, rigorous manner. But Christian theology does not allow its notions of rationality to be dictated to it from the outside. That, I think, is the great danger of third-order theological reflection (theo-

---

29. Barth, "First Commandment," p. 74.
30. Barth, "First Commandment," p. 75.
31. Randy Maddox, "Spiritual and Practical Theology: Trajectories toward Re-engagement," *Association of Practical Theology, Occasional Papers* 3 (Spring 1999): 10-16.

logical method and apologetics). Rather, even in this domain, as long as it is truly Christian theology, it seeks to know and love the One who has revealed himself in Jesus Christ, and in all creation, as Lord. And it uses methods and standards of reason that are appropriate to this goal and are likewise clear and coherent. Reason, evidence, and argument are not foreign to theology but must conform to the standards of faith and revelation to be acceptable. In this way, theology honors the God who is the source of all truth. At the same time, theology retains its proper nature as the worship and praise of God.

7 Theology, Time, and Thermodynamics

We have so far in this book developed the notion of a Christian worldview, which provided the medium whereby theology and the special sciences can influence each other in a way that does not do violence to their own distinct methodologies. In this chapter and the next, I would like to give two concrete examples that spell out this mutuality model more fully. To begin, I have chosen the topic of thermodynamics because of its intrinsic interest and because of my interest in the philosophy and theology of time.

What is time? This is one of the oldest of philosophical conundrums. St. Augustine asked this question, as did many philosophers before him including Parmenides, Plato, Aristotle, and Plotinus. We seem in some ways no closer to knowing the answers to such deep questions than those men of the past, but in one area, formerly known as natural philosophy and now called natural science, there has been a great deal of progress in our understanding of the world, including its temporality. This is in part because science limits itself to quantitative questions and answers. Even in the natural sciences, however, there is no agreement as to the true nature of time. In this chapter we will investigate what light natural science (thermodynamics in particular) can cast upon the problem of the nature of time. As a way of exemplifying the mutuality model of theology-science dialogue already developed, we will demonstrate the integration of theology and science around the topic of time.

Time seems so everyday, so ordinary, and yet at the same time so enigmatic. One of the reasons the problem of time has proven so intractable involves the many senses of the word. "Time" can mean many things, from a break in the middle of a sporting event to the so-called "fourth dimension" of our spacetime. Time has many facets, and philosophers and scientists have studied many of these different aspects. For example, there is the question of the absolute or relative character of time: does the passage of time reduce to a relationship between events and things, or can we say, with Newton, that "time of itself and from its own nature . . . flows equably without relation to anything external"?[1] Another important issue in the philosophy of time is this: is "process" (the passage of time from past to present to future) an objective part of the natural world or is it mind-dependent and subjective? Many physicists would answer that process is subjective, and what is fundamental is the geometrical spread of spacetime, which includes all events as equally real, whether or not one would call them "past" or "future" or "present" (pseudo-properties that have no measure and no physical significance). This latter view I call the stasis theory of time (though it is also known as the "tenseless" or "B" theory). Belief in objective process is called process theory.

Of the many fascinating issues in the philosophy of time, thermodynamics impinges on two issues: the beginning of time and the "arrow" of time. Since the time of Augustine or, even before him, of Origen, Christians have asked, "Does time have a beginning?" Is the initial singularity of the universe (the "Big Bang") a beginning in time? Such a question raises the distinction between physical time as we know it (what most scientists mean by time, which I call "measured time") and time plain and simple, or what we might call "pure duration."[2] Measured time is time as we know it in physics: a measurable, quantitative factor of the universe. Pure duration is what measured time is a measure *of;* time that can "go by" even though no change takes place.

On the plausible assumption that we can distinguish philosophically between time itself and the events that occur in time, the distinction between measured time and pure duration allows us to distinguish the question of their beginnings. Does the time of our

---

1. Isaac Newton, *The Mathematical Principles of Natural Philosophy,* ed. F. Cajori (Berkeley: University of California Press, 1960), p. 6.

2. For more on the nature of measured time, see Alan G. Padgett, *God, Eternity and the Nature of Time* (London: Macmillan, 1992), pp. 7-18.

universe (measured time) have a beginning? This is a separate issue from the question of whether pure duration (time in a metaphysical sense) has a beginning. As we shall see, thermodynamics can help us answer the first of these questions, although it leaves the latter untouched.

Thermodynamics is also of some help in answering the question of the "arrow" of time, that is, does time have a "direction" that it always follows? More technically, such direction is known as the anisotropy or asymmetry of time.[3] Space is isotropic: we can move freely in it, apart from some force such as gravity pulling or pushing us in some way. Time is not like that, according to our everyday experience and common sense. It only goes in one direction: physical systems cannot run backward against the clock. Or can they? The science of thermodynamics has important lessons for us in our search for an answer to this question.

Thermodynamics

One of the most interesting areas of contemporary physics is thermodynamics. Although studies in quantum mechanics, cosmology, and dynamical systems ("chaos theory") have received a great deal of attention in the popular press, and in books written for the educated general public,[4] thermodynamics deserves an equal billing. Particular interest in thermodynamics and its implications has been generated by the work of Ilya Prigogine.[5] Born in Russia in 1917, Prigogine moved with his family to Belgium, where he was schooled in the "Brussels School" of physical chemistry. A brilliant student, he eventually be-

---

3. In discussing time and thermodynamics, we should carefully distinguish between the process and stasis theories, which are about the ontological status of "nowness" or "presentness" in the physical universe, and the issue of the anisotropy or "arrow" of time. While the process theorist, who believes that nowness is objective, is committed to the anisotropy of time, the stasis theorist, for whom "past," "present," and "future" are merely subjective qualities, can consistently assert either the anisotropy or the isotropy of time.

4. A good example of this is the best-seller by Stephen Hawking, *A Brief History of Time* (New York: Bantam, 1988).

5. See his *From Being to Becoming* (San Francisco: W. H. Freeman, 1980).

came the leading researcher of this school. He received the Nobel Prize in 1977 for his work in thermodynamics and is now widely considered the world's leading expert in statistical mechanics and thermodynamics. The Center for Statistical Mechanics and Thermodynamics at the University of Texas, Austin, is named after him. The work of Prigogine and his colleagues on the thermodynamics of dissipative structures (systems that exhibit some stability, even though they are far from equilibrium and nonlinear) has greatly added to the importance of this science for physics, chemistry, and biology.

Modern physics is divided into four areas: classical physics, quantum mechanics, relativity physics, and thermodynamics. The term "thermodynamics" comes from two Greek words meaning "heat movement," and thermodynamics does indeed study heat. Perhaps this area of science is best understood as the transfer of heat and work between and within physical systems. It focuses on such measures as volume, temperature, and pressure in order to measure the amount of "work" that a system is capable of, that is, how much free energy it has to work with.

Thermodynamics arose in the nineteenth century from the study of heat and energy in steam engines and other macroscopic systems. There are four laws of thermodynamics that have arisen from such studies. The Zeroth Law states that no heat will flow between any two bodies that are at the same temperature. The First Law arises from the work of James Prescott Joule, the son of a Manchester brewing family who discovered the equivalence of heat and work. The basic unit of energy in physics, the joule, is named after him. The First Law states that energy can be neither created nor destroyed. The total energy remains conserved even when work is done; thus, energy will always be conserved in a physical process, even though it may undergo transformation from free energy to heat. The Second Law owes it origins to the work of Rudolf Clausius, a German physicist born in 1822. He noticed that while heat and work are equivalent, and energy is conserved in the exchange, they are dissimilar in that work can be fully transformed into heat but heat does not on its own turn back into useful energy for work. The Second Law is certainly the most interesting of the four laws of thermodynamics, and the best known, having wide ramifications for our everyday life. It can be stated in many ways. Clausius' statement was, "Heat does not pass spontaneously from cold to hot." A more universal expression of the Second Law is this: for isolated systems, entropy always increases.[6]

The introduction of the term "entropy" — the degree of disorder in a system, which relates to how much useful work can be extracted from that system — leads us into one of the most important concepts in thermodynamics. Thermodynamics studies heat and energy in systems, and entropy has to do with these aspects of physical systems. Although in an isolated system energy is constant over change (the First Law), the form or structure of this energy in the system is not constant. Iron will turn to rust, but rusty iron never spontaneously becomes clean again. An open bottle of perfume will send its scent into the air of a room, but the reverse process never takes place. What is lost in these processes is capacity for useful work; what is gained in each process is entropy. Entropy is difficult to describe precisely because its measure differs for different types of systems. But in each case, entropy is at a maximum at thermal equilibrium, the state of a system in which all spontaneous thermodynamic changes are at an end and all free energy has been used up. For example, an isolated system of ice and water is at thermal equilibrium when the ratio of ice to liquid water remains the same. Whatever melts, there is an equivalent amount of water that refreezes into solid form. To take another example, a marble sent spinning around in a bowl is in thermal equilibrium when the marble stops rolling around and settles to the bottom of the bowl.

According to the Second Law, whenever a change takes place in an isolated system, entropy increases and so the capacity for useful work (free energy) decreases. In the words of the title of Lord Kelvin's classic 1852 paper on the subject, the Second Law concerns "The Universal Tendency in Nature to the Dissipation of Mechanical Energy." Thus even though energy as a whole is conserved in every change in a system, the capacity for work or useful energy in the universe decreases. The implications of this for our understanding of time are our next subject.

6. The Third Law is basically about reaching zero degrees Kelvin, and will not concern us here.

Time and Thermodynamics

Since entropy is always on the increase, it is possible to give an "arrow" or direction to the time dimension. At first glance, this would not seem to be such an amazing discovery: don't we already know the direction of time from our everyday existence? But physicists and philosophers of science have argued that the "direction" of time is in fact an epiphenomenon, something that is not fundamental to physical reality. This is because the classical mechanics that Newton brilliantly formulated, and that were at one time believed to be fundamental to the universe, are time symmetric. Although equations such as "force is equal to the change in momentum over time" ($F = dp/dt$) have "time" in them, in classical mechanics the same equations can describe the same phenomenon whether "t" is positive or negative, that is, whether time is going "backward" or "forward." In the simple case of colliding billiard balls (or atoms) the equations stay the same no matter which direction time runs. It is not possible to determine the direction of time when attending only to this sort of phenomenon.

The advent of thermodynamics and entropy complicates matters. Suddenly it seems that such "time-relative" irreversible processes must boil down, ultimately, to time-symmetrical equations of classical mechanics. Or so it seemed at one time to scientists dominated by the simplified abstractions of classical Newtonian physics. In more recent times, however, scientists in a number of fields have begun to note the limitations of classical mechanics for our understanding of the rough-and-tumble, complex world of irreversible processes. According to the Heisenberg Uncertainty Principle, the exact position or energy of a particle cannot be determined. In the subatomic world, the very act of observing alters the reality being observed, meaning that there is an asymmetry in the particle system based on the "before" and "after" of the experimental intrusion. So measurement introduces irreversibility into subatomic physics, even though the equations of quantum mechanics are time symmetric. In the study of dynamical systems, or chaos theory, the smallest of differences in the initial conditions of such complex systems leads to large differences over time (weather is a good example). Our inability to predict the outcome of the system, and the complex interaction between elements of a dynamical system, lead to another kind of irreversible process. In biology, the movement from birth to full growth to death is likewise irreversible.[7]

The key philosophical issue facing those who reflect upon time in contemporary science is this: which is really fundamental? Shall we view the time-symmetrical physics of wave functions, trajectories, and classical mechanics as truly fundamental, and interpret irreversible processes in light of them? Or should we view irreversible processes such as the increase of entropy as fundamental, and view trajectories, wave functions, and classical mechanics as idealizations and simplifications? There is a growing body of science, led by Ilya Prigogine and his colleagues, arguing that the second view is the correct one.[8] The general philosophical question of which interpretation one should accept (which I will consider further below) leads to the issue of the integration of theology and science.

Time and Christian Theology

Given our quest for a systematic Christian worldview, we cannot ignore what theology and the sciences have to say on a subject. Theology and science need to be integrated, especially at the level of large-scale explanations of the universe. Time and history are important dimensions of the universe. To illustrate the manner in which theology and science can be integrated, we begin with theological perspectives on this topic. What exactly are Christians committed to with respect to time? Can we properly speak of *the* Christian view of time?

Let us recall the many issues that the philosophy of time brought up. The Christian faith is not committed to one view or the other on most of these problems. Whether time is absolute or relative, whether there is a relationship between time and change, whether the process or stasis theory is correct, or even whether measured time has a beginning — none of these is essential to the Christian faith, to the heart of the gospel. For some thinkers, the last point in particular may come as a

---

7. For a readable survey of these and other topics, see Peter Coveney and Roger Highfield, *The Arrow of Time* (London: W. H. Allen, 1990).

8. Ilya Prigogine, *From Being*, and at a more popular level, Ilya Prigogine and Isabelle Stengers, *Order out of Chaos* (London: Heinemann, 1984).

surprise. For example, Carl Sagan and Stephen Hawking both assume that "a universe with no edge in space, no beginning or end in time, [has] nothing for a creator to do."[9] In Hawking's best-seller *A Brief History of Time,* he makes the argument that the universe is just "there," adopting the stasis theory of time and incorporating some speculative elements of quantum gravitational theory to argue that the entire universe exists as a complete spacetime entity, without need of an initial bump of energy from a Creator to get it going. In fact, the universe is a kind of "free lunch."

While Sagan and Hawking may be fine scientists, as philosophers and theologians they leave something to be desired. Christian theologians like Thomas Aquinas have persuasively argued that measured time could be of infinite duration and still the Christian doctrine of "creation out of nothing" *(creatio ex nihilo)* could be true. The doctrine of creation asserts that the universe is radically contingent: the Creator's will alone is the ground of being for our universe, whether measured time has a beginning or not. Unlike Plato's Demiurge in the *Timaeus,* the Lord of Heaven and Earth did not need any "stuff" — other than his own power, love, and freedom — out of which to make the world. But we need to note that the priority of God's power and will over any and all other things is a logical or causal priority, not a temporal one. The doctrine of creation out of nothing does not necessarily imply a beginning to time. Rather, it points to the radical dependence of all other beings on the Being of God. After all, where do the laws of nature come from? Where does spacetime come from? Who ordered the delicate balance of forces in the universe that brought forth human life? Contra Hawking and Sagan, the metaphysical and scientific fact that the universe is contingent cannot be dispelled by some magic tricks in theoretical physics.[10]

Is there some aspect of time, then, which is essential to the Christian faith? I believe there is. The gospel is committed to the fact that time is linear and has a direction. There is a beginning, middle, and end to human history in biblical perspective. The Christian doctrines of

---

9. Carl Sagan, introduction to Hawking, *Brief History,* p. x.

10. For more on creation, contingency, and modern science, see the excellent collection, Ted Peters, ed., *Cosmos As Creation* (Nashville: Abingdon, 1989), and also Willem B. Drees, *Beyond the Big Bang* (La Salle, Ill.: Open Court, 1990).

creation, fall, salvation-history, Christology, soteriology, and eschatology imply a linear direction to time and history which is ineliminable from the Christian worldview. Natural religions as well as many of the philosophies of Greece and Rome did not have such a linear view of history. As Mircea Eliade points out in his fascinating book *The Myth of the Eternal Return,* "The life of archaic man . . . although it takes place in time, does not record time's irreversibility." One of the important (but not unique) contributions of Hebrew thought to Western civilization was a linear conception of history. "Christian thought," he continues, "tended to transcend, once and for all, the old themes of eternal repetition."[11] In his excellent *Christ the Meaning of History,* Hendrikus Berkhof demonstrates at length that the Christian faith is committed to the meaningfulness of the historical process, and to the once-and-for-all quality of Christ's redemption for all humanity. He rightly notes that "We must thank . . . Israel for our sense that history is goal-directed, and that as such it has meaning."[12] The Christian view of time, then, is that it has a direction and a purpose: as such, Christianity is committed to the anisotropy of the temporal process.

The Integration of Thermodynamics and Theology

Is it possible for theology and science to support each other? With care, as long as we avoid leaping to conclusions and a "God of the gaps" mentality that would find God wherever there is some unanswered scientific question, surely there can be some support and even integration between science and theology. I believe that such integration takes place most fully at the level of large-scale explanations. Despite the oft-quoted remarks of Ernan McMullin (who argued that a Big Bang model does not support the Christian doctrine of creation and that the doctrine of creation does not support a Big Bang model),[13] I find that

11. Mircea Eliade, *The Myth of the Eternal Return,* trans. Willard R. Trask (London: Routledge, 1955), citing pp. 86 and 137.

12. Hendrikus Berkhof, *Christ the Meaning of History,* trans. Lambertus Buurman (London: SCM, 1966), p. 21.

13. Ernan McMullin, "Natural Science and Belief in a Creator," in *Religion, Science, and the Search for Wisdom,* ed. D. M. Byers (Washington, D.C.: National Conference of Catholic Bishops, 1987), p. 39.

theology can support physics and vice versa.[14] According to the "mutuality model" developed earlier, there needs to be an ongoing dialogue between theology and science in which each discipline learns from the other. Of course, theology is interested in only the most general results of the special sciences, or what I have called large-scale explanations. Science, likewise, must come to its conclusions based on scientific data and methods, not on the basis of religious beliefs. Nevertheless, a coherent worldview is desired in Christian scholarship, and therefore what we learn from both theological disciplines and the sciences should be woven together into a larger picture. A rational believer who seeks a holistic worldview will not be satisfied with dividing her beliefs into separate boxes. While I agree with Ernan McMullin that science is complete on its own terms (given its methods, purpose, and limitations),[15] this does not mean that the natural sciences are in and of themselves "complete" from a theological or philosophical perspective. If we are rational, then what we believe as Christians will give shape to our views of natural science, and what we learn from the sciences will shape our theological convictions.

Both disciplines must, of course, come to their own conclusions, based on their own unique methodologies. I am certainly not proposing that we hold to scientific theories because of theology, or let theology be dictated to by science. Rather, there is room for a broader, more general attempt to put together a holistic worldview that includes what we believe both as Christians and as scientists, especially at the level of very large explanations of reality.[16] In the case of explanations of time and history, Christian theology clearly supports one particular interpretation of time in current physical science, rather than another plausible and popular view. So the Christian is reasonable in holding to that theory of time which best fits her theology, as long as both theories are equally supported by reason and evidence.

14. Part of the debate here is over the meaning of "support." McMullin makes it clear (in "Natural Science") that by support he means deductive support (implication, entailment). In this work, on the other hand, by "support" I mean inductive, indirect support.

15. McMullin, "Natural Science," pp. 14-47.

16. I assume that McMullin would also agree with this last point, given what he says about worldviews at the end of his interesting paper, "How Should Cosmology Relate to Theology?", in *The Sciences and Theology in the Twentieth Century,* ed. A. R. Peacocke (Notre Dame: University of Notre Dame Press, 1981), pp. 51f.

The Direction of Time and Irreversibility

Given that entropy is always on the increase for any changing matter-energy system in our world, the dissipation of systems provides us with a fundamental asymmetry or anisotropy for time. In the section on thermodynamics and time, above, we ended with a dilemma: either irreversible processes are the "real world" and classical dynamics and uncollapsed wave equations are a simplification of it, or the reversible world of classical dynamics and wave equations is fundamental and thermodynamics is a special, limiting case. What is important to realize is this: in either case, what is at stake is not science itself but our interpretation of science. In cases such as these, reflective believers are well within their intellectual rights in accepting that interpretation which, all other things being equal, is in line with their theological and metaphysical worldview. Given the Christian view of linear time essential to our faith, Christian philosophers of science will follow Prigogine, and a growing number of others, in finding the real world to be anisotropic and irreversible in time. At times the "dialogue" between theology and science looks like a monologue, with science doing all the talking. In this case, however, Christian theology should act as a "control belief" in guiding us to the proper interpretation of science.[17]

The End and Beginning of Time

I begin with the assumption that the universe, or better the material universe (since I do hold to a belief in nonmaterial objects), is an isolated system. Physical energy and matter are not being exchanged between our material universe and some other dimension or universe. The material universe, then, contains all the known matter and energy. In such a system, entropy will always increase. This means that the material universe, left to its own devices, will come to an end. The material universe will someday reach thermal equilibrium: all free energy will be used up, and no more "work" will take place. Whether we predict another singularity at the end of measured time (a "big crunch") or a con-

---

17. For more on "control beliefs" see Nicholas Wolterstorff, *Reason within the Bounds of Religion*, second ed. (Grand Rapids: Eerdmans, 1984).

tinual expansion of lifeless particles into empty space (a "heat death") is not of any significance.[18] The basic point remains the same from a thermodynamic perspective: entropy must increase (even if it never reaches an absolute maximum in an ever-expanding universe). The universe will come to an end.

Some scientists are uneasy with this conclusion. There are three objections to applying thermodynamics to the material universe of which I am aware. First, some have suggested that thermodynamics is questionable when applied to such large entities as an entire universe. After all, this science was developed on small steam engines, not huge galactic clusters. In response I would argue that all physical cosmological laws were developed on earth, in the study of small, simple systems. It is an axiom of astronomy and cosmology that the laws of physics apply throughout all time and space in the material universe. To try to exempt thermodynamics from such universality is simply an attempt to wiggle out of the problem. According to all we know of physics and astronomy, every single astronomical object will eventually decay, and the resultant matter and energy left over will not have the same capacity for work (free energy) as the original system. Entropy applies to everything in the material universe.

Second, Willem Drees has argued against the universal increase of entropy in the material universe by suggesting that it is not a "closed" (he no doubt means "isolated") system, in the sense necessary to apply the Second Law.[19] The expansion of the material universe, he suggests, works as if there were an "environment" into which entropy was carried away, even though there is no environment for the universe. Here I find Drees's argument rather unclear. Even the radiation given off by the universe, at the edge of its expansion, is also part of the material universe. The expansion itself is a form of thermodynamic exchange, increasing always the entropy of the whole (radiation, energy, matter) and decreasing the free energy in the material universe. Empty space is not an "environment" in the thermodynamic sense, i.e., something from which energy can be brought into the system to decrease the (local) entropy of that system. There is, I believe, no philosophical or sci-

18. For more on this topic, see S. Frautschi, "Entropy in an Expanding Universe," *Science* 217 (1982): 593-99.

19. Drees, *Beyond the Big Bang,* p. 32.

entific ground for doubting the fact that the material universe, after billions of years, will come to an end. (I count a ceaseless drifting apart of lifeless particles as an "end.")

Third, Drees also states that the Second Law is a purely statistical law. If that were the case, then perhaps this universe of low entropy is a (low probability) fluctuation in an otherwise eternal universe in thermal equilibrium.[20] Such a "fluctuation" would be very, very unlikely, but if the Second Law is merely statistical, still possible. This would allow for the material universe to be eternal, while not running counter to the Second Law. Ludwig Boltzmann suggested such a model in the nineteenth century, and Hawking's cosmology, perhaps, is of a similar kind. The problem here lies in interpreting the Second Law in a purely statistical manner. There are real forces at work in the world, which are the ground of the statistics in the Second Law. In a merely statistical interpretation, there is no answer given as to why some states are more probable (act as "attractors") than others: the fact that some are is merely asserted rather than explained. As Prigogine wrote:

> Dissipation produces entropy. But what then is the meaning of entropy? Over a century ago, Boltzmann came up with a most original idea: entropy is related to probability. . . . It is because the probability increases that entropy increases. Let me immediately emphasize that in this perspective the second law would have great practical importance but would be of no fundamental significance. . . . By improving our abilities to measure less and less unlikely events, we could reach a situation in which the second law would play as small a role as we want. This is the point of view that is often taken today, but it is difficult to maintain in the presence of the important constructive role of dissipative systems.[21]

In other words, while the merely statistical interpretation of entropy is useful and important, it is not metaphysically significant or fundamental. Dissipation, not statistics, produces entropy. "Unlikely" states of affairs, such as "fluctuations" of the age and extent of our material

20. Drees, *Beyond the Big Bang*, pp. 32 and 227.
21. Ilya Prigogine, "Irreversibility and Space-time Structure," in *Physics and the Ultimate Significance of Time*, ed. David Griffin (Albany: State University of New York Press, 1986), p. 239.

universe in an otherwise eternal thermal equilibrium, are not merely unlikely but practically impossible from a thermodynamic perspective.

Given the failure of the above objections, we can conclude that the material universe as we know it will come to an end. This therefore implies that measured time, the physical time of our universe, must have a beginning. The argument for this conclusion is a simple one. Either pure duration is of infinite or finite extension into the past. If it is finite, then time has a beginning, and thus so does measured time. If pure duration is infinite, then measured time either has a beginning, or it does not. If we begin to think that it has no beginning (i.e., it "began" an infinite time ago), we soon realize that with an *infinite* past, we should already have reached the end of measured time, since the material universe is of merely finite duration. But we have not reached the end of measured time. So measured time must have a beginning (whether pure duration also must have a beginning is another question). Yet even this result (that measured time has a beginning) is important: it adds weight to the conclusion, based on results from many areas, that the material universe is contingent. Thermodynamics therefore helps support one implication of the Christian doctrine of creation, namely, that the universe is contingent.

Conclusions

We have covered a lot of terrain in a hurry. Each major point we have made could be the subject of another chapter on its own. Still, some progress has been made toward an understanding of the relationship between thermodynamics and Christian theology. Thermodynamics supports the Christian doctrine that time is linear, while Christian doctrine supports the dynamic, irreversible view of fundamental physics. Both disciplines together lead to the conclusion that the material universe is contingent, having a beginning in time, and again in this way support each other.

In terms of the relationship between theology and science, we have seen that at least in this small area these disciplines can be integrated and can support each other (by "support" I mean indirect, inductive support). Of further methodological interest is this: in two cases *metaphysics* (that is, large-scale explanation) has served as an intermediary between theology and science. Thermodynamics supports the Christian doctrine of creation through its metaphysical implications, while the Christian doctrine of time helps us choose between rival metaphysical interpretations of basic physics with respect to the direction of time. Is not metaphysics, then, the proper meeting place of theology and science? At the very least I would suggest that our larger worldviews are the media through which various disciplines can influence each other yet still retain their own academic integrity. The next chapter will continue to press this conclusion, within the social sciences.

8 Incarnation and Historical Science

Having shown the compatibility of theology and natural science, I now move in this chapter toward the integration of theology and social science. Of course, such integration, along the suggested lines of the mutuality model, can only be hinted at in a single chapter. Our purpose is to choose a focused example that can bring out the rich possibilities for further research along these lines in the social sciences and theology. Despite the attractiveness of psychology, history has proven irresistible as a dialogue partner. Furthermore, to complement the topic of resurrection covered earlier in the book, in this chapter we will focus on the incarnation.

The message of Christmas is one of the greatest parts of the Christian gospel. The savior of the world comes to us humbly, in a manger. The God of the universe has met us face to face and resolves to love us into redemption. Nothing could be more wonderful. But is it true? Was and is the incarnation a reality? How can we know? These are deep and serious questions, which have been debated since the very beginning of Christian thought. I have no intention of giving a full answer to these questions here; rather, I want to focus on one part of the question concerning the truth of the incarnation. What role should historical studies play in our knowledge of the incarnation? In other words, we are interested in the relationship between science and religion, in this case the notion of an incarnation and scientific or critical history.[1] More specifi-

1. I will use the word "scientific" in a very broad sense, to refer to critical, academic historiography. We should resist the temptation to reduce science to physical science, which after all is only one branch of the special sciences.

cally, our question for this chapter is, what role should historical studies play in testing different theories of the incarnation? My thesis will be that historical science can and should influence theological positions adopted on the basis of revelation.

There are several possible ways in which the data of history can influence our Christology, all of which can be understood as examples of the relationship between data and theories. Broadly, there are three possible logical relationships between data and theories in theology (or any rational discipline). There is the relationship of proof (or disproof), which is the strongest possible. There is the relationship of coherence, which is the weakest possible. Both of these are formal relationships, with established meanings in logic. In between these two logical relationships between data and theory are several weaker, informal relations (all of which can be lumped together as "possibility two"). Two of these are abduction and retroduction. The purpose of this chapter is to explore these relationships between the data derived from critical history (operating within a broad Christian worldview) on the one hand, and Christian theology on the other. So this chapter is an exploration in theological method, with particular reference to informal logic.

Our discussion draws upon the discipline of history but does not take place within critical history. This is because, in my philosophy of science, historical studies deal with human explanatory schemes, not with explanation based on God's activities. Historical science, like the other sciences, investigates secondary causes (to refer again to the late medieval distinction). Theological explanation is part of theology or theistic philosophy, but not part of history itself. It is not part of historical studies, nor does it take place in biblical studies. It does, of course, draw upon conclusions and evidence from these other disciplines. I have insisted on a theistic worldview, however, simply because an atheistic historiography will finally undermine serious Christology. The critical history we have in mind is one that takes place within broad Christian presuppositions about humanity, God, the world, and history.

The main point of the chapter will be a simple one. Prior to any historical examination of the evidence, different Christologies make plausible (i.e., expect) different historical evidence. This connection between theory and evidence (a connection moving from theory *to* evidence) is called abduction, also called the method of hypothesis. Retroduction (which is also described as "inference to the best explanation") is an informal inference that the data make one theory rather than another more likely to be true. The main point of the chapter is that theologians can and should use these methods (along with others) to evaluate different Christologies in the light of history. We will examine these processes in greater detail later in this chapter.

One possible logical relationship between history and Christology has already been explored with the rise of historical biblical criticism. This is the logical relationship of coherence. The key question here is whether the implications of certain theological dogmas fit with the evidence about Jesus, as we know it from history. Theology has, for the most part, responded well to this question. The labors of Christian scholars in the field of New Testament studies in the last two centuries have demonstrated the coherence of full Christian faith and thought with outstanding biblical scholarship. Critical and Christian scholars of previous generations have demonstrated that the careful historical study of Jesus, in a pluralistic and academic setting, is coherent with Christian doctrine. Such critical history raises the question of Jesus' spiritual authority, but modern historical methods cannot answer that question. For that we need theology and philosophy to join in the conversation. In other words, once again we discover that broad religious questions that arise out of science lead to interdisciplinary studies that go beyond the sciences themselves.

Few theologians want to deny the historical character and full humanity of Jesus these days. And just as importantly, Christian scholars have demonstrated the coherence of the classical Christian faith with the best historical scholarship. "Coherence" has a clear meaning: not incoherent. In other words, two propositions are coherent if they are not logically inconsistent. Demonstrating incoherence, however, is a difficult thing to manage. Lack of incoherence, therefore, is a rather loose relationship between data and theory. In this brief chapter, we will explore a closer possible relationship between historical studies and theological reflection. Because of lack of space, this exploration will be merely methodological — we cannot develop the crucial historical evidence in a single chapter.

Having set aside coherence, what about proof? The strongest possible logical relationship between data and theory is proof (or disproof). Let us begin with a confession: I do not believe that we can, in fact, prove to a religiously pluralistic audience that an incarnation happened in the past. Even given the best historical evidence about Jesus that we have, and adding to it any possible arguments from natural theology, the preponderance of evidence will not prove that an incarnation took place. If we are not already inclined to the Christian faith, the evidence is simply not staggering enough to overturn a reasonable but non-Christian worldview. We can demonstrate that Christianity is reasonable, but not that all other options are unreasonable. In other words, in an academic and critical dialogue with any and all types of religious scholars, the public and accepted evidence about Jesus (which is quite small) combined with whatever philosophical evidence we can give to argue that there may be a God is not enough to convince a rational non-Christian thinker. The evidence about Jesus, not to mention the evidence brought forth in arguments for the existence of God, is either too slim or too controversial to do the job. I believe Tom Oden gets it right when he notes, "[Christology] is not a study that can be rightly undertaken by those who remain dogmatically committed to the assumption that nothing new can happen in history or that no events are knowable except those that can be validated under laboratory conditions. Christology is studied within the context of a worshiping community."[2] I therefore propose that we take his advice and carry on the discussion of the relationship between historical science and incarnation within the academic field of Christian systematic theology.

Even within the Christian tradition, we find many different theories of who Jesus was, that is, many different Christologies. I intend here to discuss a traditional and orthodox notion of the incarnation. By "incarnation" in this chapter we will mean a "high Christology" — that is, an event in which Jesus unites in his person both true humanity and full deity. Such issues involve a host of problems, and I am going to avoid any detailed logical defense of a high Christology. We will not spell out a particular theory of incarnation but will maintain a rather imprecise notion of Jesus as both God and human for our current purposes. Instead, I intend to focus on a rather general high Christology

---

2. Thomas C. Oden, *The Word of Life: Systematic Theology,* vol. 2 (San Francisco: Harper, 1989), p. 7. I believe William Lane Craig is too optimistic when he insists that the historical facts about Jesus will lead any careful scholar to affirm his divinity. See his book, *Apologetics: An Introduction* (Chicago: Moody Press, 1984), later published as *Reasonable Faith* (Wheaton, Ill.: Crossway, 1994), pp. 243-51.

and ask this question: what role does a critical historical examination play in our evaluation of a high Christology?

This chapter continues the work of Chapter 3 (originally given as a paper at the Resurrection Summit) on the myth of a purely historical Jesus, as well as the work of Bill Alston's paper at the same conference.[3] In particular, I take up my claim that our spiritual knowledge of the real, risen Jesus must be subject to a critical, scientific reflection and historical examination but not verification.[4] The historical sciences cannot explain a miracle, although they can evaluate the reliability of the witnesses to any purported miracle. So the resurrection cannot be subject to historical *verification*. The term "verification" is used here in a technical sense, arising from philosophy of science. It means something like "strong empirical demonstration" or perhaps even "proof." The role of history in Christology is not verification (in this limited sense) but rather historical examination and reflection. I was happy to see in Alston's paper a similar viewpoint. He wrote that "She [the Christian biblical critic] is already working within certain views on the matter" of resurrection, and "she does not take historical research to be the sole determiner of what to believe." In this way, "the historical results thus serve to shore up or weaken parts of the Christian belief system, without being allowed the presumption of completely determining even the historical parts thereof by themselves."[5] This is an important point, one that recapitulates the views of Reinhold Niebuhr and Herbert Butterfield among others.[6]

The present chapter will defend and explain this position on faith and history, with particular focus on the incarnation. We shall begin with three of the most important theologians of the past century: Karl Barth, Reinhold Niebuhr, and Wolfhart Pannenberg. Using C. S. Peirce's notion of abduction and retroduction, I will then sketch an ex-

---

3. See William P. Alston, "Biblical Criticism and the Resurrection," in *The Resurrection*, ed. Stephen T. Davis, Daniel Kendall, and Gerald O'Collins (Oxford: Oxford University Press, 1997), pp. 148-83. My essay in that volume is now updated as Chapter 3 in the present book.

4. See further my reference to Luke T. Johnson's *The Real Jesus* in Chapter 3 of the present volume, note 13.

5. Alston, "Biblical Criticism and the Resurrection," pp. 149-50.

6. See Herbert Butterfield, *Christianity and History* (London: G. Bell, 1949). I will discuss Niebuhr more fully below.

amination of the evidence for an incarnation which is based on Christian faith but which gives historical reasons and arguments for this belief. In this way we seek to avoid both fideism and rationalism in theological method.

Revelation and Scientific History

Giving up the forlorn hope for an empirical verification (i.e., proof from history) of Christology, we move to a Christian systematic theology in which the primacy of Scripture and the centrality of Christ are already accepted. In this domain, the question of how we might know that an incarnation has taken place in history involves the notion of revelation. *The* theologian of revelation in our time, and arguably the most important theologian of the twentieth century, is Karl Barth. Barth's Christology sets the stage for the development of both Protestant and Catholic theology up to the present day.

Barth was a follower, in some ways, of a position that can be traced back to Martin Kähler (1835-1912) in his famous book, *The So-Called Historical Jesus and the Historic, Biblical Christ* (1896).[7] Kähler argued that the attempt to get behind the data to the "real" Jesus is simply not possible, and in a famous phrase he concluded that "the real Christ is the preached Christ."[8] Karl Barth likewise rejected natural theology and any attempt to prove the Christian truth-claims in any area other than the revelation of God. In his early years, Barth seemingly rejected the claims of historical criticism to give us the truth about the Bible. The Scriptures, he claimed in "The Strange New World of the Bible," are not among us to impart historical knowledge but faith. "The Bible meets the lover of history with silences quite unparalleled." When God acts, "something wholly different and new begins — a history with its own distinct grounds, possibilities, and hypotheses."[9]

7. Martin Kähler, *The So-Called Historical Jesus and the Historic, Biblical Christ,* trans. Carl Braaten (Philadelphia: Fortress, 1964). Braaten has a fine introduction to Kähler, and to the book's importance.

8. Kähler, *The So-Called Historical Jesus,* p. 66.

9. Karl Barth, "The Strange New World of the Bible," in *The Word of God and the Word of Man,* trans. D. Horton (Boston: Pilgrim, 1928), pp. 36, 37.

Even in his more mature reflections, Barth insisted that faith needs no help whatsoever from history or any other source. "The dogmatic norm . . . can be no other than the revelation attested in Holy Scripture as God's Word," he wrote.[10] "[E]ven faith's presuppositions . . . belong to faith and cannot be recognized except by faith," so that "faith is related to the whole of reality" but only by faith itself, not by science, history, or philosophy.[11] Thus for Barth, "in view of God's self-demonstration in His words and works no proofs on our account are needed."[12] To be fair, Barth did use the historical critical method, and he argued that the Bible was also a human word, which must be read and studied historically *(historisch)* as a human word.[13] But this historical study was not allowed by him to affect the truth of the revelation of God's Word in the text of Scripture.

Barth has been criticized for an overemphasis on Christ and for what Dietrich Bonhoeffer called his "positivism of revelation."[14] I believe that a balanced and reasonable reply to Barth, one that is eminently British and follows in the tradition of Edwyn Hoskyns and Herbert Butterfield, has been given in recent times by Basil Mitchell.[15] Mitchell argues convincingly that criticism, the reasoned examination of argument and evidence, is itself based on some kind of trust or faith, which is part of every worldview. But at the same time, against Barth, Mitchell insists that faith also demands criticism. Faith in God as creator and redeemer in history, and as the ultimate reality and truth, leads us in our reflective moments to wonder what public evidence we might give for our Christian faith and for the gospel truths which come not from public evidence but from special revelation. This is an argument one can find in other thinkers from other times, but Mitch-

---

10. Karl Barth, *Church Dogmatics,* trans. G. W. Bromiley, ed. G. W. Bromiley and T. F. Torrance, 4 vols. in 13 parts (Edinburgh: T&T Clark, 1936-1969), I/2, p. 815.

11. Barth, *Church Dogmatics,* III/1, p. 63.

12. Barth, *Church Dogmatics,* III/2, p. 79.

13. Barth, *Church Dogmatics,* I/2, p. 464. See this entire chapter 3 (pp. 457-741): Holy Scripture.

14. Dietrich Bonhoeffer, *Letters and Papers from Prison,* trans. R. H. Fuller (New York: Macmillan, 1970), p. 168. See also, among many sources, Hendrikus Berkhof, *Two Hundred Years of Theology,* trans. J. Vriend (Grand Rapids: Eerdmans, 1989), pp. 208-28, on the theological responses to Barth.

15. Basil Mitchell, *Faith and Criticism* (Oxford: Oxford University Press, 1994).

ell is one clear representative of the position. Of course there is no question here of proving the truth of the gospel through history, science, or philosophy, nor do I seek to ground faith in rational argument.[16] It is more a matter of what Steve Davis has called "soft apologetics," that is, explaining the reasonableness of Christianity by starting with faith.[17] This, after all, represents the famous position of Anselm, *fides quaerens intellectum*. We may begin, with Barth, in faith and revelation. But at some point we will reflect critically upon our faith, and then we may seek evidence and arguments that, in Alston's words, "shore up or weaken parts of the Christian belief system."

One of Barth's severest critics was Wolfhart Pannenberg. Pannenberg argued that beginning "from above," with the Christ of dogma, as Barth's Christology does, is not possible for "us" today.[18] Pannenberg wanted to provide a Christology "from below," and to prove the resurrection from historical research. He was unhappy with any retreat into claims of faith and special revelation. He gave three reasons why a Christology from above was unacceptable. Only the first one, however, is decisive:

> A Christology from above presupposes the divinity of Jesus. The most important task of Christology is, however, precisely to present the reasons for the confession of Jesus' divinity. Instead of presupposing it, we must first inquire about how Jesus' appearance in history led to the recognition of his divinity.[19]

---

16. The error of G. E. Lessing, in his 1777 tract *On the Proof of the Spirit and of Power* (which created his famous "ugly ditch" between religion and history) was to assimilate religious truths to the "necessary truths of reason." On the contrary, religious truths are almost never logically necessary propositions. Even if "God exists" is logically necessary (as some who accept the ontological argument believe), ontological arguments for this proposition are not historical but philosophical and logical. All other religious truths are logically contingent. See H. Chadwick, ed., *Lessing's Theological Writings* (Stanford: Stanford University Press, 1956), p. 53.

17. See Stephen T. Davis, *Risen Indeed: Making Sense of the Resurrection* (Grand Rapids: Eerdmans, 1993). A similar position is advanced by William Placher in a deeply philosophical volume from a theologian: *Unapologetic Theology* (Philadelphia: Westminster, 1989).

18. Wolfhart Pannenberg, *Jesus — God and Man*, trans. Lewis L. Wilkins and Duane A. Priebe (Philadelphia: Westminster, 1968), pp. 33-37.

19. Pannenberg, *Jesus — God and Man*, p. 34.

One problem here is that Pannenberg failed in terms of pure historical science, and especially for non-Christian historians, to prove that Jesus rose from the dead. The "reasons for the confession of Jesus' divinity" are to be found within the circle of faith, not outside it. But the problem runs deep in his thought.

Pannenberg's philosophy of history in this early period was problematic. In earlier essays leading up to his major work in Christology, Pannenberg insisted that "the attempt to find a reality that is 'suprahistorical' depreciates real history."[20] In a well-known essay, "Redemptive Event and History," Pannenberg insisted that faith must be found in history itself. Any attempt to provide "the suprahistorical ground of faith" is simply a refuge from "the scientific verification of events."[21] Discussing a view similar to the one we are defending in this chapter, Pannenberg argued that "a general collapse of historical method must result if there exists alongside it another, more fruitful way to certainty about past events, or if this other method were declared to be the right historical method."[22] Independent of Pannenberg's own development over time, we should still ask the question, "Is this claim correct?"

Already in this book, I have argued that historical explanation is based on both hermeneutical understanding and causal explanations, drawn from the world of human beings, institutions, symbols, and structures. History as a scientific investigation explains events and explores meanings that human beings bring about. It does not and can not explore what God brings about: that is contrary to the focus and methods of historical investigation. I cannot agree with Pannenberg when he writes that "the question of the extent to which the historian as such may make any sort of statement about God can remain open for the time being."[23] Showing more of his true colors, he later suggests that "the concept of God" should be "really indispensable for the historian."[24] This is a misunderstanding of the goal and methods of histori-

---

20. Wolfhart Pannenberg, "Redemptive Event and History," reprinted in his *Basic Questions in Theology*, vol. 1, trans. G. Kehm (Philadelphia: Westminster, 1983), pp. 15-16.

21. Pannenberg, "Redemptive Event," p. 16.

22. Pannenberg, "Redemptive Event," p. 38. Pannenberg is discussing Erwin Reisner, *Offenbarungsglaube und historische Wissenschaft* (Berlin: Haus und Schule, 1947). This is a short pamphlet on the topic.

23. Pannenberg, "Redemptive Event," p. 66.

24. Pannenberg, "Redemptive Event," p. 76.

cal science. Critical history as such does not deal with God. It may indeed deal with human beings and their beliefs about God, or with reports of religious and other experiences, but the explanatory focus of historical science is on human agency and institutions, that is, on secondary causes.[25] For example, if I wanted to date an eclipse in the distant past, I would not consult a historian. For this knowledge, we need astronomy, not history. Just because something is a past event, it does not follow that historical science can verify or explain it. History examines the *human* past. I am not arguing that history (i.e., the past) is "closed" to divine agency. The point is about the explanatory focus and limits of historical explanation and verification. Critical history, understood as science, does not deal with God because its methods and focus look to the human world.

The position I have adopted should not be confused with "methodological naturalism." We have already found reasons to reject this way of describing scientific practice, and the very terminology is objectionable. My own position has nothing to do with naturalism of any kind. Instead, the issues are more complex. Here is a brief sketch of some of the main points we have already made in the philosophy of science which bear upon this question:

1. Scientific research is conducted within a "paradigm" or research program, which includes background criteria, values, methods, theories, and knowledge.
2. Our worldviews *(Weltanschauung)* influence any and all scientific research and argument. They provide the ultimate foundations for scientific research programs.
3. When a Christian worldview provides presuppositions, values, and the interpretive horizon for the arts and sciences, this results in Christian scholarship. The major alternative to a Christian worldview in our place and time is scientific materialism (or naturalism).

---

25. This would be true even if the evidence for the existence of God were much greater than it is. My remark is based on the aims, research methods, and paradigms of historical science, which does not concern itself with the truth about God. Historical science is about human beings (which includes the history of religions, but not theology proper). I thank Steve Davis for this question.

4. The aim of a science determines the methods, explanatory focus, and interests of that particular discipline.
5. Academic disciplines are traditional practices. Researchers are inducted into them, including their background research programs.
6. Each academic discipline has its own explanatory focus and research tradition, which circumscribes the specific aspect of reality it is competent to judge.
7. The sciences (natural and social) are rigorous and empirical investigations of secondary causes. Theology and philosophy of religion study the First Cause, that is, God.

While all the sciences aim after the truth (as Steve Evans has insisted), we must also pay attention to the particular areas of reality that specific sciences aim at. History has as its focus human institutions, events, and symbols. While there is no such thing as a fixed historical method, there are enough similarities among the best current historians to speak of a contemporary critical historical methodology. This methodology is, of course, open to change. My only claim would be that it is the best set of practices we now have, given the aims and purposes of historiography (that is, to examine the human past in terms of human and social explanations and interpretations). A full explanation of the past will always require more than history itself can provide; it will always be interdisciplinary because there is more to reality than any one discipline studies. For this reason, as David Brown insists, when historians write their popular books, they always go beyond critical history in the interpretation of the meaning of their results. This is because history (like all disciplines) raises questions that it cannot answer.[26]

The postulation of things that are "suprahistorical," then, does not denigrate history. Critical history is unconcerned with the suprahistorical. The laws of nature, for example, make historical events possible in the first place. They are not part of history yet apply throughout "history," that is, throughout time and space. While his-

---

26. These comments from Evans and Brown were made orally at the Incarnation Summit. See further, C. Stephen Evans, *The Historical Christ and the Jesus of Faith* (New York: Oxford University Press, 1996), for his views on naturalism in history.

torical events depend upon such laws, history cannot explain the truth of scientific laws. Pannenberg seems to expand "history" to encompass all of reality — a major philosophical problem in his early thought.

Ten years before Pannenberg published his first papers on history and revelation, a more moderate and reasonable position on faith and history was developed by Reinhold Niebuhr. Niebuhr's book *Faith and History* was part of a spate of books on Christian faith and history sparked by dialectical theology, especially the works of Karl Barth.[27] Niebuhr's volume anticipated many of the themes Pannenberg took up some years later. Already in 1949, Niebuhr was discussing "universal history," for example. In my view he developed an understanding of revelation and history that is superior to the views of both Barth and Pannenberg.

Like Barth, Niebuhr begins the Christian understanding of history with faith. "The truth of the Christian faith must, in fact, be apprehended in any age by repentance and faith. It is, therefore, not made acceptable by rational validation in the first instance" (p. v). I would call your attention to the words "in the first instance," for after repentance and belief in Christ, some rational exploration and defense of a Christian understanding of universal history is possible. But first we must begin with faith. "In Biblical thought," he argued, "the grace of God completes the structure of meaning beyond the limits of rational intelligibility in the realm of history" (p. 115). Why are faith and repentance necessary? Because of the "idolatrous tendencies in all human culture," repentance is necessary for a grasp of gospel truth (p. 116). "Such faith must be grounded in repentance; for it presupposes a contrite recognition of the elements of pretension and false completion in all forms of human virtue, knowledge, and achievement" (p. 171). If repentance is needed for faith, faith is needed because the "radical otherness of God is an offence to all rationalistic interpreters of life and history. Yet the worship of this God is the basis for the first genuine conception of a universal history" (p. 116). Niebuhr goes on to make an excellent point, against Pannenberg's position, that "mystery does not annul meaning, but enriches it. It prevents the realm of meaning from being reduced too simply to rational intelligibility and thereby being

---

27. Reinhold Niebuhr, *Faith and History* (New York: C. Scribner's Sons, 1949). Page references will be cited parenthetically in the text.

given a false center of meaning in a relative or contingent historical force or end" (p. 116). Theological truths must not be reduced to historical facts, however much they may be about the events that really happened in the past. Contrary to the fears of Pannenberg, Niebuhr does not retreat into subjectivism. Instead he goes on to argue, at length, for the superiority of a Christian understanding of history and its meaning. In fact there is even a chapter on "The Validation of the Christian View of Life and History."

From Reinhold Niebuhr, then, we have learned a sound and reasonable view of the relationship between faith and reason, revelation and history. Niebuhr, of course, was influenced by Karl Barth, but did not fall into the latter's overemphasis on revelation and faith. And unlike Pannenberg, Niebuhr realized that "mystery does not annul meaning, but enriches it." The dimension of faith and the "suprahistorical" does not destroy history but fulfils it.

Reasoning about an Incarnation

With the specific example of the incarnation, then, how would such a position of "faith seeking understanding" work in actual practice? Mainstream Christian faith and tradition has delivered to us the idea of a real incarnation. The real Jesus of history was and is (according to catholic, orthodox faith) both fully divine and fully human. A number of criticisms have been leveled against this idea in the last two millennia, making this orthodox belief problematic for our place and time. I believe that Christian scholars have already replied to the challenge of coherence between historical research (historical-critical methods) and theology, as remarked earlier. Despite their careful work, we still need to clarify some misunderstandings that critics have passed on to modern women and men, before we can consider this idea and develop a historical examination of it. We can then consider C. S. Peirce's method of abduction and the implications of that logic for a historical exploration of the incarnation hypothesis. This approach using abduction assumes that the issue of coherence has already been settled. But as we noted earlier, "coherence" logically turns into "lack of incoherence" — and this is a very loose relationship, since incoherence is so hard to prove.

We will treat a historical incarnation as a hypothesis, but one within the circle of Christian theological reflection and not outside it. There is no question here of seeking on the basis of historical evidence to demonstrate the truth of the Christian religion to the skeptic. Both Lessing and Hume, in the eighteenth century, rightly rejected this as an implausible program. But even the task of treating a matter of doctrine as a hypothesis raises a serious problem for some theologians and philosophers of religion. They would argue that rational criticism of the faith treats the deliberations of faith in a hypothetical way, and is thus contrary to faith. This viewpoint can be traced back through dialectical theology to Søren Kierkegaard.[28] I am a great fan of Kierkegaard, but on this point he overstates the case.[29] There are different moments and models in the life of faith. Critical reflection upon the fact that we find ourselves believing in something (or someone) is a normal part of the life of faith, once we enter upon it. Mitchell has argued this well, as we have already noted. Along the same line, Edwyn Hoskyns in 1931 rightly noted that "in consequence [of the incarnation] the Christian religion is not merely open to historical investigation, but demands it, and its piety depends on it."[30] There are ups and downs in our spiritual journey, moments of strong existential trust and moments of thoughtful reflection, times for rational argument and times for emotional worship: these facts are confirmed in the lives of many believers. Kierkegaard speaks of only one moment in the life of faith. There is another moment, that of faith seeking understanding, which demands critical and rational evaluation of our faith.

Similarly, we must defend the idea of a logical exploration of faith against certain tendencies among some followers of Wittgenstein.[31]

28. Another example would be D. Z. Phillips, following some of Wittgenstein's ideas (see Phillips, *The Concept of Prayer* [New York: Shocken, 1967], p. 14). Through his Viennese education Wittgenstein himself was influenced by Kierkegaard and Kant.

29. See for example bk. I, chap. 2, "The Speculative Viewpoint," in his *Concluding Unscientific Postscript*, trans. D. F. Swenson (Princeton, N.J.: Princeton University Press, 1941), pp. 49-55, which Kierkegaard wrote under a pseudonym (Johannes Climacus).

30. Edwyn Hoskyns and N. Davey, *The Riddle of the New Testament* (London: Faber and Faber, 1931), p. 10.

31. For two brief introductions to Wittgenstein and religion, see John Hyman, "Wittgensteinianism," in *A Companion to Philosophy of Religion,* ed. P. Quinn and C. Taliaferro (Oxford: Blackwell, 1997), pp. 150-58, and Garth Moore with Brian Davies, "Wittgenstein and the Philosophy of Religion," in *Philosophy of Religion,* ed. Brian Davies (Washington, D.C.: Georgetown University Press, 1998), pp. 27-33.

The problem here would be put in terms of the "grammar" of faith. If we treat the incarnation in a factual way, as a hypothesis, this treatment (they would argue) is contrary to the "meaning" of religious language, which is grounded in a way of life. As Wittgenstein once remarked, "In religious discourse we use such expressions as: 'I believe that so and so will happen,' and use them differently to the way in which we use them in science."[32] Belief in the incarnation, so the complaint goes, is a "grammatical remark" about living in, and making sense of, a deeply Christian way of life. It is not (for them) a factual statement, but part of a form of life, a Christian way of being in the world, which makes sense only as part of that whole picture. Wittgenstein objected to Christian philosophers who attempt to demonstrate the reasonableness of Christian faith. He remarked: "Not only is it [Christian faith] not reasonable, but it doesn't pretend to be. What seems to me ludicrous about O'Hara [a Catholic philosopher] is his making it appear to be *reasonable*."[33]

Teasing out the meaning of Wittgenstein's cryptic remarks concerning religion would take us too far afield, and his views can be interpreted in more than one way.[34] While he rightly points to religious practice and life as the space within which religious language makes sense, he seems to me (if I understand him correctly) to omit the idea that faith itself might demand some kind of critical examination, which would include factual issues drawn from other areas, perhaps even from the sciences. This is the position of Augustine and Anselm, in the tradition of *fides quaerens intellectum*. We are in good company, then, when we insist not only that the meaning of religious language is found within religion but also that the truth of religious language may include issues and criteria outside the "language-game" of religion.

My final point would be that even these "external" criteria and evidence are not "neutral" relative to faith. We can and should approach them, too, within the presupposition of a Christian worldview. Yet just as clearly, some evidence is public and pluralistic, available to any rea-

---

32. Ludwig Wittgenstein, *Lectures & Conversations on Aesthetics, Psychology, and Religious Belief*, ed. Cyril Barrett (Berkeley: University of California Press, 1966), p. 57.

33. Wittgenstein, *Lectures*, p. 58, his italics.

34. A useful beginning in this regard is James Kellenberger, *The Cognitivity of Religion* (London: Macmillan, 1985), which includes a balanced discussion of "Neo-Wittgensteinian" philosophers of religion including D. Z. Phillips.

sonable person who shares the common values and assumptions of a scientific worldview. What I am recommending, then, is a worldview that is both scientific and Christian.

Once we allow that standards of what counts as good evidence, good argument, and coherent and clear meaning can come to religious beliefs from outside religious language and practice (but not necessarily outside a Christian worldview), another problem with a real incarnation immediately arises. Philosophers have sometimes complained that the very idea of a real incarnation is logically incoherent. John Hick is famous for making just such a claim.[35] I believe this complaint has been decisively refuted by a number of philosophers in recent literature[36] and will not repeat their arguments here; we cannot consider all such issues in this chapter, and need to press forward to historical (rather than logical) considerations.

The last point does, however, call for some development of our hypothesis. To avoid confusion, we should spell out what we mean by a historical incarnation. At the very least, this implies that Jesus was a real human being and lived a true human life. At the same time, the *person* that was Jesus was identical in some way (however we define it) with God the Son. God the Son, in this case, is one member of the Blessed Trinity. Indeed, the orthodox doctrine of the incarnation depends upon the doctrine of the Trinity. With this in mind, I would argue that the orthodox, catholic view of the incarnation is committed to the reality of personal identity (as grounded in the Triune Being of God as three "persons"), but not to any one *theory* of what personal identity is.

Another point of clarification has to do with what we can expect, historically, from the consciousness of an incarnate human being. From the fact that, by definition, Jesus shares the divine nature of God the Father, it does not follow that Jesus *always knew* he was in some way identical with God the Son. It is possible to have a property without being conscious of that property. For example, I may have the power to

---

35. See John Hick, *The Myth of God Incarnate* (London: SCM, 1977), and more recently, "The Logic of God Incarnate," *Religious Studies* 25 (1989): 409-23.

36. See, e.g., Stephen T. Davis, *Logic and the Nature of God* (Grand Rapids: Eerdmans, 1983); David Brown, *The Divine Trinity* (London: Duckworth, 1985); Thomas V. Morris, *The Logic of God Incarnate* (Ithaca, N.Y.: Cornell University Press, 1986); Richard Sturch, *The Word and the Christ* (Oxford: Clarendon, 1991), and Richard G. Swinburne, *The Christian God* (Oxford: Clarendon, 1994).

fly by flapping my ears. But since I am ignorant of that property, I will never use that power. To use a somewhat less arbitrary example, a baby boy raised by wolves may have the property of being human without knowing that he is human. So there is no reason to presume that, on the hypothesis of a real incarnation, Jesus will know he shared the divine nature with God the Father. In other words, if Jesus is truly human as well as divine, there is no reason to presume that Jesus was conscious of his divinity.

One could spend an entire volume just clarifying the misunderstandings of orthodox Christology. I hope enough has been said here to at least indicate the character of the hypothesis under consideration, so that a different kind of reasoning can take place.

Abduction and Historical Evidence

Let us return to the central question of this chapter: what role does evidence from historical research play in deciding for or against a real incarnation? I have rejected the logical relationship of proof as too strong for the evidence we have from history and philosophy. We cannot prove to a pluralistic body of learned scholars that the incarnation took place, through public evidence and scientific reasoning. We have noted the logical relationship of coherence, but put that to one side as having been already explored fully. Looking at another type of logical relationship between historical evidence and theological theory, I would argue that historical considerations can help us, within Christian faith and thought, to prefer some christological theories to others. Such considerations do, of course, take place within Christian theology. They are neither history nor simply biblical studies. But in dogmatics and doctrine itself, I propose to use the method C. S. Peirce called "abduction": that is, reasoning from a hypothesis to the *measurable results that would obtain if it were true*.[37] This form of scientific, informal reasoning takes place *within a set of rival hypotheses and within a partic-*

---

37. Sometimes Peirce called this the method of hypothesis. See, for example, his *Elements of Logic,* bk. III, section B, chap. 5, in *Collected Papers of Charles Sanders Peirce,* ed. C. Hartshorne and P. Weiss, vol. 2 (Cambridge, Mass.: Harvard University Press, 1965), §641-44.

ular discipline. Next we apply what Peirce called "retroduction": given our background knowledge, we look for further evidence that (if found) would render one hypothesis rather than the other more probable.[38] If we take a criminal investigation, for example, we might look for evidence (say, a good alibi, or blood stains on clothes) that would render one person, rather than some other suspect, more likely to be guilty. This latter kind of reasoning about probable explanations and hypotheses is common in many human endeavors, and also goes under the name of inference to the best explanation. Abduction, then, moves from a theory to the (hypothetical) evidence, while retroduction moves from the evidence to a theory that best explains that evidence.

The discipline in question here is Christian systematic theology. We are not talking about all worldviews and religions but a set of ideas about Jesus within the presuppositions of Christian faith, life, and tradition. To avoid begging the question, however, we must not presuppose any one Christology. Which Christology is, given all our evidence from history, philosophy, and theology, most likely to be true? Granted that we believe in some kind of revelation in Christ and Scripture, how shall we best understand and apply that revelation, given our total evidence? As just such a juncture, issues of reason, argument, evidence, and science come into play, as we seek a coherent and reasonable Christian theology and worldview.

There are a number of systematic theories about the person of Christ. For issues of simplification and illustration (since this chapter is merely an example of using historical research in theology) we will speak broadly of three hypotheses. The first is the orthodox viewpoint

---

38. Even philosophers have sometimes misunderstood the logic of retroduction. In formal, symbolic terms (where E stands for evidence and H stands for some hypothesis), the logic of retroduction is *not:* If H1 then E1. If that were so, then retroduction would commit the fallacy of affirming the consequent. Rather the logic (in formal terms) is represented by:

> 1. If E1 then $P(H1) > P(H2)$.

Here $P(X)$ stands for "the probability of X," and > as "greater than."

> 2. If E2 then $P(H2) > P(H1)$.

The standard probability calculus puts this more eloquently as: $P(H1/E1\&K) > P(H2/E1\&K)$ where K stands for our background knowledge. See further, Richard G. Swinburne, *An Introduction to Confirmation Theory* (London: Methuen, 1973).

we have been discussing so far, that is, a real incarnation. The second broad theory is that Jesus was a great moral and religious leader whose life is an important example for all people. This theory we could call Ebionite. The third broad theory would be Arian. On this hypothesis, Jesus was a real human being, and one who occupied a special status among humans — the "firstborn of all creatures" — but he was not the one true God who is Creator and Lord of the universe. If we apply that method of scientific thinking that Peirce called abduction to these three theories, what is the result?

The area of research we are interested in is historical science. Therefore, when we are looking for measurable results of each theory, the "measurement" in question is one limited to critical historical research. Let us be clear: every element of reason and evidence, from any and all disciplines, is not under consideration here. Rather, *we limit ourselves to what we can expect historical study to reveal.* Historical science, in turn, is based on research into the human: human actions, human symbols, and the meaning and significance of events for humans and from their perspective. Albert Outler once gave a fine, brief definition of the nature of critical history: "The historian's chief business, we might perhaps agree, is the re-collection and re-presentation of selected segments of the human past, in an intelligible narration based on public data verified by scientific observation."[39] It is in this field, then, that we will seek "measurable" differences between the three hypotheses, assuming each to be true.

With respect to Arian Christology, I would recall the earlier conclusion that Jesus may not have in fact been conscious of his deity. Under this assumption, I can think of no historical evidence we might plausibly expect to find that can distinguish between Arian and orthodox Christologies. After a good deal of reflection, I have simply reached a dead-end on this topic. What measurable results (in terms of historical research) might come from one, rather than the other, being true? Given my assumptions about the consciousness of Jesus, I can find none. I suggest we simply leave Arian Christology to one side, at least for the present. Other theological points may lead to a fuller critique of this Christology, but we will not explore that issue now.

Let us examine, then, the two major options we are left with: an

39. "Theodosius' Horse," *Church History* 34 (1965): 251-61, at 253.

orthodox incarnation or an Ebionite (or liberal Protestant) Christology. What measurable, historical results can distinguish between these theories? In both cases we can expect profound moral and religious teachings that draw us closer to God and to one another. In both cases, we expect that Jesus would have a profound effect upon his followers. In both cases, we expect that he would demonstrate a powerful spiritual life and closeness to God. If we assume the truth of an incarnation, however, we have more expectations than if Jesus were merely a great teacher, prophet, and moral example. This would be true even if Jesus, while on earth, was not fully conscious of his deity.

If Jesus is in some way identical with God the Son, we would expect that he would have a mission on earth that was of supreme importance. Otherwise, why would God bother with an incarnation? This argument is based on background knowledge about God that Christians in general share over the centuries: the kind of God that creates the universe and saves Israel would not undertake an incarnation without a profound purpose. (A case could be made, however, that we could expect Christ's mission to be of supreme importance even under Ebionite Christology.) Second, given our background information about God, surely it is logical to conclude that God would ensure that this human life would have outstanding positive historical impact. God has good reasons to want the effects of this incarnation to be widely known, even if there are good reasons to allow human beings to be the means of spreading the gospel. Third, we might also expect that the Incarnate One would display some supernatural powers, perhaps over the natural world or over the forces of evil and darkness or perhaps even over death. This is quite distinct from what we would expect from a great moral exemplar and teacher. Again, the issues here are not empirical. We are not asking if, in fact, some great moral teachers have performed miracles. We are asking what, given our general knowledge as Christian believers, we have *a right to expect* from each hypothesis (if it is true). Some great moral teachers or prophets may have power over death, for example, but we should not *expect* that one will, based only on the fact that she or he is a great moral teacher or prophet. Finally, given a real incarnation, we would expect a very early *worship* of that person, even among monotheistic disciples. On an Ebionite Christology, such worship would be blasphemy for a monotheist. So there are expectations of an incarnation which go beyond our expectations of an Ebionite Christology.

Perhaps we should make the point again that if Jesus lived a real human life, he might not have known that he was in fact personally identical with God the Son. We would expect him to have a unique and always intimate relationship with God the Father and God the Holy Spirit, but that could equally well be true under the other two hypotheses. So the area of Jesus' so-called "divine self-consciousness" is shown to be irrelevant once a proper grasp of the relationship between critical history and Christology is laid out. Logically, any consciousness of divinity we expect of Jesus is based on the unexamined assumption that a real incarnation entails a divine self-consciousness: and this is false. So this area of expectation provides no distinguishing characteristics, at least for historical evidence, between our three Christologies.

Given these sorts of expectations, then, we must now turn to historical science. From this list of expectations, what can we expect critical history to actually measure? What *recoverable results* could historical research possibly uncover that might correlate with our list of expectations? The best kinds of historical evidence are eyewitness reports and conclusive archaeological remains and traces. Let us take our three historical expectations, listed above, and consider the kind of measurable evidence that (in principle) historical science could unearth. A full and complete exploration of this question would need to demonstrate (more fully than we can here) why these expectations — and not others — are being considered. I can only report here the results of that reflection, and have no space to explicate and explain it.

First, special or "supernatural" events could be witnessed by various people who reliably recorded their observations. This is the best kind of evidence we can imagine finding for supernatural events, as both Lessing and Hume recognized. It is difficult to imagine any archaeological evidence that might be recovered in this regard, although that might be possible in theory. As previously remarked, historical science cannot determine whether miracles are or are not possible. Critical history can provide good evidence for *doubting* that some supposed event really happened (for example, all stories about this event are recorded centuries after it supposedly took place); but on the positive side we can at best expect good evidence that some persons, with reliable character, witnessed supposed "miracles." Second, the strength of historical impact is something that can be measured and weighed by historical research. How important and valuable was this life, compared to other human lives, with respect to its influence on the rest of human history? While it would be quite difficult to prove that any one person had the most positive historical impact, one can imagine building a good case that some individual had a really profound positive impact upon history: as good as any other individual we know. Third, with respect to the importance of Jesus' mission, historical research can recover, at best, that the Incarnate One and his followers *believed* that mission was of worldwide spiritual significance. Whether it *actually was* of such import, history cannot decide, given its limitations and methods. Critical history can also discover whether this life did indeed have a worldwide religious impact, but that falls under number two (above) and is not a separate piece of evidence. And finally, there can be reliable evidence that early followers of the Incarnate One worshiped him even though they were monotheists.

Using the logical connections between theology and history that I am urging (abduction, retroduction), we have discovered that evidence from history does play some role in decisions within systematic theology about theological truths. This role, however, is a modest one. Historical evidence alone cannot decide which of our theological hypotheses is true. But critical history can help us make that decision, in the context of a much larger and longer argument. As we might expect, theological hypotheses are based very much on theological reasons and evidence, rather than the evidence of historical science. Nevertheless, within its limited and modest role, history does have something to say. I was myself rather surprised to see the quite limited role critical history plays in arguments about Christology. But the point remains, against Barth and Wittgenstein, that scientific results outside religious language and special revelation do have an epistemological impact on decisions concerning theological truth.

We should notice that we are dealing with a cumulative case argument here. Having applied abduction to the various hypotheses, we are now looking at the overall evidence for a best explanation (retroduction). And in this case, what counts as a best explanation will be a cumulative case argument. No one piece of evidence is decisive. We must consider the weight of them all together. Some pieces of evidence are compatible with an Ebionite Christology. The major logical point, however, will be about *what we have a right to expect* given an Ebionite Christology. Jesus being a "miracle worker" is compatible with an

Ebionite Christology, but it is simply an ad hoc addition to the Ebionite hypothesis. Given the Ebionite hypothesis, there are no grounds to expect, prior to historical considerations, that the great guru or prophet would also be a miracle worker.

I believe that a good, solid historical argument can be made for the four areas of evidence we have come to expect, through abduction, if there really was an incarnation. This will mean that, through retroduction, a real incarnation is more likely to be true. I will not attempt such a demonstration at this time. I will simply state that one could show, historically, that Jesus had a tremendous positive impact upon world culture and history after him. One could show, historically, that Jesus and his followers believed his mission was of worldwide spiritual significance. One could show historically that early, diverse, and otherwise reliable traditions concerning Jesus report that he had supernatural power over nature, over demonic forces, and even over death. Finally, one could show on good historical grounds that the early monotheistic followers of Jesus did indeed worship him. As we noted earlier and often, historical science cannot prove that such miracles (for example) occurred but only show that there are reasonable witnesses to these events. But even these limited results are illuminating. I am fascinated by the fact that, once we clarify the proper relationship between critical history and theology, historical science seems to favor (at least at first glance) an orthodox incarnation over an Ebionite theory.

The concern in this chapter has been methodological. Notice how very far the logic of this position is from the debates of the modern period exemplified by Locke, Hume, or Lessing. There is no question of historical science demonstrating the truth of the Christian religion. Rather, a proper grasp of theological method insists that we begin with faith in Christ and accept the broad traditions within Christian theology. Our argument begins within the circle of faith. But notice, too, that historical science can and does affect our systematic theology. In particular, the historical evidence seems to favor an orthodox incarnation over an Ebionite Christology. Historical evidence of this modest sort is not, however, decisive. The larger and longer argument about Christology must take place within the total evidence available to the systematic theologian.

I suspect that some readers of this chapter may feel disappointed.

All along we have assumed the Christian faith. We must start from faith, I have been arguing. Is it so surprising, then, that we arrive at results compatible with Christian faith when we look at history? Aren't we just arguing in a circle? In answer to these doubters I would say, first of all, that people do not as a rule come to their basic faith stance (whatever worldview they may hold) because of reasons, evidence, and argument. People accept the Christian faith (for example) for existential, emotional, spiritual, and fundamentally religious reasons. Second, I do think that public evidence and argument can be given for the Christian worldview, in the context of the large set of rival worldviews in our culture today. Some of this evidence will be historical and some will be philosophical. Historical evidence is of limited but real value in the rational, open, and pluralistic debate between rival worldviews and traditions. Third, the fact that we begin with faith has not, in this particular case, led to a circular argument. We begin with Christian faith, but also with a plurality of Christologies. So we have not assumed the truth of the incarnation. Thus our argument (which is actually about which Christology is true and not about the whole of Christian faith) is not a circular one.

Finally, in the minds of some, there may be a lingering doubt about the "tensions" between theology and historical science. Have we not heard, many times over, that the presuppositions of scientific history and of theological reflection are in conflict? Can the theologian also act as a critical historian? What about Lessing's "ugly ditch" between religion and history? My own view of the matter is this: the problem dissolves when we give up the Enlightenment pretensions of rationalism and "neutral" scientific research, and when we pay attention to the methodological limits of both theology and science. Since I have already argued this point at length elsewhere, there is little need to rehearse it again here.

What have we learned, then, from this methodological exercise? I have argued that we can and should avoid the twin errors of rationalism and fideism. In particular, we discovered through various logical relationships (coherence, abduction, and retroduction) the real but limited role that historical scientific results can play in theological reflection. I was myself astounded, in completing this exercise, to find that the cumulative weight of historical evidence (upon a proper conception of the relationship between theology and history) is *prima facie* in favor of a real incarnation rather than an Ebionite hypothesis. A sound historical case can be made that Jesus of Nazareth had as great and good an impact on world history as any other ancient individual. A very good case can be made that, in all the earliest traditions about Jesus, we find he was a wonder-worker with "supernatural" powers of some sort.[40] We can likewise discover, through sound historical scholarship, that both Jesus and his followers understood his mission to be of worldwide spiritual significance. Finally, there is excellent historical evidence that the early followers of Jesus worshiped him, even though they were monotheists.[41] Thus, astonishingly, the sum of historical probability is in favor of an orthodox Christology, understood as one hypothesis among others *within Christian theology*. We must remember that Christology is not a scientific discipline but a theological one. Historical evidence is only part of the picture. Remember, for example, that historical evidence cannot decide between an orthodox and an Arian Christology. Still, the methodological point remains: historical science shapes theological truth-claims. For thoughtful Christians, the nice, clean distinction between the Jesus of history and the Christ of faith should be reconsidered.

The ultimate purpose of this chapter is a humble one. We are giving one example of the "mutuality model" in which science can and should influence theology, and theology can and should influence science. Both should be integrated into an overall Christian worldview. But more than this, each of these disciplines may more directly influence our theory choice in the other. Theology may influence our theory choice in science, as we have already shown in the previous chapter. And science can and should influence our theory choice in theology, as we have demonstrated here. These, then, are all legitimate ways in which theology and science can mutually modify and enhance each other.

---

40. This claim is controversial but, on the historical evidence, eminently defensible. For a survey of the issues, see David Aune, "Magic in Early Christianity," *Aufstieg und Niedergang der römischen Welt* (Berlin, New York: de Gruyter, 1972-2000), 2/23.2, cols. 1507-37, or H. C. Kee, *Miracle in the Early Christian World* (New Haven: Yale University Press, 1983).

41. See, e.g., Larry W. Hurtado, *One God, One Lord: Early Christian Devotion and Ancient Jewish Monotheism* (Philadelphia: Fortress, 1988).

9 Seeking Truth in Theology and Science: Concluding Reflections

Coming to the conclusion of this book, we can reflect upon some overall themes that have been developed throughout these chapters. We have insisted that reasoning in each of the disciplines is traditional and contextual, based on values and criteria that are justified by the long-term success of the explanatory scheme of which they are a part. This is true in the natural sciences, the social or human sciences, and also in theology. I have also pressed the distinctness of the disciplines, because of the differences in aim, method, and explanatory focus in each. Each science has its own understanding of what counts as good evidence and good argument, in the communal process of theory evaluation. Theology is no different.

On the other hand, I have been forced by the phenomena of Christian theology itself in its traditions and modes of reasoning — in a way I did not expect before starting this project — to move theology much more fully away from the sciences. Theology is fundamentally a spiritual discipline, a means of worship, and a response to the One who creates and loves us. Thus, theology is no science, for it is spiritual as well as empirical. There is, however, an academic side or dimension to theology, which is justified as a rational discipline. It is academic theology that most obviously relates to the sciences.

We have put forward what I hope is a fruitful metaphor of collegiality between the various academic disciplines of the university. This collegial metaphor sees the disciplines all together aiming at truth. I believe that a nonreductionist understanding of truth is needed for our interdisciplinary work, and so I put forward a notion of truth as the mediated disclosure of what is real. All the sciences, and theology, are thus looking for truth and seeking to grasp something of reality, in a partial and tentative manner. The current explosion of interest in the intersection of religion and science has brought forward a number of scientists who, based on current work in science, are seeking a Creator. This knowledge comes best in a long-term, communal, and dialectical approach to truth. To this end, I have argued against rationalism in theology, and against scientism in the philosophy of science. We have presented a dialectical realism to oppose both positivism and relativism. This makes space for the mutuality model. In this model, theology and each of the sciences work together to improve our worldview. This worldview, in turn, helps us in three ways. First, it gives a larger story in which the values of science and theology make sense. Second, it provides a horizon in which the sciences, and theological truths, can be interpreted and understood more fully. This is, broadly, the hermeneutic task of any worldview. Third, our religious and scientific worldview provides a rational basis for choice between competing theories, when there is broad, temporary epistemic parity in a discipline.

The value for human flourishing of worldviews that are both fully scientific and deeply religious is hard to overestimate. For this reason, I have also argued vigorously for the importance of faith-based learning in all the sciences and arts within the university. As a Christian theologian, I am dependent upon the honest and thoughtful interpretation of experts in art, history, psychology, chemistry, and the rest — no one can be an expert at everything! But because the task of the hermeneutics of science is worldview-laden, Christian scholarship is vital to any thinking believer today. I take my hat off to all those laboring in this task, which many believers undervalue. Such anti-intellectual prejudice brings no glory to God, and inhibits the mission of the church in the world.

Philosophy has a humble but vital role to play in the current interest in the relationship between religion and science. This debate and discussion among scholars can and does take place without professional philosophers present. But philosophy is not far away, since even scientists come to such discussions with philosophical ideas and perspectives from their own philosophies of life, however tacit they may be. For all scholars in interdisciplinary work, unexamined philosophical assumptions and modes of thinking can inhibit open and honest dialogue and hinder our ability to listen and learn from one another.

In this volume I have set forth a proposal for the way in which theology and the sciences can work together, to help bring wisdom, insight, and knowledge to bear on the many problems and questions of our culture. I think that this collegial metaphor is much needed, even in our broader culture, to replace the warfare model as well as the purely independent metaphor that some scientists are now promoting.[1] I have not spelled out in detail how this is fully possible; rather, I have given two examples, drawn from thermodynamics (natural science) and critical history (social science). Some readers may feel that I have ducked the really tough issue, evolution, but this is not so. I think that setting forth a broad outline of how we should approach this rather difficult topic of science and religion is important before we enter the more emotion-laden topics such as evolution. Knowing in general how we should blend religion and science can help us avoid the many pitfalls and dead ends, extreme claims and narrow-mindedness, which plague this issue in North American popular culture. I have chosen less controversial examples in order to make my methodological points. I leave it as an exercise for the reader to develop a sophisticated and dialectical integration of theology and science on the topic of biological evolution.

I have, for the most part, also neglected historical topics in this book. The history of science is an essential part of the philosophy of science. Likewise, the history of religion and science forms an essential part of the broad topic in which we have been at work together in this book. But my task has not been to recover historical details and differences. While I have learned a great deal from such descriptive studies and reflections, my task in this book is a different one. In making a proposal for the relationship between religion and science, I do not pretend to have described the way these disciplines have connected in the past. Nor do I think that my proposal gets at the "true essence" of either religion or science. I have made suggestive distinctions, of course, but not exhaustive definitions. The mutuality model we have worked through in this volume is meant to be suggestive for future discussion, debate, and development.

1. I am thinking here of the late Stephen Jay Gould's proposal for "nonoverlapping magisteria" in religion and science. See his *Rocks of Ages* (New York: Ballantine, 1999).

For the most part, I have approached this model from a Christian perspective. I make no apologies for this focus, since this is the religious tradition I know best. The collegial metaphor is not, however, limited to Christianity. Members of other religious traditions should develop their own worldviews in dialogue with the special sciences. Many scholars from around the world are doing just that, and we can expect this trend to grow more fully in the future. All world religions, after all, are faced with the challenge of Western science and technology; science grew in the West but is now a global phenomenon.

I do think that scholars of all types need to be open to learning from other disciplines and open to adjusting their areas of specialty in the light of what they learn there. It is no dishonor to God to adjust our theology in light of science. And it is no dishonor to reason, truth, and the scientific method to go with the theory that best fits our worldview in those cases where theories are in epistemic parity — for God is the author of the book of nature and the book of Scripture (a very old metaphor indeed!). No religious believer should fear the truth, from any academic discipline. At the same time, faith-based scholarship (Christian learning for those who follow Christ) is needed to provide an interpretation and explanation of the latest developments in the special sciences. What is more, religious worldviews provide a larger story within which the assumptions and presuppositions of the special sciences make sense. This is a task that science cannot do for itself. Of course, Christian specialists may often disagree with each other on the specifics of their discipline. Christian historians, for example, may argue over the role of religion in the French Revolution, and Christian biologists may disagree about the "specified complexity" of a microbiological system. But usually these debates take place in such a manner that almost any academic can understand the arguments and make up his or her own mind among the various competing interpretations. That is part of the fun!

As part of the general task of faith-based scholarship, we have seen an amazing growth of Christian philosophy in the last thirty years. This volume has drawn upon that resource, along with serious and important theological scholarship. I am well aware that I have put forward positions, both theological and philosophical, that need to be more carefully developed and defended. But I have decided that a work written to the broad, interdisciplinary academy would do more good than yet another specialized monograph. I did indulge myself in one technical appendix, which follows this chapter: but only one!

The task of dialogue between religion and science is something theologians of all types also need to be involved in. "Theology" as I am using it here is not a narrow word but includes biblical studies, practical theology, church history, Christian ethics, and systematic and philosophical theology. Theologians can often ask important questions and explain the various theological assumptions that inform debates between Christian scholars. There is much to learn from contemporary science and technology, for these issues and ideas are helping to create the questions and quests for meaning in our day. Theologians who wholly ignore science and technology may also be ignoring their vocation.

I have no illusions as to the likely influence of just one book on the way our culture thinks about issues of faith and science — if they think about them at all! But I have tried to make a small start, and I am conscious of being part of a larger movement of scholars across the globe. Our hope rests in God, who is able to use all that we give, even our very selves and bodies, for the redemption of all creation.

To him who sits on the throne and to the Lamb
Be praise and honor and glory and power,
For ever and ever.
And the four living creatures said, "Amen."

Induction after Foundationalism:
Four Theses on Informal Inference

As a philosopher I have long been interested in the traditional problem of induction, especially in light of recent moves in epistemology after the collapse of classical foundationalism. I believe both theology as an academic discipline and all the special sciences depend upon informal reasoning for their epistemic warrant. In this appendix, I present four theses on informal reasoning for discussion and critique, without pretending to prove or discuss each one fully. My purpose is to provide some further philosophical grounding for the mutuality model developed in this book, and especially for some of the claims made in the chapter on dialectical realism. These topics are more specialized, and of mainly philosophical interest.

The Nature of the Problem

Ever since the work of Hume philosophers have wondered just how it is that induction really works. No one, not even Hume, has really questioned the fact that induction is a normal part of our everyday reasoning processes.[1] It is in many ways a part of our common sense. I assume

---

1. Witness, for example, this well-known passage from Hume: "When he [the Pyrrhonian skeptic] awakes from his dream, he will be the first to join in the laugh against himself and to confess that all his objections are mere amusement, and can have no other tendency than to show the whimsical condition of mankind, who must act and reason and believe, though they are not able, by their most diligent inquiry, to satisfy themselves concerning the foundation of these operations or to remove the objections which may be raised against them" (*An Inquiry Concerning Human Understanding*, §XII, part II, ed. C. W. Hendel [Indianapolis: Bobbs-Merrill, 1955], pp. 168f).

water, which I needed to live yesterday, does not become poison today. I look for a penny in the general area where I heard it drop. Based on theory and careful experiment, I believe that matter is made up of tiny particles that cannot be directly observed. Not one of these argument forms (real or implied) is deductive, and they all go beyond direct experience. Examples could be multiplied a thousandfold. We do live by inductive reasoning. Hume challenges us to find a justification for such reasoning. In this overview, I take up Hume's challenge.[2] Thomas Reid, Hume's fellow countryman and contemporary, gave the best response to Hume's challenge during his own lifetime. My own reply will follow, in broad outline, Reid's reply to Hume.[3] In particular, I follow Reid when it comes to our everyday experiences. We depend upon our common sense and our prior, pre-philosophical assumptions to justify our everyday inductions concerning the world around us. But does that also apply to the special case of academic disciplines? Can our commonsense, everyday reasoning sustain the special sciences?

This further question is the topic of this appendix. I hope to make some improvements on Reid's "commonsense" approach. I will argue that the collapse of classical foundationalism in recent epistemology provides the philosophical horizon for improving upon his solution to Hume's problem.

Henry Kyburg usefully distinguished between two types of problems for induction: the problem of description and the problem of justification.[4] The descriptive problem is one of spelling out the general principles we use in good inductive arguments. For the most part, I shall ignore the specifics of that problem in this appendix. The problem of justification is one of giving reasons or grounds for the rationality of inductive principles. This is Hume's challenge, and our central focus.

---

2. For a careful analysis of Hume's argument against induction, see D. C. Stove, *Probability and Hume's Inductive Scepticism* (Oxford: Clarendon, 1973).

3. I have been led to Reid by William P. Alston, among others. See, for example, his essay "Thomas Reid on Epistemic Principles," *History of Philosophy Quarterly* 2 (1985): 435-52.

4. Henry E. Kyburg Jr., *Probability and Inductive Logic* (New York: Macmillan, 1970), p. 126. See also Peter Lipton, *Inference to the Best Explanation* (New York: Routledge, 1991), pp. 6-10.

Reid's Commonsense Realism

Reid's response to the challenge of Hume was to appeal to our "common sense."[5] Reid recognized that the problem of induction is a philosopher's puzzle. The fact that logicians have not, so far, been able to solve this puzzle does not imply that induction is unreliable.[6] We are justified in relying on induction because of its pervasive role in our everyday life, and because it plays a part in the common sense of humanity. As Reid wrote in his 1764 treatise, *An Inquiry into the Human Mind,*

> If there are certain principles, as I think there are, which the constitution of our nature leads us to believe, and which we are under a necessity to take for granted in the common concerns of life, without being able to give a reason for them — these are what we call the principles of common sense; and what is manifestly contrary to them, is what we call absurd.[7]

Reid recognized, along with Kant, that there are certain principles of inductive argument which provide justification for our assessment of particular informal arguments.[8] (From now on, I shall use the term "informal" instead of "inductive," for reasons that will soon become clear.) Some of the principles of informal inference may be propositions, while others are criteria for theory choice, which are perhaps best understood as epistemic value judgments. These latter can be spelled out as propositions, but are typically discussed in simpler format, often a single word (e.g., fruitfulness or parsimony).

5. For brief introductions to Reid's philosophy, see the article on Reid by Robert Gallie in the *Routledge Encyclopedia of Philosophy* (London: Routledge, 1998), 8:171-80, or Colin Brown, *Christianity and Western Thought,* vol. 1 (Downers Grove, Ill.: InterVarsity, 1990), pp. 259-68. For Reid on induction, see Peter Anstey, "Reid on the Problem of Induction," *History of Philosophy Quarterly* 12 (1995): 77-93. For a fuller general discussion, see the excellent volume by Keith Lehrer, *Thomas Reid* (Boston: Routledge, 1989).

6. See James Cargile, "The Problem of Induction," *Philosophy* 73 (1998): 247-75, who makes a similar argument.

7. Thomas Reid, *An Inquiry into the Human Mind,* chap. 2, §6; reprinted in Reid's *Inquiry and Essays,* ed. R. E. Beanblossom and Keith Lehrer (Indianapolis: Hackett, 1983), p. 20.

8. See the chapter "The First Principles of Contingent Truths," chap. 5, essay 6 of his *Essays on the Intellectual Powers of Man* (Beanblossom ed., pp. 266-84).

Reid's point that the problem of induction is a philosopher's puzzle, rather than a problem that undermines our reliance on induction, has been clarified in the recent debate between externalism and internalism in epistemology. We should distinguish between a person being justified in believing that *p* is true, and a person consciously seeking warrant (or justification) for the belief that *p* is true. A person may in fact be warranted (or justified) for accepting some proposition, without being able to articulate that warrant.[9] In other words, we need to distinguish justification as an activity (internal) from the state of being justified (external). I take it that not only Reid but most externalist or reliabilist epistemologists would accept this point. And there is surely something right here.

There is a problem with the justification of informal inference, however, in those infrequent cases when I may have cause to doubt some commonsense principle (or perhaps, the manner in which I have brought common sense into language). A young boy raised in a very honest small community will come to rationally rely upon the principle of testimony. All other things being equal, we should accept as true the sincere report of people regarding some matter they are in good position to know. Without such a principle, or something like it, we would know almost nothing, in fact. The boy grows up, however, and moves to the metropolis, where liars and con artists soon teach him to modify the principle. He may now wonder: is this principle in fact a reliable one, epistemically? In seeking warrant for the principles of informal arguments, we are in fact consciously seeking warrant for our beliefs. I do not recommend this as a systematic program, *à la* Descartes, but there are situations (such as when there is incoherence among principles, or the case of our young friend) that call for the investigation of our warrant for accepting these principles. In such situations, even if one is rational to rely upon the deliverances of some informal inference, we will want to investigate further to see why it is rational to rely upon them. I believe this is particularly true in the academic disciplines. The development of special interests and explanatory focus may

9. Reid articulates this principle in the chapter cited just above. I follow Alvin Plantinga in calling "warrant" that thing (or "quantity") which, when added to true belief, makes for knowledge. See his *Warrant: The Current Debate* (New York: Oxford University Press, 1993).

call us to question our "commonsense" assumptions. The history of quantum mechanics in the twentieth century is a well-known example of what I have in mind.

Hume challenged us to discover why it is we believe these commonsense principles, that is, to find the grounds for our rational reliance on informal arguments to provide us with knowledge. The fact that informal inferences are reliable for an individual in our everyday settings is not at issue. Informal inferences can be reliable for a particular person in a "normal" setting, even though logicians may not be able to discover why they are reliable. The logician's puzzle is: what warrant (if any) can we give for our reliance on patterns of informal inference *when they are called into question?* I am particularly interested, in this appendix, in the justification of informal reasoning within academic disciplines. I believe this is an important problem for philosophy of science even if we are rational to normally rely upon our commonsense informal inferences. Notice that this question should come in a particular, rather than in a general, form. To make any headway in this area, however, we will need to clarify what an informal argument is.

The Nature of Informal Inference

Some good arguments are formal or deductive in character. These arguments are such that, if their premises are true, then their conclusions must (logically must) be true. Arguments like this in ordinary language can, in principle at least, be expressed in a formal and symbolic manner that demonstrates their deductive character. I say "in principle" because there is no universal, agreed upon logic accepted by all cultures. The logics we do have, moreover, have not always been known. I will call all deductive arguments "formal" even if they are not so expressed, because of this in-principle deductive structure. All other good arguments are informal (that is, not formal or nondeductive).

In order to clarify this distinction, we need a notion different from the standards of validity and soundness, which are well-formed notions in formal logic.[10] I should like to add the idea of the "assessment" of an argument, to discover the epistemic support that the pre-

---

10. An argument is sound when the premises are true and the inference is valid.

mises (if true) give to the conclusion. The sign of a good formal argument, then, will be that the epistemic support is the strongest possible one: logically necessary. On the other hand, a good informal argument will give epistemic support to its conclusion without logically determining it. Let us call this "cogency."[11] Cogent informal arguments increase the likelihood that their conclusions are true, but do not make them logically necessary.[12] By the "assessment" of an argument, then, in this technical sense, I will mean the investigation of the strength of epistemic support that the premises give to the conclusion.

In the sweep of Western cultural history, philosophers from Plato and Pythagoras to Russell and Husserl have given priority to demonstrative, formal reasoning. The model for such reasoning has been mathematics. I believe that, as part of the rejection of classical or radical foundationalism, we should learn to appreciate degrees of knowledge that are less than logically necessary. By "classical foundationalism" we mean that epistemological program, at the heart of so much Western philosophy, which sought to ground our knowledge-claims upon "basic beliefs" (beliefs not founded upon other beliefs) that are "self-evident or incorrigible or evident to the senses."[13] This is the program that Richard Rorty attacks under the name "epistemology" in his *Philosophy and the Mirror of Nature.*[14] Of course, there are more types of epistemology, even in classical Western philosophy, than classical foundationalism — which is a good thing, since classical foundationalism is in trouble. I will simply assume, rather than argue, that classical foundationalism should be abandoned in epistemology.

But if classical foundationalism should be rejected, so should the

11. I thank Bruce Reichenbach for this term. See his *An Introduction to Critical Thinking* (New York: McGraw-Hill, 2000).

12. I assume that argument to the conclusion that P is false will be support for the truth of this larger proposition, "it is false that P."

13. I borrow the term "classical foundationalism" from Alvin Plantinga. See the well-known collection of essays, ed. Plantinga and Nicholas Wolterstorff, *Faith and Rationality* (Notre Dame, Ind.: University of Notre Dame Press, 1983), quoting p. 72.

14. Richard Rorty, *Philosophy and the Mirror of Nature* (Princeton, N.J.: Princeton University Press, 1979). For other criticism of classical foundationalism, see Fredrick Will, *Induction and Justification* (Ithaca, N.Y.: Cornell University Press, 1974); or Plantinga and Wolterstorff, *Faith and Rationality.* A. J. Ayer rejected the view that something must be certain in order to be known, in his *The Problem of Knowledge* (Harmondsworth: Penguin, 1956).

privileging of demonstrative reasoning over probable reasoning. After all, certain knowledge is notoriously difficult to attain. In areas of philosophy important for human flourishing, such as the philosophies of ethics, religion, science, politics, and beauty, almost all of our knowledge is probable and fallible, rather than deductive. One could claim that probable knowledge is far more important for human life than deductive knowledge. So why can we not begin to value such knowledge, *alongside* deductive truths?[15]

Once we give up the opinion that only formal, deductive arguments are *real* arguments, many of the so-called "problems" associated with induction disappear. A formal argument is one whose validity depends upon the (in principle) logical structure of the argument, on purely formal grounds. These arguments can be given symbolic structure. Informal arguments, however, are *not formal*. A full assessment of such an argument cannot be carried out merely by attention to its structure or symbolic form. The conclusion of an informal argument trades upon the content of the premises the way that a deductive argument trades upon the formal logical structure. To assess informal arguments, therefore, we must pay attention to the meaning of the premises and our background knowledge concerning their content, in order to determine whether the argument is cogent. The structure or form of an argument is important, of course; I am not denying this. But structure alone is not sufficient in the case of informal arguments. This follows from the very fact that such arguments are informal. And yet, so many "problems with induction" have arisen because philosophers trained in symbolic logic have complained that the formal (symbolic) structure of informal arguments is not formally valid.[16] Of course it is not! All good informal arguments must (logically must) be formally invalid. If they were formally valid, they would be formal (deductive) arguments. To re-

15. In *Proofs and Refutations: The Logic of Mathematical Discovery* (Cambridge: Cambridge University Press, 1976), Imre Lakatos argued that even mathematics is based in the long run on informal reasoning. "An investigation of *informal* mathematics will yield a rich situational logic for working mathematicians, a situational logic which is neither mechanical nor irrational, but which cannot be recognized and still less, stimulated, by the formalist philosophy" (p. 4, his italics).

16. Many of the points I am making here, about the nature of informal inference, follow the work of D. C. Stove, *The Rationality of Induction* (Oxford: Clarendon, 1983), and Will, *Induction and Justification*.

mind us of these facts, I call inductive reasoning "informal," hoping the name will press home the point that informal reasoning cannot be assimilated to thinking along formal lines.

Let us take an example of this problem. Carl Hempel often discussed a paradox of induction called the "black raven paradox" or simply the Hempel Paradox.[17] J. L. Mackie once called this the paradox of confirmation. The paradox arises from assuming that (in an informal argument) "[i]f observations confirm one formulation of a hypothesis they confirm any logically equivalent formulation."[18] Add to this the further assumption that "There is a black raven" is to be understood as a material conditional (if x is a raven then x is black). It then follows that the supposed general law that "All ravens are black" is supported not only by "There is a black raven" but also by, "There is a non-black non-raven" (for example, "There is a blue car"). But our common sense tells us that "There is a blue car" does not help confirm the law in question about black ravens.

The problem here lies in importing an idea from symbolic logic, namely the material conditional, and imposing it upon the informal logic of simple induction. Since evaluating an informal inference depends upon knowing not only the content of the statements but also an often-complex background of related knowledge, the way the hypothesis is stated is important to our assessment of the argument. Hempel's paradox rests upon a common problem. He assimilates rules from formal logic into his analysis of what is best understood as an informal argument. And this is just to misjudge the differences between formal and informal logics. I am not arguing that cogent informal arguments may contain logical contradictions. We are talking instead of standards for assessing the epistemological weight that premises give to conclusions (evaluation). The rules for inference from one premise

17. See, for example, Carl Hempel, "Recent Problems of Induction," in *Mind and Cosmos: Essays in Contemporary Science and Philosophy,* ed. R. G. Colodny (Pittsburgh: University of Pittsburgh Press, 1966). This work in turn depends upon, and is critical of, the inductive criteria of Jean Nicod, *Foundations of Geometry and Induction* (New York: Harcourt, 1930).

18. "The Paradox of Confirmation," *British Journal for the Philosophy of Science* 13 (1963): 265-77; reprinted in P. H. Nidditch, ed., *The Philosophy of Science* (Oxford: Oxford University Press, 1968), quoting p. 165.

to the next (i.e., derivation) are often quite different in formal and informal arguments.

It also follows logically from a proper definition of informal inference that, for all good informal inferences, the premises will only make their conclusion likely to be true. Even if all the premises were true the conclusion could still be false. Notice that this fact follows from the very definition of "informal argument." So this fact is not, and cannot be, a "problem of induction." On the contrary, it is a logical truth. In the philosophy of science, for example, theories are supported by evidence through informal arguments.[19] This means that theories will *always* be "underdetermined" by the data. It is logically necessary that, if the sciences are based on informal patterns of inference, their theories will be underdetermined by the evidence. If the evidence (premises) *determined* the theory (conclusion) by logical necessity, then we would have a formal (deductive) argument.

Good informal arguments, then, cannot be fully assessed on the basis of their structure alone. Two informal arguments can have the same structure, and one can be cogent while the other is not. Assessing informal arguments often depends crucially upon the semantics of the argument, not its syntax. Of course, clarifying the syntax or form of any argument is important in the analysis of it. But to assess an informal argument, I need to know both the meaning of the premises and something of what the argument is about. Perhaps it is time for an example. Consider the following argument:

1. Over the years, I have observed that when I fail to water my lawn in the summer, the grass dies.
2. While on summer vacation out of state, I learn that the lawn was not watered the whole summer.
3. I infer that, more likely than not, the grass on my lawn is dead, even though I have not observed it (yet).

To assess the argument, I need to know some things about grass, water, lawns, and summers. Abstract reasoning about "All F's are G" is not re-

---

19. At least, that is the view many hold, including the present writer. See further Ernan McMullin, *The Inference That Makes Science* (Milwaukee: Marquette University Press, 1992).

ally of any use, as becomes clear if we consider the symbolic version of this argument:

4. Some G's (observed unwatered lawns during the summers) are F (dead).
5. Therefore, all G's are F.
6. M (my lawn back home) is G.
7. Therefore M is F.

But this is not a formally valid argument, because of the step from (4) to (5). Although (7) does follow from (5) and (6), (5) itself does not follow deductively from (4). Yet this is *not* a "problem of induction." Good informal arguments should not be assessed as one would a formal argument.

An interesting corollary to the right understanding of the nature of informal inference has to do with probability calculus. Some philosophers, following Thomas Bayes, respond to Hume by turning to the mathematics of probability.[20] But the probability calculus, when used properly, is a kind of mathematical argument whose conclusions must (logically must) be true. So the probability calculus is a kind of formal argument. The conclusion of a valid, symbolic argument in the mathematics of probability must be true if the premises are true. So such arguments are formal, not informal, patterns of inference. If I know that 10 percent of all Methodists are Canadians, and if about all I know about Debbie is that she is a Methodist, then I know with logical certainly that the probability she is a Canadian is 0.1. This is a formal (not an informal) argument, even though it is about probability. Perhaps we should use the term "likelihood" for informal support for conclusions, rather than probability, to avoid confusing them. In any case, in Bayesian terms, a full assessment of an informal argument must include the *specific reasons* why evidence E makes one hypothesis (H1) rather than another (H2) probable. Merely knowing in the abstract that $P(H1/E\&K) > P(H2/E\&K)$ does not allow me to assess the argument fully. The starting probabilities in a Bayesian argument are usually known on informal grounds. So while the Bayesian calculus may well

---

20. See further John Earman, *Bayes or Bust?: A Critical Examination of Bayesian Confirmation Theory* (Cambridge, Mass.: MIT Press, 1992).

be helpful in some areas, we cannot rely upon it alone to assess informal arguments.[21]

I have stated that in order to assess an informal argument, like the one given about my unfortunate lawn, we need to know something about the subject of the argument. That is, in informal arguments we need background knowledge about the premises and the objects being discussed, in order to assess the likelihood that the conclusion is true.[22] How likely is it, for example, that there might have been enough rain over the summer to keep my lawn alive? And that is not all we need to know. We also need to have a good grasp of the principles of informal inference. These principles, I will argue, differ slightly from discipline to discipline. So chemists, for example, need to be trained in the practice of natural scientific reasoning, just as detectives need to be trained in the science of good detective work. This brings us, then, to the principles of "common sense," which Reid believed included the principles of sound reasoning.

Tradition and Reason in the Principles of Informal Inference: Postfoundational Theses

There are four theses that I will propose concerning the "principles of induction" which go beyond Reid's position on the "self-evident" character of the principles of reason.[23] The positions I present for discus-

---

21. This would be true even if we agree with the Bayesian that the objective, epistemic weight which evidence (E) gives a conclusion (H) is a necessary truth. When we are seeking justification for a particular informal inference, we are seeking human knowledge, that is, something that we are going to believe. In order for us to come to know the (relative) epistemic weight that evidence gives a conclusion (which is infrequently expressible in numerical terms), I need to understand the evidence and the conclusion. Only then can we judge the soundness of the argument.

22. See, among others, Dennis Temple, "Grue-Green and Some Mistakes in Confirmation Theory," *Dialectica* 228 (1974): 197-210, who argues that we may need "total information" to fully decide between grue (a time-indexed color) and green as properties.

23. Althought Reid was a fallibilist in general, I am not sure he was a fallibilist with respect to first principles. For example, he wrote that "one of the surest marks of a first principle" is that "no man ever pretended to prove it, and yet no man in his wits calls it into question" (*Intellectual Powers,* essay 6, chap. 5, point 3, p. 270).

sion presuppose the collapse of classical foundationalism.[24] At the same time, I do seek some kind of ground or basis for our acceptance of these principles and propositions, even if not classical foundations. Is that not a contradiction?

The Fallibilist Thesis and Noetic Warrant

In the presence of a reason for doubt, rational people will seek justification or warrant for a belief. The Cartesian program of radical doubt should be avoided, but in the presence of reasonable doubt, some further analysis makes sense. This seeking of grounds or reasons is not classical foundationalism, because I believe that these grounds may be fallible. Nevertheless, given some reason for doubting a belief, it is reasonable to ask the question, "Why should I believe it?" I should like to present two fallible grounds upon which we might seek justification for informal principles of reasoning within academic disciplines. *Broadly speaking, these grounds will be reason and tradition.* Let us begin with reason.

One problem with Hume's criticism of informal reasoning is that in looking at the grounds for our faith in informal reasoning, he overlooked a possible ground for the principles of informal inference. Hume presents us with only two options, when in fact a third possibility exists. Thus, his argument commits the fallacy of a false dilemma. Hume's argument relies on the claim that knowledge is based either on deduction *à la* mathematics or on impressions (sensations). But it is surely possible that inductive arguments are based on principles that are known by rational intuition but that are not necessary truths like mathematics. This was the view of both Kant and Reid, in their response to Hume. This option is one that I believe is fruitful for understanding the bases of inductive reasoning.

I suggest we develop a fallibilist notion of rational insight as warrant or justification,[25] which I will call "noetic warrant." Leibniz,

---

24. I do not claim that all types of foundationalism should collapse, just the classical variety.

25. Such a conception is in the air these days: see, e.g., Donna Summerfield, "Modest A Priori Knowledge," *Philosophy and Phenomenological Research* 51 (1991): 39-66; M. Giaquinto,

Hume, Kant, and other philosophers assimilate principles of reason to the example of mathematics (or in more modern cases, symbolic logic). In this they surely do philosophy a disservice. Our claim to know something by reason does not imply that the idea is necessary and universally applicable, at least not in every case. Some principles may not be logically necessary, while others may be limited in the kinds of circumstances in which they apply. I propose that we find another category of rational judgment at the foundation of our acceptance of informal argument.[26] Let us call a "noetic concept" any idea that we accept on the basis of *a priori* or noetic warrant. Noetic concepts may be propositions, epistemic values, definitions, or criteria. The warrant for a proposed noetic concept comes (at least in part) from rational intuition. This implies a *process* of seeking warrant for such propositions or principles. Noetic warrant makes a claim to knowledge that (1) may arise in the context of experience but (2) goes beyond the deliverances of experience, strictly understood, to assert an insight or intuition into the subject based on reason. In addition, (3) what is known in this way does not have to be necessary and universal,[27] and (4) the claims we make to noetic warrant may be wrong.

On this fallibilist understanding of noetic warrant, we have moved from *all* to *some:* some appeal to rational insight makes the warrant for our concept noetic, even if it is mixed with an appeal to experience. Of course, it may be that all of the warrant is purely rational, but it need not be that way. Given this mixed idea of noetic warrant, it

---

"Non-Analytic Conceptual Knowledge," *Mind* 105 (1996): 249-68; Noah Lemos, "Common Sense and A Priori Epistemology," *The Monist* 81 (1998): 473-87; or most recently Laurence BonJour, *In Defense of Pure Reason* (Cambridge: Cambridge University Press, 1998).

26. I am hardly alone in finding insight or intuition at the basis of rationality. Aristotle held that the basic truths *(arche)* upon which scientific or demonstrative reasoning was based were known through rational intuition *(nous)*. See *Posterior Analytics* II.xix (99B-100B). This was also Reid's position. See in more recent times, e.g., Bernard Lonergan, *Insight* (London: Longman, Green, 1957), or for induction, Donald Williams, *The Ground of Induction* (Cambridge, Mass.: Harvard University Press, 1947), and BonJour, *In Defense of Pure Reason.*

27. I have been influenced in my thinking about noetic warrant and concepts by Hilary Putnam, "Analycity and Apriority," *Midwest Studies in Philosophy* 4 (1979): 423-71; reprinted in *A Priori Knowledge,* ed. Paul K. Moser (Oxford: Oxford University Press, 1987); and by Saul A. Kripke, *Naming and Necessity* (Cambridge, Mass.: Harvard University Press, 1980).

makes sense to test, examine, and explore supposed noetic concepts. This is the sort of reasoning that is typical concerning moral first principles. I believe that Hilary Putnam points us in the right direction when he argues that (so-called) *a priori* truths — which I call noetic concepts — "have the character of *maxims* — general principles that are not, or at least may not be, exceptionless, and they involve 'generic', or somewhat pre-theoretical, notions rather than the (supposedly) perfectly precise notions of an ideal theory in the exact sciences."[28]

It is points (1), (3), and (4) that make this notion of noetic warrant different from Hume's "relations of ideas" and Kant's "*a priori* judgment." Examples of such noetic concepts would be logical truths like *modus ponens,* the principle that only real things have causal efficacy, rational criteria for theory choice, or basic moral truths. On the other hand, I agree that sometimes epistemic warrant is based fully upon experience. So another category would be "empirical warrant" — in other words, *a posteriori* warrant for some proposition.

The typical claim, since Leibniz, is that the truths of reason must be necessary. But Saul Kripke has, I believe, given us good reasons to affirm that some noetic concepts may be about contingent things. Richard Swinburne, in a careful reply to Kripke, gives several possible definitions of "necessity" and "*a priori,*" and this seems right.[29] There is indeed more than one meaning to these words. I am willing to accept the proposal that all noetic warrant is based on "necessity," given the large and flexible definitions of necessity that Swinburne develops. Reid certainly had, for example, a much larger conception of necessity than logical necessity.[30] Perhaps we will develop our notions of necessity even more over time. But I am not committed to this thesis. I suggest that we simply look and see. What I wish to deny, however, is that all noetic concepts are "necessary" in the sense of *logically* necessary.

A noetic concept, then, does not have to be an analytic proposition. The fact that "every colored object takes up space" is something known to be true on the basis of noetic warrant, and not simply from experience alone. We can state this fact in different words ("All colored

28. In Moser, *A Priori Knowledge,* p. 104.

29. Richard G. Swinburne, "Analycity, Necessity, and Apriority," *Mind* 84 (1975): 225-43, also reprinted in Moser, *A Priori Knowledge.*

30. This point is made in Louise Marcil-Lacost, *Claude Buffier and Thomas Reid* (Montreal: McGill-Queen's University Press, 1982), p. 117.

things are spatial things," etc.), but any argument for it assumes its truth in some way. Nevertheless, it is not an analytic truth, in the strict sense of "contained in the meaning of the words." The meaning of "colored" does not logically include the notion of "spatial." It is reasonable, on the other hand, to assume that this noetic concept is a metaphysical truth. In any possible world story, whenever we instantiate the property of being colored, we likewise instantiate (by implication) "being spatial." But this noetic concept is not an analytic truth, because "being colored" does not include in its meaning "being spatial." This conclusion is hardly surprising, however, since being analytic is a logical property, while "known to be true on the basis of noetic warrant" is an epistemological property.[31]

Noetic warrant is not based on logical arguments, nor simply on the accumulation of experiences (although it may arise from and be stimulated by our encounter with the world). The warrant by which we agree that proposed noetic concepts are true comes from rational reflection upon the proposition (criterion, etc.) This rational reflection is what I call noetic warrant. How do we know when some proposition is genuinely noetic, rather than empirical? Two signs point the way. First, any attempt to explain our concept ends up assuming it (or something like it). To draw another example from ethics, it is very hard to explain why doing and being ethically good is to be pursued without assuming this to be true already. In other words, careful analysis of why a person should believe this proposed noetic concept shows that it is not based simply on cumulative experience, nor on some argument. Second, our grounds for knowing the concept have the air of rational insight, intuition, or appeal to reason. To take an example from logic, when we reflect upon why we believe the law of noncontradiction, we find ourselves appealing to rational insight and not to cumulative experience. Another way of putting this same point is, the quality that makes this true belief qualify as *knowledge* is rational-plus-empirical, not merely empirical alone.

The claim to know some truth noetically is not an arbitrary one. Since noetic concepts are not always logically necessary, it makes sense to test and explore our noetic warrant. For example, some statements we hold to be true through noetic warrant will be analytic, and others

---

31. Paul Moser makes this point in *A Priori Knowledge,* pp. 7-9.

will be synthetic. Only by exploring the nature of our noetic concepts can we know if one is synthetic or analytic. Once this is determined, then we can also explore the truth of our proposed concept. This exploration or assessment is not a kind of verification or proof. Herbert Feigl made the important distinction, concerning the rational exploration of the first principles of reason, between *verification* and *vindication*.[32] While basic principles cannot be verified, since they are at the foundations of rationality, they can be vindicated. They can be explained by being clarified and set within a system of ideas, which expands upon them and demonstrates their use.[33] I am proposing, then, that we seek vindication for the principles of informal inference.

In one place, Reid seems to have understood this point. He wrote, "The most simple operations of the mind, admit not of a logical definition: all we can do is to describe them, so as to lead those who are conscious of them in themselves, to attend to them, and reflect upon them; and it is often very difficult to describe them so as to answer this intention."[34] This notion of needing to further clarify and define the "simple operations of the mind" is part of what a good vindication does. We may also, along the way, need to correct our noetic concepts.

There are at least three ways in which our acceptance of a noetic concept can be made more sure. One is by further empirical exploration. Are there other areas of knowledge and experience, not originally considered, that help us to believe (or disbelieve) the principle under consideration? Such empirical considerations help our sense of surety about our warrant but should not mean that the noetic warrant is based on experience alone. If we find that, after all, the warrant is based on experience alone, then we discover that it is not noetic, but empirical, warrant. Second, the principle can be placed within a larger system of which it is a part, and which helps make sense of it. To the extent that the larger system is credible, so too will our principle be. Sometimes basic principles of a worldview can be tested only in experience,

32. This kind of exploration does not validate the noetic warrant, but it can vindicate it. See, on this distinction, Herbert Feigl, "De principiis non disputandum . . . ?" in *Philosophical Analysis,* ed. Max Black (Ithaca, N.Y.: Cornell University Press, 1950).

33. This procedure should satisfy Larry Laudan's complaint against all intuitionist meta-methodologies, namely, that an intuition is not subject to further correction. See his "Some Problems Facing Intuitionist Meta-methodologies," *Synthese* 67 (1986): 115-29.

34. Reid, *An Inquiry,* chap. 6, §20 (p. 83).

over a long history, and in dialogue — even conflict — with rival traditions and worldviews.[35] Third, we can explore the implications of our principle, given our other beliefs, and examine these implications. So, for example, *modus ponens* is as secure a noetic concept as any. One can, of course, test it to see if it makes sense in terms of ordinary reasoning processes. We can place it in a larger system of formal logic, and see its implication for other forms of reasoning, examining these implications as well. So too the moral principle that "it is good to help those in need" or something like it (say the principle of benevolence) can be tested by comparison with standard examples of goodness. It can be placed in a larger frame of ethical theory, and its implications can be questioned by borderline cases. Claims to noetic truth, then, may fail the test: what we thought was based on reason may not have been.

Hard-nosed skeptics may be thinking something along these lines: "Very well. You have defined a type of reasoning that, if there is any such, improves upon Reid's solution to the problem of induction. But are there any of these 'noetic concepts' which are synthetic? If so, show me!" Let us take, then, an example from scientific reasoning. One type of informal argument is the inference to the best explanation (or better, inference that an explanation is best), and one criterion for a good explanation is that of comprehensiveness. The best explanation covers all the relevant data. Is this criterion empirical? Have we looked at lots and lots of good explanations to come to this conclusion? Of course not. It is a rational requirement, not an empirical conclusion. So the criterion of comprehensiveness is noetic. Perhaps, then, it is analytic; yet its denial is coherent and possible, and its truth does not come from the meaning of the words in the sentence. Only an arbitrary, ad hoc definition of "good explanation" as "covering all the data" can possibly validate an argument that this criterion is analytic. I can prove any statement is analytic with such logic! "The moon is made of green cheese," for example, is analytic when we define the moon as "a verdant heavenly body composed of moldy milk products." One will have to argue that we use "good explanation" to always mean "covers all the data" — but that is

---

35. Imre Lakatos argued this for research programs in the natural sciences, in *The Methodology of Scientific Research Programmes: Philosophical Papers*, vol. 1 (Cambridge: Cambridge University Press, 1977), while Alasdair MacIntyre makes a similar argument for first principles in moral philosophy in *First Principles, Final Ends, and Contemporary Philosophical Issues* (Aquinas Lecture; Milwaukee: Marquette University Press, 1990).

not true to our use of this term in science and philosophy.[36] Sometimes a "good explanation" is one that satisfies the questioner, for example. The criterion, then, is not analytic. So it is synthetic. The criterion of comprehensiveness, then, is a synthetic noetic concept.

The principles that underlie induction, therefore, may be justified (in part) by noetic warrants. Some of these noetic concepts may be necessary propositions; others may not. In this way we can advance Reid's solution to the problem of induction and also avoid the objections to "apriorism" voiced by many philosophers of science today who are heirs to Hume.

The Tradition Thesis

To recap: From the definition of informal inference, I have argued that we need to know the content of the argument (its formal and informal character, its semantics and its syntax) in order to assess the strength of the argument. This further requires both a background knowledge concerning the subject(s) of the argument and some grasp of the standards of informal inference relevant for that subject. These standards must be learned, just like the background knowledge. To become an excellent chemist, for example, is not only to learn the facts and theories of chemistry; it is to be inducted into a particular history and tradition of standards of argument.

Pierre Duhem, early in the last century, gave an oft-quoted example of a visitor to a physics lab. A scientist is engaged in an experiment to measure electric resistance, but the visitor (who is not a scientist) only sees the oscillations of an iron bar that carries a mirror. The visitor asks the scientist what he is up to. "Measuring electric resistance," the scientist answers. When the visitor asks the scientist what mirrors and iron bars have to do with electric resistance, he is told to take a course in electricity: the explanation would be a very long one![37] In

36. I assume my opponent will agree that the meaning of a term comes from its use in a language-game.

37. Pierre Duhem, *La théorie physique* (Paris: Chevalier & Rivière, 1906), p. 218, cited in N. R. Hanson, *Patterns of Discovery* (Cambridge: Cambridge University Press, 1961), p. 16. This work was translated into English by Philip P. Wiener as *The Aim and Structure of Physical Theory* (Princeton: Princeton University Press, 1954).

cases like these, we can see that informal arguments (about electricity or other things) depend crucially upon important training. As N. R. Hanson rightly argued, "physical science is not just a systematic exposure of the senses to the world; it is also a way of thinking about the world, of forming conceptions."[38] In a similar way, Stephen Toulmin argued in *The Uses of Argument* that our standards of good argument are "field-dependent."[39] To learn the sciences is, in part, to be trained in a particular way of forming conceptions. Lawyers, too, go through such training. But the kind of informal thinking typical of law is quite different from that of natural science. Both practices are rational, yet they are not identical in their standards of what counts as good informal argument.

Perhaps the whole of Kuhn's philosophy of science cannot be accepted, yet he wrote one of the most influential academic books of the last century. His notion of "paradigms" at the basis of scientific practice and rationality has been widely accepted, and rightly so. But a paradigm includes background facts and theories as well as standards of rationality. Since Kuhn notoriously failed to give a precise definition of "paradigm" (a word he borrowed from Wittgenstein), perhaps I ought to indicate how I use the word. To students I explain that a scientific paradigm rests between a "theory" and an entire "worldview," and includes elements of both. Paradigms ground the traditions of rational inquiry in the humanities and sciences, including background knowledge and value judgments. Almost all of my students find this a helpful comment, even though it is not a definition either. Still, by a careful definition of "theory" in science, along with "worldview," we can use this concept of "between" to specify somewhat what a paradigm is.

The role of paradigms in scientific inference would indicate that we learn such standards, along with facts and theories, when we are initiated into a particular academic discipline. Imre Lakatos developed this notion further with his theory of rival "research programmes" that have conflicting histories of development, conjecture, theories, and practices within a particular science or academic discipline.[40] I believe

38. Hanson, *Patterns of Discovery,* p. 30.

39. Stephen Toulmin, *The Uses of Argument* (Cambridge: Cambridge University Press, 1964), p. 15.

40. Lakatos explains himself most clearly in his radio lecture for the Open University, published as "Science and Pseudoscience" in his *Methodology.*

that Lakatos is right when he claims that his theory of research programs is superior to the philosophy of science of both Kuhn and Karl Popper. Larry Laudan has developed these ideas in helpful directions, correcting Lakatos at some crucial points;[41] but in broad terms, the point for our thesis is that such research programs are (among other things) traditions of inquiry. Call them paradigms or research programs, scientific reasoning comes in traditional packages.[42] We may wish to borrow the term "doxastic practice" from William Alston to speak of such traditional, learned rationality.[43] This includes the standards of informal reasoning accepted within a particular tradition.

The implications of this for the "problem of induction" are significant: if a particular standard of good informal inference is an established part of a successful, progressive, and long-term research program, that standard has *prima facie* justification. We will need some reason to doubt that standard before we spend our precious time exploring the warrant for our belief in that standard. But what are these standards of informal inference?

The Diversity Thesis

Reid believed that there are a few principles and faculties belonging to common sense that are at the foundation of our faith in perception and informal reasoning.[44] Despite the work of logicians such as Mill and Russell, no one has made a convincing and complete list of such

41. See most recently, Larry Laudan, *Beyond Positivism and Relativism: Theory, Method, and Evidence* (Boulder, Col.: Westview, 1996), which contains frequent references to Lakatos.

42. See also Alasdair MacIntyre, "Epistemological Crises, Dramatic Narrative, and the Philosophy of Science," *The Monist* 60 (1977): 453-72, reprinted in *Why Narrative?*, ed. Stanley Hauerwas and L. Gregory Jones (Grand Rapids: Eerdmans, 1989).

43. William P. Alston, "A 'Doxastic Practice' Approach to Epistemology," in *Knowledge and Skepticism*, ed. Marjorie Clay and Keith Lehrer (Boulder, Col.: Westview, 1989).

44. See his "Cura Prima," printed in Marcil-Lacoste, *Claude Buffier*, p. 197. In an unpublished letter Reid noted, "That there may be innumerable self-evident Propositions I acknowledge; but the greater part of these will be found to be trifling propositions as Mr. Locke very justly calls them" (Birkwood Collection, T. Reid 2131.6 (II) (6); cited in Marcil-Lacoste, *Claude Buffier*, p. 68 n.).

principles, and I propose we give up the quest for a shortlist of self-evident principles. Instead, let us accept the fact that informal inference is a very varied practice, with many basic principles that guide good inference.[45] Since there are so many different kinds and patterns of informal inference, why should we think that there is some simple list of principles that underlies all informal reasoning? In the examination of particular forms of informal inference, we may find some similarities; but I expect we will discover a number of differences as well. Only careful and sustained exploration will clarify the number and scope of the principles of induction, and indeed we may never discover them all. Informal inference is certainly not based on some simplistic principle, like "the uniformity of nature."

There may in fact be more than one explanation for why we accept a particular informal argument. Let us take an example from Nelson Goodman:

1. All observed emeralds have been green.
2. Probably, the greenness of emeralds is a product of the chemical makeup of the mineral.
3. The chemical makeup of a mineral is stable across time and space.
4. Probably, all emeralds are green.

The meaning of "probably" in these statements is: more likely to be true than any alternative hypothesis. What reasons can we give for accepting this particular informal argument? First, we should note that (2) is a proposed explanation for (1). So the first move is an instance of what Peirce called "retroduction," in other words, inference that some explanation is better than rival hypotheses. Assessing the likelihood of this first step in the argument would require a good deal of chemical evidence and background knowledge. We would need to know the physical basis for color as well as the chemical analysis of emeralds. Given all the data, we could argue for (2), using the standards of argument found in the central research programs of physical chemistry.

Notice how our evaluation, so far, vindicates our major points al-

---

45. This point, which is basically Wittgensteinian, has been made by many authors, including Will, *Induction and Justification.*

ready made in this appendix. Assessing this informal argument required knowledge of the particular things and properties the argument is about. Merely formal issues may be necessary, but they are not sufficient. The argument that (2) is the best explanation for the fact of (1) will not be based on data alone. It will also include principles for theory assessment in chemistry, and in general the "paradigm" of current chemical science. We may need to rely upon a principle of simplicity for physical properties within proposed chemical theories, for example, in order to rule out colors such as "grue" for minerals.[46] It is hard to specify in advance all of the principles and criteria we might need to substantiate the truth of (2) based (in part) upon (1). So our example also validates our diversity thesis.

Some have argued that there could be a nearly infinite number of hypotheses that fit the same facts. This is logically possible, but once again smuggles standards of argument from formal logic into the consideration of informal inference. In the actual practice of chemistry, there will be a limited number of hypotheses to explain a focused and limited amount of chemical data concerning some material. *We do not, in informal inference, have to argue against all logically possible hypotheses,* but merely against those actual hypotheses that investigators (including oneself), trained in the same traditions of inquiry, put forward.[47] This places a difficult burden on those who would reject some theory in science: propose a better one! Simply poking holes in the current theories, without a new proposal, will not advance science in the long run.[48]

Let us assume that, in a context of actual rival chemical hypotheses, we have given a good argument for (2) based upon (1). What about the next step? Here there are a number of metaphysical commitments that we rely upon in our move from (2) to (4). For example, we assert in

---

46. Grue is a very complex color which is time-indexed. See Nelson Goodman, *Fact, Fiction and Forecast* (Cambridge, Mass.: Harvard University Press, 1955), p. 74. For a good defense and explanation of the principle of simplicity, see Richard G. Swinburne, *Simplicity As Evidence of Truth* (Milwaukee: Marquette University Press, 1997).

47. In other words, an inference that an explanation is "best" takes place against the background of rival hypotheses. See Dennis Temple, "The Contrast Theory of Why-Questions," *Philosophy of Science* 55 (1988): 141-51; Peter Lipton, "The Contrastive Explanation and Causal Triangulation," *Philosophy of Science* 58 (1991): 687-97, and his *Inference to the Best Explanation,* pp. 32-55.

48. Of course, in the short run it may well be quite useful.

(3) that central features of the chemical makeup of a mineral are part of the essential properties of that mineral. The standard example among philosophers of science is "water is H_2O." We also assume that, in this particular case, the color green is a symptom of those essential properties. Now it is certainly logically possible that we may be wrong. Yet an important point must be made, in order to avoid a modal fallacy. Just because it is logically possible that I may be wrong, it does not follow that I am wrong. This is a modal fallacy, which some critics of induction need to avoid. What we need is some reason to believe that (4) is false, given (2) and (3). *The mere logical possibility of error is simply a part of the very nature of informal inference, and should be ignored.* "Somewhere within the realm of logical possibility may be lurking a defeater, but until it rears its ugly head, we need pay it no mind."[49] Of course, the critic may feel that anything less than logical certainty does not count as knowledge: but this is an opinion we have already discussed and rejected along with other elements of classical foundationalism.

The reasons, then, that (2) and (3) are good evidence for (4) are diverse. There is no simple principle at work here, but a detailed knowledge of the chemical makeup of emeralds, in the context of broad chemical knowledge concerning crystals, colors, and the doxastic practices of our chemical paradigm.

The Contextual Thesis

One important reason there is great diversity among the principles of informal inference is the great variety of such patterns of reasoning. Another reason, however, has to do with the many areas of research in which we use informal inference. If rationality is a traditional practice, it follows that there may well be principles of good informal argument which differ from science to science and from discipline to discipline. Toulmin argued for this some time ago, following some of the insights of Wittgenstein. The principle of simplicity, for example, is one example of a principle of informal inference. But simplicity of theory in mathematics will be quite different from simplicity of theory in biology.

49. From private correspondence with Charles Hughes concerning an earlier version of this appendix.

To take another example, Sherlock Holmes once remarked (concerning criminal investigations) that once we eliminate all options but one as impossible, whatever is left, however improbable, must be true.[50] This principle is one that may help us decide who committed some crime. But it is of doubtful use in other areas of investigation, say, concerning theories of the origin of life. In the case of Sherlock's principle, one can reasonably assume we have a complete list of all possible explanations for the crime. Given the evidence of the crime, we can create a reasonable list of all possible suspects and means. If we can eliminate some as impossible, the remaining one must (if our assumptions are true) be the answer. This principle can, in fact, be verified by deductive logic. But this principle cannot be used universally. In the area of prebiotic evolution, which falls in the discipline of chemistry, we have no reason whatsoever to believe that we know all the possible ways in which life could possibly arise. Eliminating some theories as impossible, in this case, does not mean that whatever is left, however improbable, must be true.

The principle of contextuality does not claim that these principles are invalid because they are not universally applicable. Instead, contextuality follows from the fact that we must know about the objects and properties involved in an informal argument in order to assess its soundness or cogency. The more we understand about the things the premises are asserting and assuming, the better able we are to assess the strength of the argument. If different disciplines and traditions of argument are involved in assessing informal arguments, it should not be surprising that criteria for what counts as a good inductive argument may differ from discipline to discipline. There are indeed general and abstract principles of inductive argument that apply to all disciplines; these are usually discussed in textbooks about critical thinking and formal logic. The law of noncontradiction, applied to what counts as a good theory, would be an example of such a general rule. But even these will need to be contextualized to spell out their significance for the particular argument being assessed. And there will be plenty of room for argument about the *meaning* of these principles for

50. "Eliminate all other factors and the one which remains must be the truth." See the beginning of the first chapter, entitled "The Science of Deduction," in Arthur Conan Doyle's story *The Sign of Four.*

particular arguments. Finally, in addition to these general principles there will be special principles that have been developed within each discipline.

Thomas Kuhn is one philosopher of science who famously argued for the contextual thesis.[51] "[E]ach paradigm will be shown to satisfy more or less criteria that it dictates for itself and to fall short of those dictated by its opponents."[52] This led him to conclude that choice between paradigms is a matter of "a mixture of objective and subjective factors, or of shared and individual criteria."[53] Here I think we should distinguish between contextualism and relativism. I do not hold to the relativist position of radical incommensurability between paradigms. The historical fact that different scientists have been able to argue together, for example, would indicate that a strong principle of incommensurability is contrary to the actual practice of scientific debate. A good example of this would be the debate between Galileo and his Aristotelian critics. They were able to debate the issues just because their paradigms were not radically incommensurable. Members of the two paradigms in astronomy understood each other, even though they also meant slightly different things by the same words. As Kuhn himself notes, this kind of trans-paradigm dialogue is possible, but "for that we must go native, discover that one is thinking and working in, not simply translating out of, a language that was previously foreign."[54]

With respect to the criteria for standards of good informal inference, I would continue to hold to a diversity approach. Some standards may indeed be relevant only to a particular discipline, or even a particular research program in that discipline. But there are surely a large number of criteria and propositions that guide informal argument, are largely similar, and overlap the different paradigms. Kuhn called these

51. David B. Annis uses this name in a different way in "A Contextualist Theory of Epistemic Justification," *American Philosophical Quarterly* 15 (1978): 213-19. I discuss the view sometimes called contextualism under the rubrics of fallibilism and diversity, above.

52. Thomas Kuhn, *The Essential Tension* (Chicago: University of Chicago Press, 1977), p. 325.

53. Thomas Kuhn, *The Structure of Scientific Revolutions* (Chicago: University of Chicago Press, 1962), pp. 108f.

54. Kuhn, *Structure,* p. 204.

"shared values."[55] The more a standard or epistemic value appears to be based on reason and common human experience, the more it may be a standard that can be shared between paradigms. For example, our criterion of comprehensiveness would be a standard for informal inference which can be used in a variety of contexts. The contextual thesis, however, insists that the meaning and application of these general criteria or propositions *must be contextualized to be fully of use* in any given research program.

Perhaps philosophy of science, at this point, should borrow a page from the philosophy of Thomas Aquinas. Shared criteria of informal inference, which overlap between several research programs, may not have univocal meaning in all contexts, but that does not imply that their different uses are equivocal. The similarities and differences between "simplicity" and "comprehensiveness" in different disciplines may best be described as analogous. This provides for a *weak* incommensurability thesis, and yet allows for criteria of good informal reasoning that are not relative to particular traditions of inquiry.

Some Objections

I suspect that a number of questions and objections to this "postmodern" approach to Reid's solution to the problem of induction may already have occurred to you. One can be immediately laid to rest: have I really tackled the problem of induction, you may ask? After all, the problem is usually set forth in formal, logical terms. And I have not answered the problem in those terms. Instead, my approach has been to argue that *in these terms* there may not be a problem at all. Formal logic may be of limited use, of course, but not of central import for evaluating informal arguments.

There are, however, informal fallacies of reasoning as well as formal ones. Charges such as incoherence or circularity apply to both kinds of arguments. If, as is often maintained, the principles of informal reasoning are *circular* in nature, then there will be a genuine problem with the justification of our principles of informal inference. A circular argument is one that states its conclusion as a premise, often in a

---

55. Kuhn, *Essential Tension*, pp. 321-22.

disguised manner. If there is at least one principle for informal infer- ence whose justification is not based on itself nor on any other infor- mal principle of reasoning, then it will be false that all of the principles of informal inference are circular in nature. We therefore need only one noncircular argument to refute the claim that all the principles are cir- cular. I have already argued, above, that accepting the principle of com- prehensiveness in theory choice is not based on experience, nor on in- formal argument. So there is at least one principle of informal inference that is not based on any other. Therefore, they cannot all be circular.

What we really need here is a particular argument that a specific principle of informal inference is either circular or perhaps baseless. We can then look and see if that is the case. Wholesale arguments to this conclusion are not very convincing. Typically, we justify a principle of informal argument by appeal to our background knowledge and/or our common sense. Here I think Reid is right. For example, it is a prin- ciple of textual criticism that (all other things being equal) the more difficult reading is more original. Asked to justify this practice, the tex- tual critic might point to our knowledge of the way that ancient texts were copied, and the fact that scribes would be more likely to smooth over a difficult reading than to make it more complicated. If pressed further, the textual critic would supply evidence from historical manu- scripts describing the practices of ancient scribes, and so forth. What would not be appealed to is the principle itself, in its own justification. It is unlikely, as this example shows, that warrant for a principle of in- formal inference will circle back upon itself *as a general rule.*

I have also suggested that some of the principles of informal in- ference from specific traditions of inquiry may be justified by appeal to noetic warrant. Are there not serious problems with such an appeal? Some philosophers may complain that supposed rational intuitions are merely arbitrary. One philosopher's intuition is another philoso- pher's nonsense. I have tried, above, to give good reasons why that need not be so. In particular, there seem to be signs or symptoms of times when an appeal to reason is legitimate and to be expected. Moreover, the process of vindication would cut down on any arbitrariness. This objection loses its force when we open up proposed noetic concepts to revision and criticism. Other philosophers might complain that truths of reason are not subject to correction at all, yet this complaint assumes we have a true, complete, and clear expression of the truth, and this often may not be the case. Our particular way of expressing our rational insight may need revision; or, upon further investigation, it may not turn out to be true at all. We can talk only about proposed noetic concepts that have been subject to careful critique. These are fallible, however well established, and subject to further refinement. I should also make clear that what we are aiming for here is truth, not "agreement" nor "consensus" nor something "noncontroversial."

Finally, some philosophers seem to be afraid of anything that smacks of the postmodern or the postfoundational. I should clarify, then, that I have rejected classical foundationalism. The alternative is not relativism; at least that is not my conclusion. I am open to a humble and modest form of "foundation" or ground for epistemic criteria.[56] Indeed, the concept of noetic warrant developed here could qualify as just that.

---

56. Such as that defended by William Alston. See his *Epistemic Justification* (Ithaca, N.Y.: Cornell University Press, 1989).

Bibliography

Abelard, Peter. *Dialectica.* Trans. L. M. de Rijk. Assen: Van Gorcum, 1956.

———. *Sic et Non.* Ed. B. B. Boyer and R. McKeon. Chicago: University of Chicago Press, 1977.

Abraham, W. J., and S. W. Holtzer, eds. *The Rationality of Religious Belief.* Oxford: Oxford University Press, 1987.

Adorno, T. W. *Negative Dialectics.* Trans. E. B. Ashton. New York: Seabury, 1973.

Allport, F. H. *Social Psychology.* New York: Houghton Mifflin, 1924.

Alston, William P. "Biblical Criticism and the Resurrection." In *The Resurrection,* ed. Stephen T. Davis, Daniel Kendall, and Gerald O'Collins. Oxford: Oxford University Press, 1997.

———. "A 'Doxastic Practice' Approach to Epistemology." In *Knowledge and Skepticism,* ed. Marjorie Clay and Keith Lehrer. Boulder, Col.: Westview, 1989.

———. *Epistemic Justification.* Ithaca, N.Y.: Cornell University Press, 1989.

———. *A Realist Theory of Truth.* Ithaca, N.Y.: Cornell University Press, 1996.

———. "Thomas Reid on Epistemic Principles." *History of Philosophy Quarterly* 2 (1985): 435-52.

Annis, David B. "A Contextualist Theory of Epistemic Justification." *American Philosophical Quarterly* 15 (1978): 213-19.

Anstey, Peter. "Reid on the Problem of Induction." *History of Philosophy Quarterly* 12 (1995): 77-93.

Aquinas, Thomas. *Summa Theologiae.* Ed. T. Gilby et al. 61 vols. New York: McGraw-Hill, 1964-1990.

Aristotle. *Complete Works of Aristotle.* Ed. J. Barnes. 2 vols. Princeton, N.J.: Princeton University Press, 1984.

Augustine. *Augustine: Early Writings.* Ed. J. H. S. Burleigh. Philadelphia: Westminster, 1953.

———. *City of God.* 7 vols. Cambridge, Mass: Harvard University Press, 1957-1972.

———. *De Doctrina Christiana.* Ed. R. P. H. Green. Oxford: Oxford University Press, 1995.

————. *De Vera Religione.* In *Opera, pars IV.1.* Corpus Christianorum: Series Latina, vol. 32. Turnholti: Brepols, 1962.

Aune, David. "Magic in Early Christianity." *Aufstieg und Niedergang der römischen Welt* 2/23.2, cols. 1507-37. Berlin, New York: de Gruyter, 1982.

Ayer, A. J. *The Problem of Knowledge.* Harmondsworth: Penguin, 1956.

Banner, Michael. *The Justification of Science and the Rationality of Religious Belief.* Oxford: Oxford University Press, 1990.

Barbour, Ian. *Issues in Science and Religion.* London: SCM, 1966.

————. *Myths, Models and Paradigms.* New York: Harper and Row, 1974.

————. *Religion in an Age of Science.* San Francisco: Harper and Row, 1990.

————. *When Science Meets Religion.* San Francisco: Harper, 2000.

————, ed. *Science and Religion.* London: SCM, 1968.

Barth, Karl. *Church Dogmatics.* Ed. G. W. Bromiley and T. F. Torrance. Trans. G. W. Bromiley. 4 vols. in 13 parts. Edinburgh: T&T Clark, 1936-1975.

————. "Das erste Gebot als theologisches Axiom." *Theologische Fragen und Antworten: Gesamelte Vorträge.* Vol. 3. Zürich: Theologischer Verlag Zürich, 1957.

————. "Philosophie und Theologie." In *Philosophie und christliche Existenz,* ed. Gerhard Huber. Basel: Helbing und Lichtenhahn, 1960.

————. *The Way of Theology in Karl Barth.* Ed. and trans. H. M. Rumscheidt. Allison Park, Pa.: Pickwick, 1986.

————. *The Word of God and the Word of Man.* Trans. D. Horton. Boston: Pilgrim, 1928.

Benton, Ted. "Naturalism in Social Science." *Routledge Encyclopedia of Philosophy.* London: Routledge, 1998. 6:717-20.

Berger, Peter. *The Sacred Canopy.* New York: Doubleday, 1967. Anchor Books ed., 1990.

Bernstein, Richard J. *Beyond Objectivism and Relativism.* Oxford: Blackwell, 1983.

Berkhof, Hendrikus. *Christ the Meaning of History.* London: SCM, 1966.

————. *Two Hundred Years of Theology.* Trans. J. Vriend. Grand Rapids: Eerdmans, 1989.

Bhaskar, Roy. *Dialectics: The Pulse of Freedom.* London: Verso, 1993.

Birch, L. Charles. "Creation and the Creator." *Journal of Religion* 37 (1957): 85-98. (Also in Barbour, ed., *Science and Religion.*)

Black, Max, ed. *Philosophical Analysis.* Ithaca, N.Y.: Cornell University Press, 1950.

Borg, Marcus. *Jesus in Contemporary Scholarship.* Valley Forge, Pa.: Trinity Press International, 1993.

Bonhoeffer, Dietrich. *Letters and Papers from Prison.* Trans. R. H. Fuller. New York: Macmillan, 1970.

BonJour, Laurence. *In Defense of Pure Reason.* Cambridge: Cambridge University Press, 1998.

Bromberger, Sylvian. "Why Questions." In *Mind and Cosmos,* ed. Robert G. Colodny. Pittsburgh: University of Pittsburgh Press, 1966.

Brown, Colin. *Christianity and Western Thought.* Vol. 1. Downers Grove, Ill.: InterVarsity, 1990.

Brümmer, Vincent. *Speaking of a Personal God.* Cambridge: Cambridge University Press, 1992.

Bultmann, Rudolf. *Existence and Faith.* Trans. Schubert M. Ogden. Cleveland: Meridian, 1960.

Butterfield, Herbert. *Christianity and History.* London: G. Bell, 1949.

Byers, David M., ed. *Religion, Science, and the Search for Wisdom.* Washington, D.C.: National Conference of Catholic Bishops, 1987.

Cargile, James. "The Problem of Induction." *Philosophy* 73 (1998): 247-75.

Carnley, Peter. *The Structure of Resurrection Belief.* Oxford: Oxford University Press, 1987.

Charry, Ellen. *By the Renewing of Your Mind.* New York: Oxford University Press, 1998.

Churchland, Patricia. *Neurophilosophy.* Cambridge, Mass.: MIT Press, 1986.

Clayton, Philip. *Explanation from Physics to Theology.* New Haven: Yale University Press, 1989.

Clement of Alexandria. *Stromateis.* In *Alexandrian Christianity.* Ed. J. E. L. Oulton and H. Chadwick. Philadelphia: Westminster, 1954.

Cobb, John B., Jr. *A Christian Natural Theology.* Philadelphia: Westminster, 1965.

———. *Grace and Responsibility.* Nashville: Abingdon, 1995.

Cobb, John B., Jr., and David Ray Griffin. *Process Theology.* Philadelphia: Westminster, 1976.

Colodny, Robert G., ed. *Mind and Cosmos.* Pittsburgh: University of Pittsburgh Press, 1966.

Coveney, Peter, and Roger Highfield. *The Arrow of Time.* London: W. H. Allen, 1990.

Craig, William L. *Apologetics: An Introduction.* Chicago: Moody, 1984.

———. *Reasonable Faith.* Wheaton, Ill.: Crossway, 1994.

Danto, A. C. "Naturalism." *Encyclopedia of Philosophy.* Ed. P. Edwards. New York: Macmillan, 1967. 5:488-450.

Davaney, Sheila, ed. *Theology at the End of Modernity.* Philadelphia: Trinity Press International, 1991.

Davies, Brian, ed. *Philosophy of Religion.* Washington, D.C.: Georgetown University Press, 1998.

Davies, Paul. *The Mind of God.* Harmondsworth: Penguin, 1993.

Davis, Stephen T. "Doubting the Resurrection: A Reply to James A. Keller." *Faith and Philosophy* 7 (1990): 99-111.

———. "Is It Possible to Know That Jesus Was Raised from the Dead?" *Faith and Philosophy* 1 (1984): 147-59.

———. *Logic and the Nature of God.* Grand Rapids: Eerdmans, 1983.

———. "Naturalism and Resurrection: A Reply to Habermas." *Faith and Philosophy* 2 (1985): 303-8.

———. *Risen Indeed: Making Sense of the Resurrection.* Grand Rapids: Eerdmans, 1993.

Davis, Stephen T., Daniel Kendall, and Gerald O'Collins, eds. *The Resurrection.* Oxford: Oxford University Press, 1997.

Dembski, William. *Intelligent Design.* Downers Grove, Ill.: InterVarsity, 1999.

Descartes, René. *Philosophical Writings of Descartes.* Trans. J. Cottingham et al. 3 vols. Cambridge: Cambridge University Press, 1984-1991.

De Vries, Paul. "Naturalism in the Natural Sciences." *Christian Scholar's Review* 15 (1986): 388-96.

Dewey, John. *The Quest for Certainty.* London: Allen and Unwin, 1930.

Dilthey, Wilhelm. *Selected Writings.* Ed. H. P. Rickman. Cambridge: Cambridge University Press, 1976.

Dionysius the Pseudo-Areopagite. *Pseudo-Dionysius: The Complete Works.* Trans. Colm Luibheid. New York: Paulist, 1988.

Douven, I., and L. Horsten, eds. *Realism in Science.* Leuven: Leuven University Press, 1996.

Drake, Durant, et al. *Essays in Critical Realism.* London: Macmillan, 1920.

Drake, Stillman. *Galileo Studies.* Ann Arbor: University of Michigan Press, 1970.

Drees, Willem B. *Beyond the Big Bang.* La Salle, Ill.: Open Court, 1990.

———. *Religion, Science and Naturalism.* Cambridge: Cambridge University Press, 1996.

Duhem, Pierre. *The Aim and Structure of Physical Theory.* 1906. Eng. trans., Princeton, N.J.: Princeton University Press, 1954.

Dungan, David L., ed. *The Interrelations of the Gospels.* BETL 95. Leuven: Leuven University Press, 1990.

Dupre, John. *The Disorder of Things: Metaphysical Foundations of the Disunity of Science.* Cambridge, Mass.: Harvard University Press, 1993.

Earman, John. *Bayes or Bust? A Critical Examination of Bayesian Confirmation Theory.* Cambridge, Mass.: MIT Press, 1992.

Eddy, Paul. "Jesus as Diogenes?" *Journal of Biblical Literature* 115 (1996): 425-45.

Eliade, Mircea. *The Myth of the Eternal Return.* Trans. Willard R. Trask. London: Routledge, 1955.

Enç, B. "Paradigm." *Cambridge Dictionary of Philosophy.*

Evans, C. Stephen. *The Historical Christ and the Jesus of Faith.* New York: Oxford University Press, 1996.

Farley, Edward. *Theologia.* Philadelphia: Fortress, 1983.

Feigl, Herbert. "De principiis non disputandum . . . ?" In *Philosophical Analysis,* ed. Max Black. Ithaca, N.Y.: Cornell University Press, 1950.

Feyerabend, Paul. *Conquest of Abundance.* Chicago: University of Chicago Press, 1999.

Fodor, J. A. "Special Sciences." *Synthese* 28 (1974): 97-115.

Frautschi, S. "Entropy in an Expanding Universe." *Science* 217 (1982): 593-99.

Funk, Robert, et al., eds. *The Five Gospels.* New York: Macmillan, 1993.

Gadamer, Hans-Georg. *Truth and Method.* Second English ed. New York: Continuum, 1991.

Galilei, Galileo. *Dialogue Concerning the Two Chief World Systems.* Trans. S. Drake. Berkeley: University of California Press, 1953.

———. *Discoveries and Opinions of Galileo.* Trans. and ed. S. Drake. Garden City: Doubleday, 1957.

Gallie, Robert. "Reid, Thomas." *Routledge Encyclopedia of Philosophy.* London: Routledge, 1998. 8:171-80.

Giaquinto, M. "Non-Analytic Conceptual Knowledge." *Mind* 105 (1996): 249-68.

Goldingay, John. *Models for Interpretation of Scripture.* Grand Rapids: Eerdmans, 1995.

Goodman, Nelson. *Fact, Fiction and Forecast.* Cambridge, Mass.: Harvard University Press, 1955.

Gould, Stephen Jay. *Rocks of Ages.* New York: Ballantine, 1999.

Grant, Ed. *The Foundations of Modern Science in the Middle Ages.* Cambridge: Cambridge University Press, 1996.

Gregersen, Niels, and J. Wentzel van Huyssteen, eds. *Rethinking Theology and Science.* Grand Rapids: Eerdmans, 1998.

Griffin, David R. *Religion and Scientific Naturalism.* Albany: State University of New York Press, 2000.

———, ed. *Physics and the Ultimate Significance of Time.* Albany: State University of New York Press, 1986.

Gruner, Rolf. "Science, Nature and Christianity." *Journal of Theological Studies* 26 (1975): 55-81.

Gunter, W. Stephen, ed. *Wesley and the Quadrilateral.* Nashville: Abingdon, 1997.

Habermas, Gary. *Ancient Evidence for the Life of Jesus.* Nashville: Nelson, 1984.

———. "Knowing that Jesus' Resurrection Occurred: A Response to Davis." *Faith and Philosophy* 2 (1985): 295-302.

Hall, Norman F., and Lucia Hall. "Is the War Between Science and Religion Over?" *The Humanist* 46, no. 3 (May/June 1986): 26-28.

Hamilton, William. *The Quest for a Post-Historical Jesus.* New York: Continuum, 1994.

Hardy, Dan, and David Ford. *Praising and Knowing God.* Philadelphia: Westminster, 1985.

Hart, Trevor. *Faith Thinking.* London: SPCK, 1995.

Hartshorne, Charles. *Wisdom As Moderation: A Philosophy of the Middle Way.* Albany: State University of New York Press, 1987.

Harvey, Van. *The Historian and the Believer.* New York: Macmillan, 1966. Second edition: Urbana: University of Illinois Press, 1996.

Hasker, William. "Evolution and Alvin Plantinga." *Perspectives on Science and Christian Faith* 44 (1992): 150-62.

———. "Should Natural Science Include Revealed Truth? A Response to Plantinga." *Perspectives on Science and Christian Faith* 45 (1994): 57-59.

Hauerwas, Stanley, and L. Gregory Jones, eds. *Why Narrative?* Grand Rapids: Eerdmans, 1989.

Hawking, Stephen. *A Brief History of Time.* New York: Bantam, 1988.

Hegel, G. F. W. *The Encyclopedia of Logic.* Trans. T. F. Geraets. Indianapolis: Hackett, 1991.

Heidegger, Martin. *Being and Time.* Trans. J. Macquarrie and E. Robinson. London: SCM Press, 1962. Also trans. Joan Stambaugh. Albany: State University of New York Press, 1996.

———. *Existence and Being.* Trans. W. Brock. Chicago: Regnery, 1949.

———. *Identity and Difference.* Trans. Joan Stambaugh. New York: Harper and Row, 1969.

———. *Introduction to Metaphysics.* Trans. R. Manheim. London: Oxford University Press, 1959.

———. *On the Way to Language.* Trans. P. D. Hertz. New York: Harper and Row, 1971.

———. *Phänomenologie und Theologie.* Frankfurt am Main: Klostermann, 1970.

———. *The Piety of Thinking.* Trans. J. G. Hart and J. C. Maraldo. Bloomington: Indiana University Press, 1976.

———. *Sein und Zeit.* Tübingen: Max Niemeyer, 1953.

Hempel, Carl. *Philosophy of Natural Science: Essays in Contemporary Science and Philosophy.* Englewood Cliffs: Prentice-Hall, 1966.

———. "Recent Problems of Induction." In *Mind and Cosmos,* ed. R. G. Colodny. Pittsburgh: University of Pittsburgh Press, 1966.

Hick, John. "The Logic of God Incarnate." *Religious Studies* 25 (1989): 409-23.

———. *The Myth of God Incarnate.* London: SCM, 1977.

Hilgevoord, Jan, ed. *Physics and Our View of the World.* Cambridge: Cambridge University Press, 1994.

Hoskyns, Edwyn, and N. Davey. *The Riddle of the New Testament.* London: Faber and Faber, 1931.

Huber, Gerhard, ed. *Philosophie und christliche Existenz.* Basel: Helbing und Lichtenhahn, 1960.

Hume, David. *An Inquiry Concerning Human Understanding.* Ed. C. W. Hendel. Indianapolis: Bobbs-Merrill, 1955.

Hurst, L. D., and N. T. Wright, eds. *The Glory of Christ in the New Testament.* Oxford: Oxford University Press, 1987.

Hurtado, Larry W. *One God, One Lord: Early Christian Devotion and Ancient Jewish Monotheism*. Philadelphia: Fortress, 1988.

Jaki, Stanley. *The Road of Science and the Ways to God*. Chicago: University of Chicago Press, 1978.

Jeeves, Malcolm. *The Scientific Enterprise and Christian Faith*. Downers Grove, Ill.: InterVarsity, 1969.

Johnson, Luke T. *The Real Jesus*. San Francisco: Harper, 1995.

Johnson, Phillip. *Reason in the Balance*. Downers Grove, Ill.: InterVarsity, 1995.

Kähler, Martin. *The So-Called Historical Jesus and the Historic, Biblical Christ*. Trans. C. Braaten. Philadelphia: Fortress, 1964.

Kallenberg, Brad. "The Gospel Truth of Relativism." *Scottish Journal of Theology* 53 (2000): 177-211.

Kant, Immanuel. *Critique of Judgement*. Trans. James Creed Meredith. Oxford: Oxford University Press, 1952.

————. *Critique of Pure Reason*. Trans. N. K. Smith. New York: St. Martin's, 1956.

————. *Gesammelte Schriften*. Edited by the Akademie der Wissenschaften. 30 vols. Berlin: de Gruyter, 1902-1999.

Kaufman, Gordon. *An Essay on Theological Method*. Third ed. Atlanta: Scholars Press, 1995.

Keck, Lelander. *The Future of the Historical Jesus*. Nashville: Abingdon, 1971.

Kee, H. C. *Miracle in the Early Christian World*. New Haven: Yale University Press, 1983.

Kellenberger, James. *The Cognitivity of Religion*. London: Macmillan, 1985.

Keller, James A. "Contemporary Christian Doubts about the Resurrection." *Faith and Philosophy* 5 (1988): 40-60.

Kelsey, David. *Between Athens and Berlin*. Grand Rapids: Eerdmans, 1993.

————. *To Understand God Truly*. Louisville, Ky.: Westminster John Knox, 1992.

Kierkegaard, Søren. *Concluding Unscientific Postscript*. Trans. D. F. Swenson. Princeton, N.J.: Princeton University Press, 1941.

————. *The Sickness unto Death*. Trans. W. Lowrie. Princeton, N.J.: Princeton University Press, 1941.

Kitcher, Philip. *The Advancement of Science*. Oxford: Oxford University Press, 1993.

Kripke, Saul A. *Naming and Necessity*. Cambridge, Mass.: Harvard University Press, 1980.

Kuhn, Thomas. *The Copernican Revolution*. Cambridge, Mass.: Harvard University Press, 1957.

————. *The Essential Tension*. Chicago: University of Chicago Press, 1977.

————. *The Structure of Scientific Revolutions*. Second ed. Chicago: University of Chicago Press, 1970.

Kyburg, H. E. *Probability and Inductive Logic*. New York: Macmillan, 1970.

Lakatos, Imre. *The Methodology of Scientific Research Programmes: Philosophical Papers*. Vol. 1. Cambridge: Cambridge University Press, 1977.

————. *Proofs and Refutations: The Logic of Mathematical Discovery.* Cambridge: Cambridge University Press, 1976.

Langford, Jerome. *Galileo, Science and the Church.* New York: Desclee, 1966.

Laudan, Larry. *Beyond Positivism and Relativism: Theory, Method, and Evidence.* Boulder, Col.: Westview, 1996.

————. "Some Problems Facing Intuitionist Meta-methodologies." *Synthese* 67 (1986): 115-29.

Lehrer, Keith. *Thomas Reid.* London: Routledge, 1989.

Lemos, Noah. "Common Sense and A Priori Epistemology." *The Monist* 81 (1998): 473-87.

Lessing, G. E. *Lessing's Theological Writings.* H. Chadwick, ed. Stanford: Stanford University Press, 1956.

Lindberg, David. *The Beginnings of Western Science.* Chicago: University of Chicago Press, 1992.

Lindberg, David, and Ronald Numbers, eds. *God and Nature.* Berkeley: University of California Press, 1986.

Lipton, Peter. "The Contrastive Explanation and Causal Triangulation." *Philosophy of Science* 58 (1991): 687-97.

————. *Inference to the Best Explanation.* London: Routledge, 1991.

Lonergan, Bernard. *Insight.* London: Longman, Green, 1957.

————. *Method in Theology.* London: Darton, Longman and Todd, 1972.

Lundin, Roger, et al. *The Responsibility of Hermeneutics.* Grand Rapids: Eerdmans, 1985.

MacIntyre, Alasdair. "Epistemological Crises, Dramatic Narrative, and the Philosophy of Science." *The Monist* 60 (1977): 453-72. Reprinted in *Why Narrative?* ed. Stanley Hauerwas and L. Gregory Jones. Grand Rapids: Eerdmans, 1989.

————. *First Principles, Final Ends and Contemporary Philosophical Issues.* Milwaukee: Marquette University Press, 1990.

————. *Three Rival Versions of Moral Enquiry.* Notre Dame, Ind.: University of Notre Dame Press, 1990.

Mack, Burton. *A Myth of Innocence: Mark and Christian Origins.* Philadelphia: Fortress, 1988.

————. *The Lost Gospel: The Book of Q and Christian Origins.* San Francisco: Harper, 1993.

MacKay, D. M. *The Clockwork Image.* Downers Grove, Ill.: InterVarsity, 1974.

————. "'Complementarity' in Scientific and Theological Thinking." *Zygon* 9 (1974): 225-44.

Mackie, J. L. "The Paradox of Confirmation." *British Journal for the Philosophy of Science* 13 (1963): 265-77. Reprinted in *Philosophy of Science,* ed. P. H. Nidditch. Oxford: Oxford University Press, 1968.

Maddox, Randy. "Spiritual and Practical Theology." *Association of Practical Theology, Occasional Papers* 3 (Spring 1999): 10-16.

————, ed. *Rethinking Wesley's Theology.* Nashville: Kingswood, 1998.

Marcil-Lacost, Louise. *Claude Buffier and Thomas Reid.* Montreal: McGill-Queen's University Press, 1982.

Marsden, George. *The Outrageous Idea of Christian Scholarship.* New York: Oxford University Press, 1997.

Marxsen, Willi. *Jesus and Easter.* Trans. Victor Paul Furnish. Nashville: Abingdon, 1990.

Maximus the Confessor. *Selected Writings.* Trans. G. C. Berthold. New York: Paulist, 1985.

McDonald, M. J. "Exploring 'Levels of Explanation' Concepts," I and II. *Perspectives on Science and Christian Faith* 41 (1989): 194-205 and 42 (1990): 23-33.

McMullin, Ernan. "Epistemic Virtue and Theory Appraisal." In *Realism in Science,* ed. I. Douven and L. Horsten. Leuven: Leuven University Press, 1996.

————. "The Goals of Natural Science." *Proceedings of the American Philosophical Association* 58 (1984): 37-64.

————. "How Should Cosmology Relate to Theology?" In *The Sciences and Theology in the Twentieth Century,* ed. A. R. Peacocke. Notre Dame, Ind.: University of Notre Dame Press, 1981.

————. *The Inference That Makes Science.* Milwaukee: Marquette University Press, 1992.

————. "Natural Science and Belief in a Creator." In *Religion, Science, and the Search for Wisdom,* ed. D. M. Byers. Washington, D.C.: National Conference of Catholic Bishops, 1987.

Meier, John P. *A Marginal Jew.* 2 vols. Garden City: Doubleday, 1991, 1994.

Merleau-Ponty, M. *Phenomenology of Perception.* London: Routledge, 1962.

Meyer, Ben. *Critical Realism and the New Testament.* Allison Park, Pa.: Pickwick, 1989.

Midgley, Mary. *Science As Salvation.* London: Routledge, 1992.

Mitchell, Basil. *Faith and Criticism.* Oxford: Oxford University Press, 1994.

Moreland, J. P. *Christianity and the Nature of Science.* Grand Rapids: Baker, 1989.

————, ed. *The Creation Hypothesis.* Downers Grove, Ill.: InterVarsity, 1994.

Morgan, Robert, ed. *The Nature of New Testament Theology.* Studies in Biblical Theology, Second Series, 25. London: SCM, 1973.

Morris, Thomas V. *The Logic of God Incarnate.* Ithaca, N.Y.: Cornell University Press, 1986.

Moser, Paul K., ed. *A Priori Knowledge.* Oxford: Oxford University Press, 1987.

Murphy, Nancey. *Theology in an Age of Scientific Reasoning.* Ithaca, N.Y.: Cornell University Press, 1990.

————. *Reconciling Theology and Science.* Kitchener, Ont.: Pandora, 1997.

Murphy, Nancey, and George Ellis. *On the Moral Nature of the Universe.* Minneapolis: Fortress, 1996.

Myro, George. "Aspects of Acceptability." In *Naturalism: A Critical Appraisal,* ed. Stephen J. Warner and R. Wagner. Notre Dame, Ind.: University of Notre Dame Press, 1993.

Nagel, Thomas. *The View from Nowhere.* Oxford: Oxford University Press, 1985.

Newton, Isaac. *The Mathematical Principles of Natural Philosophy.* Ed. F. Cajori. Berkeley: University of California Press, 1960.

Nicod, Jean. *Foundations of Geometry and Induction.* New York: Harcourt, 1930.

Nidditch, P. H., ed. *The Philosophy of Science.* Oxford: Oxford University Press, 1968.

Niebuhr, Reinhold. *Faith and History.* New York: C. Scribner's Sons, 1949.

Niebuhr, Richard R. *Resurrection and Historical Reason.* New York: Scribner, 1957.

Nielsen, Kai. *Naturalism without Foundations.* Buffalo: Prometheus, 1996.

O'Collins, Gerald. *Jesus Risen.* Mahwah, N.J.: Paulist, 1987.

Oden, Thomas C. *After Modernity — What? Agenda for Theology.* Grand Rapids: Zondervan, 1990.

————. *Agenda for Theology.* San Francisco: Harper and Row, 1979.

————. *The Word of Life: Systematic Theology,* vol. 2. San Francisco: Harper, 1989.

Ogden, Schubert M. *On Theology.* San Francisco: Harper and Row, 1986.

————. *The Point of Christology.* San Francisco: Harper and Row, 1982.

————. "Process Theology and the Wesleyan Witness." *Perkins Journal* 37 (1984): 18-33.

Orr, James. *A Christian View of God and the World.* Edinburgh: A. Elliot, 1893.

Oulton, J. E. L., and H. Chadwick, eds. *Alexandrian Christianity.* Philadelphia: Westminster, 1954.

Outler, Albert. "Theodosius' Horse." *Church History* 34 (1965): 251-61.

Owens, David. "Levels of Explanation." *Mind* 98 (1984): 59-79.

Padgett, Alan G. "The Roots of the Concept 'Laws of Nature': From the Greeks to Newton." *Perspectives on Science and Christian Faith* 55 (2003): 212-21.

————. *God, Eternity and the Nature of Time.* London: Macmillan, 1992; Eugene, Ore.: Wipf and Stock, 2000.

————. "The Mutuality of Theology and Science." *Christian Scholar's Review* 26 (1998): 12-35.

Palmer, G. E. H., et al., eds. *Philokalia.* Vol. 1. London: Faber and Faber, 1979.

Pannenberg, Wolfhart. *Basic Questions in Theology,* vol. 1. Trans. G. Kehm. Philadelphia: Westminster, 1983.

————. *Jesus — God and Man.* Trans. Lewis L. Wilkins and Duane A. Priebe. Philadelphia: Westminster, 1968.

————. *Theology and the Philosophy of Science.* Trans. F. McDonagh. Philadelphia: Westminster, 1976.

Patar, Benoit, ed. *Ioannis Buridani Expositio et Quaestiones in Aristotelis De Caelo.* Louvain: Peeters, 1996.

Patterson, Sue. *Realist Christian Theology in a Postmodern Age.* Cambridge: Cambridge University Press, 1999.

Peacocke, A. R. *Creation and the World of Science.* Oxford: Oxford University Press, 1979.

————. *Intimations of Reality.* Notre Dame, Ind.: University of Notre Dame Press, 1984.

————. *Theology for a Scientific Age.* Minneapolis: Fortress, 1993.

————, ed. *The Sciences and Theology in the Twentieth Century.* Notre Dame, Ind.: University of Notre Dame Press, 1981.

Peerman, Dean, ed. *Frontline Theology.* London: SCM Press, 1967.

Peirce, C. S. *The Collected Papers of Charles Sanders Peirce.* 5 vols. C. Hartshorne and P. Weiss, eds. Cambridge, Mass.: Harvard University Press, 1965.

Perkins, Pheme. "Jesus before Christianity: Cynic or Sage?" *Christian Century* 110 (July 28–August 4, 1993): 749-51.

Peters, Ted, ed. *Cosmos As Creation.* Nashville: Abingdon, 1989.

————. *Science and Theology: The New Consonance.* Boulder, Col.: Westview, 1998.

Phillips, D. Z. *The Concept of Prayer.* New York: Shocken, 1967.

————. *Religion without Explanation.* Oxford: Blackwell, 1976.

Placher, William. *Unapologetic Theology.* Philadelphia: Westminster, 1989.

Plantinga, Alvin. "Methodological Naturalism?" In *Facets of Faith and Science,* ed. Jitse van der Meer. Vol. 1. Lanham, Md.: University Press of America, 1996.

————. "On Rejecting the Theory of Common Ancestry: A Reply to Hasker." *Perspectives on Science and Christian Faith* 44 (1992): 258-63.

————. *Warrant: The Current Debate.* New York: Oxford University Press, 1993.

————. *Warranted Christian Belief.* New York: Oxford University Press, 2000.

————. "When Faith and Reason Clash." *Christian Scholar's Review* 21 (1991): 8-32.

Plantinga, Alvin, and Nicholas Wolterstorff, eds. *Faith and Rationality.* Notre Dame, Ind.: University of Notre Dame Press, 1983.

Plato. *Collected Dialogues.* Ed. E. Hamilton and H. Cairns. Princeton, N.J.: Princeton University Press, 1961.

Polanyi, Michael. *Personal Knowledge.* Chicago: University of Chicago Press, 1962.

Polkinghorne, John. *Belief in God in an Age of Science.* New Haven: Yale University Press, 1998.

————. *One World.* London: SPCK, 1986.

————. *Reason and Reality.* London: SPCK, 1991.

————. *Science and Creation.* London: SPCK, 1988.

————. *Science and Providence.* London: SPCK, 1989.

Popper, Karl R. *The Logic of Scientific Discovery.* Tenth ed. London: Hutchinson, 1980.

Prevost, Robert. *Probability and Theistic Explanation.* Oxford: Oxford University Press, 1990.

Prigogine, Ilya. *From Being to Becoming.* San Francisco: W. H. Freeman, 1980.

———. "Irreversibility and Space-time Structure." In *Physics and the Ultimate Significance of Time,* ed. David R. Griffin. Albany: State University of New York Press, 1986.

Prigogine, Ilya, and Isabelle Stengers. *Order out of Chaos.* London: Heinemann, 1984.

Putnam, Hilary. "Analycity and Apriority." *Midwest Studies in Philosophy* 4 (1979): 423-71. Reprinted in *A Priori Knowledge,* ed. Paul K. Moser. Oxford: Oxford University Press, 1987.

———. *Reason, Truth and History.* Cambridge: Cambridge University Press, 1981.

———. *The Threefold Cord: Mind, Body, World.* New York: Columbia University Press, 1999.

Quine, W. V. *Theories and Things.* Cambridge, Mass.: Harvard University Press, 1981.

Quinn, P., and C. Taliaferro, eds. *A Companion to the Philosophy of Religion.* Oxford: Blackwell, 1997.

Ramsey, I. T. *Models and Mystery.* Oxford: Oxford University Press, 1963.

Ratzsch, Del. *Science and Its Limits.* Downers Grove, Ill.: InterVarsity, 1999.

———. *Nature, Design and Science.* Albany: State University of New York Press, 2001.

Reichenbach, Bruce. *An Introduction to Critical Thinking.* New York: McGraw-Hill, 2000.

———. *The Law of Karma.* Honolulu: University of Hawaii Press, 1990.

Reid, Thomas. *Inquiry and Essays.* Ed. Ronald E. Beanblossom and Keith Lehrer. Indianapolis: Hackett, 1983.

Reimarus, Hermann Samuel. *Fragments.* Ed. C. H. Talbert. London: SCM, 1971.

Reisner, Erwin. *Offenbarungsglaube und historische Wissenschaft.* Berlin: Haus und Schule, 1947.

Richardson, Alan. *Christian Apologetics.* London: SCM, 1947.

Robinson, James, and John B. Cobb Jr., eds. *The Later Heidegger and Theology.* New York: Harper and Row, 1963.

Roberts, R. C. *Rudolf Bultmann's Theology.* Grand Rapids: Eerdmans, 1976.

Rorty, Richard. *Philosophy and the Mirror of Nature.* Princeton, N.J.: Princeton University Press, 1979.

Ruben, David-Hillel. *Explaining Explanation.* London: Routledge, 1990.

Runyan, Theodore, ed. *Wesleyan Theology Today.* Nashville: Kingswood, 1985.

Runzo, Joseph. *Worldviews and Perceiving God.* London: Macmillan, 1993.

Ruse, Michael. *Darwinism Defended.* Reading, Mass.: Addison-Wesley, 1982.

———. *Mystery of Mysteries: Is Evolution a Social Construct?* Cambridge, Mass.: Harvard University Press, 1999.

Russell, R. J., N. Murphy, and A. R. Peacocke, eds. *Chaos and Complexity: Scientific Perspectives on Divine Action.* Second ed. Vatican City: Vatican Observatory, 2000.

Russell, R. J., W. R. Stoeger and G. V. Coyne, eds. *Physics, Philosophy and Theology.* Vatican City: Vatican Observatory, 1988.

Sanders, E. P. *Jesus and Judaism.* Philadelphia: Fortress, 1985.

Schermer, Michael. *How We Believe.* New York: W. H. Freeman, 2000.

Schleiermacher, F. D. E. *On the Glaubenslehre.* Trans. J. Duke and F. S. Fiorenza. Chico, Calif.: Scholars Press, 1981.

Schoen, Edward L. *Religious Explanations.* London: Routledge, 1985.

Shermer, Michael. *How We Believe: The Search for God in an Age of Science.* New York: W. H. Freeman, 2000.

Sellars, Roy. *Critical Realism.* Chicago: Rand, McNally, 1916.

Soskice, Janet Martin. *Metaphor and Religious Language.* Oxford: Oxford University Press, 1985.

————. "Theological Realism." In *The Rationality of Religious Belief,* ed. W. J. Abraham and S. W. Holtzer. Oxford: Oxford University Press, 1987.

Stanton, G. N. "Presuppositions in New Testament Criticism." In *New Testament Interpretation,* ed. I. H. Marshall. Exeter: Paternoster, 1977.

Stone, Bryan, and Thomas Oord, eds. *Thy Nature and Thy Name Is Love.* Nashville: Kingswood, 2001.

Stove, D. C. *Probability and Hume's Inductive Scepticism.* Oxford: Oxford University Press, 1973.

————. *The Rationality of Induction.* Oxford: Oxford University Press, 1986.

Strauss, David F. *The Life of Jesus Critically Examined.* Trans. George Eliot. London: SCM, 1973.

Sturch, Richard. *The Word and the Christ.* Oxford: Oxford University Press, 1991.

Suchocki, Marjorie. *The Fall to Violence.* New York: Continuum, 1995.

Summerfield, Donna. "Modest A Priori Knowledge." *Philosophy and Phenomenological Research* 51 (1991): 39-66.

Swinburne, Richard G. "Analycity, Necessity and Apriority." *Mind* 84 (1975): 225-43. Reprinted *A Priori Knowledge,* ed. Paul K. Moser. Oxford: Oxford University Press, 1987.

————. *The Christian God.* Oxford: Oxford University Press, 1994.

————. *The Coherence of Theism.* Oxford: Oxford University Press, 1977.

————. *The Concept of Miracle.* London: Macmillan, 1970.

————. *The Existence of God.* Rev. ed. Oxford: Oxford University Press, 1991.

————. *An Introduction to Confirmation Theory.* London: Methuen, 1973.

————. *Simplicity As Evidence of Truth.* Milwaukee: Marquette University Press, 1997.

————. ed. *The Justification of Induction.* Oxford: Oxford University Press, 1979.

Temple, Dennis. "The Contrast Theory of Why-Questions." *Philosophy of Science* 55 (1988): 141-51.

————. "Grue-Green and Some Mistakes in Confirmation Theory." *Dialectica* 228 (1974): 197-210.

Thiselton, Anthony C. *New Horizons in Hermeneutics.* London: HarperCollins, 1992.

―――. *The Two Horizons.* Grand Rapids: Eerdmans, 1980.

Thorsen, Donald. *The Wesleyan Quadrilateral.* Grand Rapids: Zondervan, 1990.

Tillich, Paul. *Systematic Theology,* Volume I. Chicago: University of Chicago Press, 1951.

Torrance, T. F. *Divine Meaning: Studies in Patristic Hermeneutics.* Edinburgh: T&T Clark, 1995.

―――. *Reality and Scientific Theology.* Edinburgh: Scottish Academic Press, 1985.

―――. *Theological Science.* Oxford: Oxford University Press, 1969.

―――. *Theology in Reconstruction.* Grand Rapids: Eerdmans, 1965.

Toulmin, Stephen. *Foresight and Understanding.* Bloomington: Indiana University Press, 1961.

―――. *The Uses of Argument.* Cambridge: Cambridge University Press, 1964.

Tracy, David. *The Analogical Imagination.* New York: Crossroad, 1981.

Trigg, Roger. *Rationality and Religion.* Oxford: Blackwell, 1998.

―――. *Rationality and Science.* Oxford: Blackwell, 1993.

―――. *Reality at Risk.* Second ed. New York: Harvester, 1989.

Troeltsch, Ernst. "Historiography." In *Encyclopedia of Religion and Ethics,* ed. J. Hastings, 6:716-23. Edinburgh: T&T Clark, 1913.

―――. *Reason in History.* Trans. J. L. Adams and W. F. Bense. Minneapolis: Fortress, 1991.

Van der Meer, Jitse, ed. *Facets of Faith and Science.* 4 vols. Lanham, Md.: University Press of America, 1996.

Van Beeck, Frans Josef. *God Encountered,* vol. 1: *Understanding the Christian Faith.* Collegeville, Minn.: Liturgical Press, 1989.

Van Fraasen, Bas. *The Scientific Image.* Oxford: Oxford University Press, 1980.

Vanhoozer, Kevin. *Is There a Meaning in This Text?* Grand Rapids: Zondervan, 1998.

Van Huyssteen, J. Wentzel. *Duet or Duel?* London: SCM, 1998.

―――. *Essays in Postfoundational Theology.* Grand Rapids: Eerdmans, 1997.

―――. *The Shaping of Rationality.* Grand Rapids: Eerdmans, 1999.

―――. *Theology and the Justification of Faith.* Grand Rapids: Eerdmans, 1989.

Van Till, Howard. "Basil, Augustine and the Doctrine of Creation's Functional Integrity." *Science and Christian Belief* 8 (1996): 21-38.

―――. "The Creation." *Theology Today* 5 (1998): 344-64.

―――. "The Fully Gifted Creation." In *Three Views on Creation and Evolution,* ed. J. P. Moreland and J. M. Reynolds. Grand Rapids: Zondervan, 1999.

―――. "When Faith and Reason Cooperate." *Christian Scholar's Review* 21 (1991): 33-45.

Van Till, Howard, et al. *Portraits of Creation.* Grand Rapids: Eerdmans, 1990.

Volf, Miroslav, ed. *A Passion for God's Reign.* Grand Rapids: Eerdmans, 1998.

Wainwright, Geoffrey. *Doxology.* New York: Oxford University Press, 1980.

Ward, Keith. *Religion and Revelation.* Oxford: Oxford University Press, 1994.

Warner, Stephen J., and R. Wagner, eds. *Naturalism: A Critical Appraisal.* Notre Dame, Ind.: University of Notre Dame Press, 1993.

Webb, Stephen. *Taking Religion to School.* Grand Rapids: Brazos, 2000.

White, Andrew D. *A History of the Warfare of Science with Theology.* 2 vols. Reprint: New York: Dover, 1960.

Whitehead, Alfred North. *Process and Reality: An Essay in Cosmology.* New York: Macmillan, 1929. Corrected edition, ed. David Ray Griffin and Donald W. Sherburne. New York: Free Press, 1978.

————. *Science and the Modern World.* New York: Macmillan, 1925.

Will, Fredrick. *Induction and Justification.* Ithaca, N.Y.: Cornell University Press, 1974.

Williams, D. C. *The Ground of Induction.* Cambridge, Mass.: Harvard University Press, 1947.

Wittgenstein, Ludwig. *Culture and Value.* Oxford: Blackwell, 1980.

————. *Lectures and Conversations on Aesthetics, Psychology and Religious Belief.* Ed. C. Barrett. Berkeley: University of California Press, 1966.

————. *Philosophical Investigations.* Oxford: Blackwell, 1967.

Wolterstorff, Nicholas. *Divine Discourse.* Cambridge: Cambridge University Press, 1995.

————. "Public Theology or Christian Learning?" In *A Passion for God's Reign,* ed. Miroslav Volf. Grand Rapids: Eerdmans, 1998.

————. *Reason within the Bounds of Religion.* Second ed. Grand Rapids: Eerdmans, 1984.

Wykstra, Stephen. "Have Worldviews Shaped Science?" In *Facets of Faith and Science,* ed. Jitse van der Meer. 4 vols. Lanham, Md.: University Press of America.

————. "Should Worldviews Shape Science?" In *Facets of Faith and Science,* ed. Jitse van der Meer. 4 vols. Lanham, Md.: University Press of America.

Index

CPSIA information can be obtained at www.ICGtesting.com
Printed in the USA
LVOW12s1526080115

422026LV00003B/658/P